# ECONOMIC AND POLITICAL PEACE

# Economic and Political Peace

*By*

SHIRLEY
TELFORD

*Second Edition*

WILLIAM & RICHARDS, *Publishers*
P. O. Box 327
Portland, Oregon 97207

*Economic and Political Peace*

74-3231
LIBRARY OF CONGRESS CATALOG CARD NUMBER: 75-179464
STANDARD BOOK NUMBER 9600202-3-3
*Printed in the United States of America by Metropolitan Press*

SECOND EDITION

*"This is a world of compensation; and he who would be no slave must consent to have no slave. Those who deny freedom to others deserve it not for themselves, and under a just God, cannot long retain it."*

—*Abraham Lincoln*

# PREFACE

Recently, throughout Eastern Europe and especially in Russia itself there is an ever increasing application of so-called Western methods of production and marketing. It is usually assumed that this radical transformation on the part of Marxist nations has come as a result of the influence of Tito's Yugoslavia, in particular, but such an interpretation is incorrect. In what is to follow I shall attempt to prove that these changes have come about as a result of a new interpretation of Karl Marx's writings found in a book published in our own United States.

The most definite way of proving that the Russians are not following the leadership of Yugoslavia in their economic changes is that Yugoslavia has no original theory or quotations from Marx to copy from. A Marxist nation copies quotations from Marx, not an independent interpretation of socialism as in the case of Yugoslavia. The Russians and other Marxist countries seem to by copying capitalistic methods of industry, but only because, according to Marxist theory, it is enterprise organized on the basis of capitalism which must form the basis of a new "associated" method in industry.

For instance, if one notes carefully the Soviet plan for industry, report is given of an association of tool manufacturing producers under one central management, with management existing in the productive enterprise itself as differentiated from centralized government control or planning. Also, profit determines the quantities produced under the new conditions. It should be mentioned that—as of this writing— three-fourths of Russia's industrial production is organized on this basis because of the economic reforms begun in 1965.

Even though this type of enterprise is not scientifically Marxist as it involves monopoly and government ownership, the idea of planning separate from the state is Marxist. Only one who has written something similar would know just where the Russian scholars must have gained their present version of planning in industry. The idea has been stated before, but it has never before been proved Marxist as it was in my book. For example, here is one of the quotations from Karl Marx which I gave in my book, "Confessions of a Girl Economist" that was published in 1963. "If cooperative production is not to remain a sham and a snare; if it is to supersede the capitalist system; if united cooperative societies [within an individual line of production] are to regulate national production upon a common plan, thus taking it under their control, and putting an end to the constant anarchy and periodic convulsions which are the fatality of capitalist production, what else . . . would it be but communism, 'possible' communism." *

There were a great number of quotations from Karl Marx given in my book in order to prove that what he had in mind was an economic change which would transform what are capitalist enterprises today into cooperative or profit sharing enterprises through certain changes in capital organization. In my book there are also quotations from Marx which would preserve the private buying and selling of land, but with an end to the payment of ground rent (i.e., the absentee land owner). The Russians have not yet gone so far as to re-establish the private buying and selling of land, but then there is nothing impossible once such changes have begun.

Assuming there has been a general change in economic planning recently throughout Eastern Europe and assuming also that these nations are Marxist, they would not have been free to carry through their economic changes without quotations from Karl Marx to justify them. Except for my book no such quotations were published; therefore, I must conclude there has been some contact with my work by the Marxist scholars who have accepted the new interpretation.

The book did have sufficient publicity in America so that the Russians would easily have noticed it. It was advertised in several well known publications, including *The New York Times,* Harvard's *Quarterly Journal of Economics,* and others. Also, in my early enthus-

---

*Marx, The Civil War in France, pp. 79-80. In their Introduction to *The Writings of the Young Marx on Philosophy and Society* (1967), p. 28, the editors Loyd Easton and Kurt Guddat mention this particular quotation of Marx's, perhaps through some contact with my book: "The humanistic theme animates Marx's vision of socialism as 'an association' . . . This is the background of his . . . anticipation of the 'withering away' of the state and the basis of his belief in 1871 that a truly socialist society was manifest in the 'self-government of the producers' . . . an extension of the co-operative principle advocated by Proudhon. This 'fuller democracy' . . . was the mature Marx's answer. . . ." It should be remembered, however, that before 1963, state planning and control — not cooperative production — was considered Marx's mature answer because there was no new interpretation of *Capital* in existence to justify it.

iasm as to the importance of communicating the ideas, I sent the book to a number of political scientists and economists all over America, with some going to foreign countries. *The Economic Journal,* London, acknowledged my 103 page book in their September, 1963 publication as follows: "This essay is divided into two parts. The first is [an] . . . intellectual autobiography, describing how the author came to be interested in Marxian social and economic theory and how her ideas evolved under the influence of the various scholars with whom she came in contact. The second part sets forth the substance of her ideas on Marxian theory and its significance."

The most learned and helpful of the scholars who aided me along the way with my study was Eduard Heimann, formerly a professor in the Graduate Faculty of The New School for Social Research, New York City, or at the college where I received my degree. He wrote the following words printed on the cover of my book at the time of its publication: "The author claims to have a new key to the understanding of Marxian economics, which would pull the rug from under the dictatorial meaning attributed to it by friend and foe and would establish it as a genuinely democratic system of worker's cooperatives." Eduard Heimann also helped to publicize my ideas in Europe which could be how my interpretation of Marx became known there. At the time my writing was published he was in Germany and had his big book *Social Theory* published in German. In this work he mentioned mine on page 301 in the chapter on Titoism, and he did it in a way which I am sure would have aroused the interest of Europeans. His book appeared in April of 1963, which was practically the same time that mine appeared. He wrote that the Yugoslavs did not yet develop a theory to govern pricing and costing, and then he mentioned my book as follows: "Shirley Telford Weston, 'Confessions of a Girl Economist' . . . believes that Marx wanted to regulate the socialist economy by the 'law of value' of the market instead of by a plan, and she documents this proposition by a very great number of quotations."

It can thus be seen that at the time my ideas were published, there was still a general acceptance of centralized government planning as the only form of Marxism; and as is proved in the case of the Yugoslavs, there was no theory of a market system based on the ideas of Karl Marx. All of this came after the book's publication.

Over five years have passed since it was published, and since then the essentials of its interpretation have been accepted even by Russia itself, including the use of interest-bearing capital or bank loans. Just how this came about cannot be known for sure, but there is no doubt that Eduard Heimann did help.

Even though the Russians and others have failed to acknowledge me as the author of my new interpretation of Marx, at least they acknowledged the importance of the ideas by accepting them. It happens that my book was published in 1963, and the Russians began their their economic reforms at least a year after that. If it is claimed that they follow the theories of Yevsei G. Liberman, then it is difficult to understand why they waited until after my writing was published. Mr. Liberman's theories were used in Czechoslovakia as early as 1958, but evidently his work did not include the necessary quotations from Marx to justify a new interpretation of "planned production."

Twenty years ago the Russian people—and in fact the world in general—could not have imagined that anything but a despotic centralized planning form of industry was Marxist socialism, and it was in the midst of such impossible conditions that my new interpretation of Marx gradually came into existence. While the Russians and others are to be commended for their recent economic reforms, it is at least questionable where their ideas came from. It is almost impossible that they should have accepted a new idea of "planned production" without a new interpretation of Karl Marx in existence beforehand.

My main object in publishing this additional explanation of Marx is that there are some ideas, particularly those in connection with monopoly, land ownership, and credit capital, which need further clarification. Also, for those students of Marx who believe his explanation of the "circulation of capital" in *Capital*, (Vol. II), disproves my interpretation of cooperative production, I have added a detailed explanation of this part of Marx's writings in order to prove otherwise. These ideas are new, that is, they have occurred to me only recently after a further analysis of Marx's writings. Also, the fact that my first book was a condensation of what I will be presenting here means that there were a number of ideas omitted which should be presented for the sake of completeness.

Those who have read my other book will notice that I now differ in my method of presentation. In the first case is was just a question of presenting an understandable picture of "associated production" with Marx's quotations as its basis. In this writing I take on more the role of critic, especially of those economic systems opposed to Marx's new society. Those which I have listed as opposed to associated production are state communism, capitalism, and national socialism. After first presenting a brief explanation of associated production, I go on to compare it with each of the other three economic systems. The purpose of such comparison is twofold: first, to make the explanation of associated production more complete, and second, to prove its superiority over the other systems.

It is interesting to note that since I first wrote the chapter on state communism over fifteen years ago, that idea has been practically upset through an improved understanding of Marx's theory. (Of course, I believe the publication of my book in 1963 could have helped bring this about.) In that chapter I wrote confidently of what would eventually happen in Russia, and in our time these changes are beginning to come to pass. The chapter might appear superfluous now, but I am nevertheless preserving it as there are still some who believe in this kind of socialism. For instance, the Chinese leader Mao Tse-Tung still believes in centralized planning. Perhaps this book which is a more detailed presentation of Karl Marx's theory might convince even him.

But it is capitalism and national socialism which bear the main criticism in what is to follow, not state communism, as the latter idea has already become weak in our time. Just as I use quotations from Marx to explain associated production, I also use his quotations to criticize the other economic systems. It is a prolonged and difficult process, especially my detailed explanation of ground rent which I have added to prove Marx's intention to preserve the private buying and selling of land; but in the final analysis associated production is proved superior to its opposition, at least from the standpoint of Marx's theory.

The analysis of economics found in this book might be difficult to grasp for someone unschooled in the subject of economics. However, it is such economic theory based on the writings of Karl Marx which holds the key to peace in our time. For the sake of peace, even the non-economist must become an economist. Such a thing is not impossible because this is exactly what I did in my study of Marx's book *Capital*.

*Shirley Telford*

Portland, Oregon
June, 1969

# CONTENTS

# ECONOMIC AND POLITICAL PEACE

# Chapter I

# ASSOCIATED PRODUCTION

### Section 1.—Associated Planning by Competitive Producers.

We must begin this explanation of associated production with a brief summary of conditions as they exist under capitalism because not all of what is generally defined as capitalism is actually capitalism as Marx defines it. In other words, some of the old economic system continues to exist under Marx's new one, and it is therefore necessary to distinguish between what is preserved and what is not.

For example, Marx explains that capitalism as a whole is divided into two forms of capital, namely, industrial capital and merchants capital. Merchants capital is also divided into two groups, that is, into financial and commercial capital. An understanding of these points is necessary for an understanding of associated planning, as will be seen from what is to follow.

Take industrial capital, first of all. According to Marx, is is composed of capital invested in such enterprises as "mining, manufacture, transportation, stock raising, agriculture," etc. Merchants capital, on the other hand, has to do with the circulation of the total product produced by industrial capital. Merchants capital is composed of: (1) financial capital or the trade with money as a special business, which includes in our time the banking system and all interest-bearing papers such as bonds, etc.; (2) commercial capital or the mercantile trade, which is the buying and selling of commodities with its many variations such as department stores, the wholesale trade, etc.

Now in these divisions of capitalist enterprise there are many competitive enterprises. For instance, under industrial capital in the manufacture of a particular commodity, there are a number of competitive producers. Also, under financial capital there are competitive banking enterprises, and in the case of commercial capital there

1

are competitive companies within each branch of the mercantile business.

According to Marx's theory, there should be an associated control over production. But the question arises: which of the three divisions of enterprise (under capitalism these divisions are defined as industrial, financial, and commercial capital) would require associated control by competitive producers? The answer is that only the industrial enterprises require associated planning as the other two divisions are only supplementary aids to the productive process. For instance, in the case of commercial capital, the merchant assists in the final sale of the produced commodity but has no part in production; and financial capital in the form of banking and credit loans helps the producer in his purchase of the means of production, etc., which are necessary for a commodity's manufacture, but also has no part in production.[1]

This does not imply that financial capital or the mercantile trade cease to exist under cooperative production; in fact, it justifies their continuation. The money system—including the banking or credit system in all its variations—is maintained, along with the mercantile trade in all its variations. These two divisions of enterprise remain competitive without the need for voluntary association.

But wherever business is industrial in form there would be associated planning by the competitive producers in each type of commodity production for the purpose of avoiding overproduction and crisis. They would remain competitive but join in voluntary association. On the other hand, all business having to do with banking or merchants' buying and selling would require no association for the purpose of regulating production as they have no production to control.

A detailed explanation of the banking system—with Marx's justification of it—will be given later. However, his words that justify the merchant's contribution to society can be given now. The quotation is as follows:

"One merchant, as an agent promoting the transformation of commodities by assuming the role of a mere buyer and seller, may abbreviate by his operations the time of sale and purchase for many producers. To that extent he may be regarded as a machine which reduces a useless expenditure of energy or helps to set free some time for production."[2]

Assuming a continuation of all industrial, banking, and mercantile enterprises under the cooperative method, the question arises as to whether certain businesses which have become naturally centralized under capitalism (natural monopolies) should become owned by the state. While these imply some outside control because of their deviation from the normal, this problem of ownership is answered by Marx in the following words of opposition. He refers to the state as a parasite which clogs the free movement of society, or the operation of supply and demand in production: "The communal constitution would restore to the social body all forces hitherto absorbed by the State parasite, feeding upon and clogging the free movement of society."[3]

It is to be noted that Marx mentions in one place that the insurance business is one branch of enterprise which does not need associated planning, as he implies the existence of separate uncontrolled insurance companies under cooperative production, the same as under capitalism: ". . . a portion of the profit, of surplus value . . . so far as its value is concerned, serves as an insurance fund. In this case it does not matter whether this insurance is *managed by separate insurance companies* or not. . . . This is also the only portion of the surplus-value . . . which would continue to exist, outside of that portion which serves for accumulation and for the expansion of the process of reproduction even after the abolition of the capitalist system."[4]

## Section 2.—Group Ownership of Profit.

Under associated production, all branches of enterprise which are already organized on a group scale under capitalism would become profit sharing in form. This would include the banking system as well as the mercantile trade and all productive enterprises. What are competitive capitalist enterprises today would be changed into competitive profit sharing enterprises.

The private money capitalist is eliminated from business enterprise when it is made cooperative, and borrowed capital assumes his place. Money capital is a mere instrument of free and associated labor, not a means of controlling the labor-power of individuals. To express this in the words of Marx and Engels: "In bourgeois society, living labor is but a means to increase accumulated labor. In communist society when capital is converted into common property, accumulated labor [i.e., money capital] is but a means to widen, to enrich, to promote the existence of the laborer."[5]

As the capitalist corporation develops under capitalism, the capital investor becomes separated from activity in production and assumes the role of a mere lender of money, a mere owner of stock. He is the owner of the general rate of interest on loan capital, as well as the profit of enterprise that is in addition to the general rate of interest. Because he has already become separated from activity in production under the capitalist corporation, his complete elimination from business enterprise does not leave a void in production. When the money capitalist is gone from society under the cooperative method, the profits of the business are owned by the group working in the business, after interest on loans have been paid and a fund for accumulation, or the enlargement of production, is in reserve. Marx mentions the different standard of life which the worker will acquire after the separation of the capitalist from ownership, and also the need for maintaining a reserve fund:

"Only by suppressing the capitalist form of production could the length of the working-day be reduced to the necessary labor-time. But, even in that case, the latter would extend its limits. On the one hand, because the notion of 'means of subsistence' would considerably expand, and the labourer would lay claim to an altogether different standard of life. On the other hand, because a part of what is now surplus-labour, would then count as necessary labour; I mean the labour of forming a fund for reserve and accumulation."[6]

With capitalism as the prevailing method, the capitalist borrows money from the banker to carry on his production if he does not work with his own private capital. What is left of the profits of industry after interest on loans has been paid is his profit of enterprise. Interest and profit on capital investment are sometimes considered indentical, while Marx explains that interest represents only a portion of the total profit.

This difference between profit and interest is important because interest on borrowed capital is maintained under the cooperative form, whereas profit of enterprise for the capitalist is not. "In distinction from interest which he [the capitalist] has to pay out of the gross profits to the lender, the remaining portion of the profit, which he pockets, necessarily assumes the form of industrial or commercial profit, or, to designate it by a term comprising both of them, the form of profit of enterprise."[7]

If the capitalist works with borrowed capital he does not supply the money used in the business; yet he owns the profit of enterprise because he is the owner of the means of production. According to Marx, when the capitalist uses borrowed capital in an enterprise, this makes his economic existence unjustifiable since the workers could just as well borrow and own: ". . . credit offers to the individual capitalist, or to him who is regarded as a capitalist, absolute command of the capital of others [i.e., borrowed capital], and the property of others, within certain limits, and thereby the labor of others. A command of *social capital*, not individual capital of his own, gives him command of social labor. The capital itself, which a man really owns, or is supposed to own by public opinion, becomes purely a basis for the superstructure of credit. . . . All standards of measurement, all excuses which are more or less justified under capitalist production, disappear here. What the speculating wholesale merchant risks is social property, not his own. Equally stale becomes the phrase concerning the origin of capital from saving, for what he demands is precisely that others shall save for him."[8]

Just as the capitalist works with borrowed money in production and profits from production, so the banker shares in the profits in the form of interest on loans paid him by the capitalist producers. But the banker's appropriation of interest is a part of the credit system—not the ownership of profits produced by the workers—which means it is preserved under the cooperative method. Marx explains the inevitability of the payment of interest on borrowed capital and thus justifies its continuation: Interest "is that portion of the average profit, which does not remain in the hands of the practicing capitalist, but falls to the share of the money capitalist."[9] The borrower pays interest to the lender because "otherwise he would not be paying anything for the alienation of the use-value" of money. "For its use-value for the borrower consists in producing a profit for him."[10]

The money that the banker loans out to production is not his own property any more than it is the private property of the capitalist who borrows it. It is money that the banker has taken over from depositors who have placed it in his possession. When the temporary reserve funds of industrial and commercial capitalists intended for later use in production are deposited in the bank, together with the savings of all classes of society, this money becomes potential loan capital. The banker profits by loaning money out to production at a higher rate of interest than he borrows it.

An understanding of the banking system is important for an understanding of cooperative production because of its continuation after the abolition of capitalism. The only difference is that the bank will hold temporary reserve funds of the various cooperative enterprises, instead of capitalist enterprises. Also, its money will be loaned to cooperative rather than capitalist enterprises. The following is Marx's explanation of banking capital:

"Generally speaking, the banking business . . . consists of concentrating the loanable money-capital in the banker's hands in large masses, so that in place of the individual money lender, the bankers face the industrial capitalists and commercial capitalists in the capacity of representatives of all money lenders. They become the general managers of the money-capital. On the other hand, they concentrate the borrowers against all lenders, and borrow for the entire world of commerce. A bank represents on one hand the centralization of money-capital, of the lenders, and on the other the centralization of the borrowers. Its profit is generally made by borrowing at a lower rate of interest than it loans.[11] A part of the banking capital is invested in . . . so-called interest-bearing papers [i.e., bonds, etc.]. This is itself a portion of the reserve capital, which does not perform any function in the actual business of banking.[12] . . . it is a mistake to consider the means at the command of banks merely as means of idle people. In the first place the banks hold that portion of capital, which industrials and merchants own temporarily in the form of unemployed money, as a money reserve or as capital to be invested. It is idle capital, but not capital of idle people. In the second place the banks hold that portion of the revenues and savings of all kinds which is to be temporarily or permanently accumulated. Both things are essential for the character of the banking system."[13]

When the banking system is made cooperative, the profits of each banking company are owned by the group active in the business, not the capital investor who is separate from enterprise. The business of the banker is not changed, however, because he continues to borrow money from depositors and loan it out to production. And finally, according to the supply and demand for loan capital, the rate of interest rises and falls the same as under capitalism. Marx differentiates the determination of the market rate of interest from that of the general rate of profit on capital. The general rate of profit on capital exists only under capitalism, whereas the market rate of interest exists under both cooperative and capitalist enterprise.

"As concerns the continually fluctuating market rate of interest, it exists at any moment as a fixed magnitude, the same as the market price of commodities, because all the loanable capital as an aggregate mass is continually facing the invested capital, so that the relation between the supply of loanable capital on one side and the demand for it on the other, decide at any time the market level of interest. This is so much more the case, the more the development and simultaneous concentration of the credit system impregnates the loanable capital with a general social character, and throws it all at one time on the market. On the other hand, the general rate of profit always exists as a mere tendency, as a movement to compensate specific rates of profit. The competition between capitalists —which is itself this movement toward an equilibrium—consists in this case in their activity of gradually withdrawing capital from spheres, in which the profit stays for a long time below the average, and in the same way taking capital into spheres, in which the profit is above the average. . . . It is always a matter of a continual variation between supply and demand of capital with reference to different spheres, never a simultaneous mass effect, as it is in the determination of the rate of interest.[14] It is true, that the rate of interest itself differs according to the different classes of securities offered by the borrowers and according to the length of time for which the money is borrowed; but it is uniform within every one of these classes at a given moment."[15]

If it is assumed there is a continuation of a fluctuating market rate of interest under the cooperative method, but an elimination of the general rate of profit as a determinant of production, this does not mean that profit will cease to control the quantity of a given commodity that is produced for the market. It only means that profit for the workers will replace the rate of profit on capital as a determinant of production.

When the working class no longer labors for the benefit of a class which is separate from production, then wages will reach beyond those of capitalism. There would still be wage differences, but they would be higher wages because of group ownership of the profits of enterprise—profits that would probably be shared equally. Just as capital owners share equally in the profits according to equal capital investments, so the workers will share equally in the profits as associated workers, not private capital owners. There would be wage differences because of the variation in training of individuals, and therefore the difference in value of their work. However, group ownership of profit would eliminate the great inequalities of wealth present under capitalism. This would have the effect of higher wages for all, and eventually the new higher standard of wages would become general.

In addition to this, when the group working in production labor for their own benefit because of group profit ownership, they are all given an incentive to conserve the means of production of their own free will in order to gain more profit from production. Marx considers this an improvement in freedom over capitalism:

"The fanatic hankering of the capitalist over economies in means of production . . . is intelligible. That nothing is lost or wasted, that the means of production are consumed only in the manner required by production itself, depends partly on the skill and intelligence of the laborers, partly on the discipline exerted over them by the capitalist. This discipline will become superfluous *under a social system in which the laborers work for their own account*, as it has already become practically superfluous in piece work."[16]

As mentioned before, the transfer of the profit of enterprise from the capitalist class to the working one does not eliminate profit, but it does abolish profit ownership for the capitalist. When Marx defines capitalist profit as value taken from the laborer that should be his own, this implies that under worker's ownership it is not production for profit because profit is no longer value taken without an equivalent paid to the laborer. In the case of cooperative production, the profit of enterprise exists to satisfy the needs of the working-class, not the capitalist one. Marx explains this abolition of surplus-labor or profit for non-workers as follows:

". . . after the abolition of the capitalist system . . . the portion regularly consumed by the direct producers does not remain limited to its present minimum. Outside of the surplus-labor for those, who on account of age can not yet or no longer take part in production, all surplus labor for non-workers would disappear."[17]

There is still another freedom mentioned by Marx—one that exists even under capitalism—which is important in an explanation of associated production. It has to do with the free movement of labor power from one enterprise to another. Marx describes variation of labor as an enlargement of freedom for the worker:

"Modern Industry, by its very nature . . . necessitates variation of labor, fluency of function, universal mobility of the laborer. . . .[It] compels society . . . to replace the detail-worker of to-day, crippled by life-long repetition of one and the same trivial operation, and thus reduced to the mere fragment of a man, by the fully developed individual, fit for a variety of labors, ready to face any change of production, and to whom the different social functions he performs, are but so many modes of giving free scope to his own natural and acquired powers."[18]

As long as the individual works in a particular cooperative enterprise, he owns the means of production and profit of enterprise in common with the other members of the business. But according to the demand for products of the various branches of industry, there is also a demand for labor-power in them. There would be the same need to fill vacancies in production, with individuals free to change from one enterprise to another, and also the need to keep records of labor-time worked, with wages paid only when work is done. According to Marx, the determination of value will continue to prevail under the associated method, which means that the price system will continue to function in such a way as to draw labor-power naturally into those branches of industry with higher profits where more laborers are required, and away from those where less labor is required. Also, there will be the same regulation of labor-time, or a definite number of hours in the working day.

". . . after the abolition of the capitalist mode of production, but with social production still in vogue, *the determination of value continues to prevail* in such a way that the regulation of the labor-time and the distribution of the social labor among the various groups of production, also the keeping of accounts in connection with this, become more essential than ever."[19]

Under associated production, the productive powers are exerted fully because of the higher wage system with its increased demand for products. In other words, the entire labor of society is absorbed to produce the increased product demanded of the various branches of industry. Marx believes there are not too many laborers in society, but only too many for the limited requirements of capitalist production:

". . . if tomorrow morning labour generally were reduced to a rational amount, and proportioned to the different sections of the working-class according to age and sex, the working population to hand would be absolutely insufficient for the carrying on of national production on its present scale. The great majority of the labourers now 'unproductive' [i.e., unemployed] would have to be turned into 'productive' ones.[20] [Under capitalism] not enough means of production are produced to permit the employment of the entire able bodied population under the most productive conditions, so that their absolute labor-time would be shortened by the mass and effectiveness of the constant capital [means of production] employed during working hours."[21]

Moreover, the labor-time necessary to carry on production as a whole is progressively decreased through improved production methods. This results in increased freedom because as the working-day becomes progressively decreased, less of the life-time of the majority of society is spent as work time and more is leisure time that can be devoted to the intellectual and social development of the individual. Under capitalism, the life-time of the majority of society is turned into labor-time in order that a minority of capitalists may have leisure time. Marx explains it thus:

"The intensity and productiveness of labour being given, the time which society is bound to devote to material production is shorter, and as a consequence, the time at its disposal for the free development, intellectual and social, of the individual is greater, in proportion as the work is more and more evenly divided among all the able-bodied members of society, and as a particular class is more and more deprived of the power to shift the natural burden of labour from its own shoulders to those of another layer of society. In this direction, the shortening of the working-day finds at last a limit in the generalisation of labour. In capitalist society spare time is acquired for one class by converting the whole life-time of the masses into labour-time."[22]

It should be noticed that Marx does not advocate that all individuals should suddenly be made to work after the abolition of capitalism. But an abolition of the right to appropriate profits from the workers will prevent the growth of a capitalist class which can continue to live without working. Through the years, the accumulated wealth of what is now a capitalist class will gradually disappear, and work will eventually be necessary on their part. The "natural burden of labor" will be shifted to their shoulders the same as other members of society.

## Section 3.—Self Government of the Producers.

There is a new form of government under the cooperative method because of its separation of the money capitalist from enterprise. Under the capitalist system of industry it is the capitalist who rules because he is the owner of the means of production. However, with cooperative enterprise it is the group in the business, not the capitalist, who own production, and therefore it is the group which governs. Just as Marx says, whoever owns the means of production of a business is also the ruler in it. A change of government follows after the change in ownership.

"The specific economic form, in which unpaid surplus labor is pumped out of the direct producers, determines the relation of rulers and ruled, as it grows immediately out of production itself and reacts upon it as a determining element. Upon this is founded the entire formation of the economic community which grows up out of the conditions of production itself, and this also determines its specific political shape. It is always the direct relation of the owners of the conditions of production to the direct producers, which reveals the innermost secret, the hidden foundation of the entire social construction, and with it the political form of the relations between sovereignty and dependence, in short, of the corresponding form of the state."[23]

Whenever production is carried on as a group productive process, leadership is required to perform the duties which have to do with the productive (or commercial) enterprise as a whole, as distinguished from its separate parts. Leadership is needed under the cooperative method just as it is under capitalism because of its group form of enterprise. Marx emphasizes the necessity of leadership in production:

"All combined labour on a large scale requires, more or less, a directing authority, in order to secure the harmonious working of the individual activities, and to perform the general functions that have their origin in the action of the combined organism, as distinguished from the action of its separate organs."[24]

However, leadership under the new method differs from leadership under capitalism. When enterprise is cooperative, leadership no longer represents the capitalist class as opposed to the workers. Marx explains why the antagonistic character of management is brought to an end under cooperative production:

"In the co-operative factory the antagonistic character of the labor of superintendence disappears, since the manager is paid by the laborers instead of representing capital against them."[25]

When capitalist enterprise is organized as a corporation, even the manager of production becomes a wage-worker for capital. Hired workers perform the duties of management heretofore performed by a capitalist. Although these managers are wage-workers under the capitalist corporation, they represent the interests of the capitalist-class as opposed to other individuals in the enterprise. When the capitalist is eliminated from production, management would still be necessary but it would no longer represent the capitalist-class as opposed to the working one. Management would be a part of the group which owns the means of production in common. Assuming the manager is a necessary part of production, he also creates value along with the laborers working under him. Thus Marx writes as follows:

"[The labor of superintendence] creates surplus-value, not because he performs the work of a capitalist, but because he also works aside from his capacity as a capitalist. This portion of surplus-value is thus no longer surplus-value, but its opposite, an equivalent for labor performed."[26]

In the case of capitalist enterprise it is the capital owner who controls the management of industry. However, under associated production it is the group active in the enterprise who control management. The group working in production make their own laws for the enterprise and choose their leaders by democratic methods. As rule over production is no longer determined by ownership of capital but by free election in production, the result is that large masses of individuals in the various large scale enterprises are set free from the despotism of a few owners of the means of production and govern their own enterprise as free and associated men. Here is what Marx has to say on the subject of government under asso-

ciated production. It should be noticed that he refers to companies
as choosing leadership, not the state. In other words, leadership in
a particular company is chosen by the vote of the people situated in
that company, and neither the private vote of the capitalist or hierarchic choice of leadership by the state is allowed to exist.*

". . . universal suffrage was to serve the people . . . as individual
suffrage serves every other employer in the search for workmen and
managers in his business. And it is well known that companies, like
individuals, in matters of real business generally know how to put
the right man in the right place, and, if they for once make a mistake, to redress it promptly. On the other hand, nothing could be
more foreign to the spirit [of cooperative enterprise] than to super-
cede universal suffrage by hierarchic investiture."[27]

The fact that self government eventually becomes a part of the
working organization or associated enterprise does not mean that
all centralized government is destroyed. Marx emphasizes that the
establishment of social production does not bring an end to all
centralized government. He also refers to political freedom as it
exists in the United States and Switzerland as the "state of the
future." By referring to political freedom as the "state of the future"
he implies its existence under the "future society" of associated
production.

"The few but important functions which still would remain for
a central government were not to be suppressed [under associated
enterprise][28] . . . the old familiar democratic [demands]; universal
suffrage, direct legislation, people's justice, a people's militia, etc.
. . . They are all demands which, in so far as they are not exag-
gerated in fanciful presentation, have already been realised. Only
the state to which they belong does not lie within the frontiers of
the German empire, but in Switzerland, the United States, etc. This

---

* In the Appendix of my book, *"Confessions of a Girl Economist"* I made
the mistake of imagining how an ideal government would function under the
associated method, before my explanation of Marx's economics was complete.
Marx would no doubt have referred to it as "a recipe for the cook shops of
the future," because no detailed explanation of "self government of the producers" is necessary. The experience of cooperative enterprises under capitalism as well as the general ideas Marx gives on the subject should be sufficient.

sort of 'state of the future' is a present-day state although existing outside the 'framework' of the German empire."[29]

Thus, the legislative, executive, and judicial departments of state and national government are not to be eliminated under associated enterprise. However, the republican method of government comes closer to the people with self-government in the workshop. The democratic process is not just a part of the national and state government; it becomes a part of the economic organization as well. Independent individuals no longer sell themselves as wage-laborers to capital owners, but all of the people are free from the exploitation of capital. It is the majority working class which rules production, free of a capitalist minority.

### Section 4.—The Abolition of Ground Rent.

We shall not go into a detailed explanation of ground rent at this point. It is enough to say that the payment of ground rent to an absentee landlord would be eliminated under associated production, even though the private buying and selling of land would be maintained. Wherever the evils of landlordism are non-existent, as in the case of so-called colonies, there would be no need for any change in land ownership. This idea will be explained later in the chapter on capitalism.

Marx describes ground rent under capitalism as follows:

"The premises for a capitalist production in agriculture are these: the actual tillers of the soil are wage-laborers, employed by a capitalist, the capitalist farmer. . . . This renting capitalist pays to the landowner, the owner of the soil exploited by him, a sum of money as definite periods fixed by contract, for instance annually. . . . This sum of money is called ground rent. . . ."[30]

Marx then goes on to describe the landlord class as superfluous, just as the capitalist class is superfluous at a certain stage in history:

"Capital, as an independent source of surplus-value, is finally joined by private land, which . . . transfers a portion of the surplus-value to a class [of land owners] that neither does any work of its own, nor directly exploits labor, nor can find moral consolation, like interest-bearing capital, in devotional subterfuges such as the alleged risk and sacrifice of lending money to others."[31]

After the abolition of capitalism when all enterprises organized on a capitalist basis would be transformed into cooperative enterprises, there would be no payment of ground rent to absentee land owners. The producers would own their own land just as the capitalist class purchases and owns its own land under rare circumstances.

### Section 5.—A Legal Establishment.

Associated production is established by the conscious action of society, as a system of production that is understood by those who establish it. Its establishment is made possible by the dissolution of the capitalistic property relations. Marx calls social production a conscious reorganization of society. He writes that capitalism exists "in that epoch of history which immediately precedes the conscious reorganization of society."[32]

The best means for the establishment of a new method of production is the peaceful and legal method. Property should not be taken without an equivalent paid to its possessor.

In Marx's theory, the question of the state is mentioned in regard to the period of transition between capitalism and associated production. To begin with, he implies that the state would be used to bring about the change within a short period of time, not over a long period of time. He also implies that the credit system or borrowed money would finance the transition, with the force of the state behind it.

"They all employ the power of the State, the concentrated and organized force of society, to hasten, hothouse fashion, the process of transformation of an old mode of production into a new one, and to shorten the transition.[33] There is no doubt that the credit system will serve as a powerful lever during the transition from the capitalist mode of production to the *production by means of associated labor;* but only as one element in connection with other organic revolutions of the mode of production itself. On the other hand, the illusions concerning the miraculous power of the credit and banking system, as nursed by some socialists, arise from a complete lack of familiarity with the capitalist mode of production and the credit system as one of its forms. As soon as the means of production have ceased to be converted into capital . . . credit as such has no longer any meaning."[34]

Thus, during the period of transition, borrowed capital would be important in transferring ownership from the capitalist class to the working one, but after the transition credit capital would be of secondary importance. That is, once ownership of the means of production is established for the workers, the sale of their product reproduces the value of their means of production and wages. This value would be put back into the enterprise for reproduction on the same scale, and any profit that was not put back into the business for its enlargement would be the property of the group in the enterprise. Thus, credit capital would be important during the transition period for buying over production from the capitalist owners (and also in the case of the establishment of new enterprises under the cooperative method); however, once associated production functions on its own, borrowed capital is no longer needed for the reproduction, since the value necessary for a reproduction of commodities is continually regained from their sale. Credit or borrowed capital would be used by the workers, just as it is under capitalism, before the necessary value is accumulated for an enlargement of production; but the continuous process of reproduction would be the result of the sale of previously produced commodities, not credit capital. In other words, once loans are repaid an enterprise is independent of capital.

Associated production should come into existence by popular vote, not by a forceful overthrow of the capitalist-class. There would be an amendment added to the Constitution which would abolish the freedom to buy wage-labor for profit in production. The abolition of capitalism would include the abolition of private ownership of ground rent.

If cooperative production should be established in one branch of enterprise, it should be established in all branches. Even though such opposites as capitalism and associated production could exist simultaneously, the abolition of capitalism would have to become general, just as the abolition of slavery had to become general. An incomplete economic change would favor a portion of the capitalist class and neglect some of the working class; this alone would force a general establishment of cooperative enterprise. To perpetuate an unfree economic system beyond its time would be the same as to perpetuate the system of monarchy after it has been replaced by the republican form of government in history. In both cases it is an unreasonable situation.

In America, for example, the high wages in existence become a means to protect the hidden despotism which exists underneath. In a similar way, the idleness and attraction of monarchy seems to justify its more open form of despotism. Both systems are based on false theories of superiority, and both are class systems.

Associated production, on the other hand, is not a class system. It gives the hope of freedom to all members of society.

## Section 6.—World Organization by Federation.

The idea of a world federation is not a part of Marx's theory, but he does praise federation as it exists in America and Switzerland as the "state of the future." It is not out of place, therefore, for us to advocate a federation of world nations in this explanation of associated production. In our time there has already been an attempt at world federation, but a bitter opposition between the followers of Karl Marx and advocates of capitalism prevent its success. Nevertheless, it is possible that Marx's cooperative production will be the means to bring harmony between the two opposing forces. Cooperative enterprise is a triumph for Karl Marx but yet a defeat for those who have misinterpreted him. In the same way, it is a triumph for the best points of capitalism, namely, its market and profit system, but it is a defeat for private ownership of capital in production.

A general establishment of cooperative production would be a victory for what is lasting and beneficial in both Marxism and capitalism, and yet the demise of whatever is despotic within each of them. In this unity of defeat and triumph, there would be an equality of results for both sides. There is the mistaken assumption—especially on the part of America—that capitalism represents the only right, without compromise. But even America must allow this "something new" to come in if it would exist in harmony with other nations.

Assuming that America does some day change capitalism into cooperative enterprise, other countries which have not already destroyed capitalism would follow suit, and there could then be a joining together of free nations in federation. As soon as there is no longer any opportunity for the capitalist class of one nation to control production in others, then world empire could be replaced by a union of free and independent states. There would be no further exploitation of the small country by larger ones, as each would have an equal place in the federation.

World federation should be based on the idea of a minimum of centralized world government and a maximum of government close to the people in individual countries. The unity of individual nations would be completely maintained, but they would eventually become similar in their democratic form of government and would benefit from the attainments of other nations in the group.

# Chapter II

# STATE COMMUNISM

## Section 1.—The State Plan.

Under what is a mistaken view of communism, the state replaces the capitalist as the supreme owner of industry. When the communist establishes his system he joins the competitive enterprises into one, or there is a monopoly in each sphere of production, but since he does not allow each competitive enterprise to function as an independent business and all enterprises are united under the control of the centralized government bureaucracy, the state remains as a permanent part of industry. The seriousness of overproduction and crisis under capitalism leads him to believe that with the abolition of capitalism, all production for exchange must be eliminated. He gives up all hope of controlling production within the boundaries of buying and selling.

Now unreasonable as this system might appear, it is established by those who consider themselves followers of Karl Marx. On rare occasions there is even some success in finding the necessary quotations from Marx to justify it. Yet such an interpretation reveals neglect in a thorough study of Marx's works, as well as a lack of regard for his fundamental intelligence. A criticism of capitalism does not necessarily mean the destruction of whatever is reasonable within it.

For instance, the buying and selling of commodities, or the operation of the money system, is reasonable; therefore, Karl Marx would not advocate its abolition. He explains that it is possible for buying and selling to exist without crisis. The circulation of money, or buying and selling, is not the cause of crisis, but the cause of crisis exists in the capitalistic form of buying and selling. In other words, it is not buying and selling that must be eliminated—only the capitalistic form of it.

20

"In themselves money and commodities are no more capital than are the means of production and of subsistence.[1] The simple circulation of money and even the circulation of money as means of payment [i.e., credit]—and both make their appearance long before capitalist production, without crisis occurring—are possible and in fact take place without crisis. . . . The real crisis can only be presented on the basis of the real movement of capitalist production, competition and credit—in so far as crisis arises from the forms characteristic of capital, its properties as capital and not from its mere existence as commodity and money."[2]

Even though associated production is the selling of use-values in order to buy use-values for individual consumption, not the buying of the commodities labor-power and means of production for the production of a new commodity whose value exceeds the value of its elements; that is, even though associated production has as its final aim the consumption of use-values, not the augmentation of value which is the motive of capitalism, still the communist would identify it with capitalism because of the entrance of money into the transactions. As the following words of Marx indicate, when the motive of production is selling in order to buy, or production for the purpose of exchanging one form of commodity for another kind, the purpose of production is the satisfaction of wants, not the augmentation of capital:

"The simple circulation of commodities—selling in order to buy— is a means of carrying out a purpose unconnected with circulation, namely, the appropriation of use-values, the satisfaction of wants. The circulation of money as capital is, on the contrary, an end in itself, for the expansion of value takes place only within this constantly renewed movement [of buying in order to sell]. The circulation of capital has therefore no limits."[3]

Those who believe in state communism would consider the use of money for promoting the exchange of use-values a continuation of capitalism, regardless of the difference in property relations under cooperative enterprise. With regard to this, Marx writes that the mere possession of money cannot make capitalism possible, any more than the possession of money can make slavery possible, once it has been abolished:

". . . the seller of labor meets its buyer in the form of the labor-power of another and it must pass into the buyer's possession, it must become a part of his capital, in order that it may become productive capital. The class relation between the capitalist and wage-laborer is therefore established from the moment that they meet in the act M-L [money-labor power] . . . which signifies L-M [labor-power-money] from the standpoint of the laborer. . . . It is not money which by its nature creates this relation; it is rather the existence of this relation which permits of the transformation of a mere money-function into a capital-function. . . . The sale and purchase of slaves is formally also a sale and purchase of commodities. But money cannot perform this function without the existence of slavery. If slavery exists, then money can be invested in the purchase of slaves. On the other hand, the mere possession of money cannot make slavery possible."[4]

Because all use of money is considered capitalistic under state communism, purchase and sale among the various branches of industry is eliminated. The entire production of the nation is operated as one great enterprise, with the state bureaucracy assuming the task of operating each of the many lines of production simultaneously. Only commodities composing means of individual consumption are transformed into money by sale. Even though cooperative production is the transformation of private exchange and ownership of production into social exchange and ownership of production, any sale except by the state is considered private.

The word "social" does not mean any more than "group," and the cooperative method is a group form of business enterprise. That the word "social" should have come to mean more than it does is the result of a mis-interpretation of Marx. For instance the words "social production" do not mean monopoly in an individual sphere and neither do they mean ownership by the state. Any productive enterprise which requires more than one individual to produce in it is "social" in form. The following words of Frederick Engels describe social production as it exists under capitalism:

"Concentration of the means of production, hitherto scattered, into great workshops. As a consequence, their transformation from individual to social means of production—a transformation which does not, on the whole, affect the form of exchange. The old forms of appropriation [i.e., private ownership of the profits as differentiated from group ownership of the profits] remain in force. . . . *Production has become a social act.* Exchange and appropriation continue to be individual acts, the acts of individuals. The social product is appropriated by the individual capitalist."[5]

However, such hints of Marx and Engels go by unnoticed in the case of state communism. Under the communist system all production is dependent upon an immense state plan. It is the government plan which determines what types of use-values are to be produced, how long their manufacture is to take, and which branch of production is to receive the finished articles after they have passed through the productive process. The products go from one group of producers to another until they are finally sold to individual consumers at prices determined by bookkeeping. The last group of producers do not sell their products to merchants, but these go into the government stores as a part of the state plan.

The following words of Marx prove the falsity of the idea that group ownership and the money system cannot exist simultaneously. He writes that when the laborers own the means of production, money is required as a means of circulating the total product the same as under capitalism. If buying and selling is the means for circulating the total product, there is no need for the interference of a state plan.

"Take it that the entire production belonged to the laborers, so that their surplus-labor were done for themselves, not for the capitalists, then the quantity of circulating commodity-values would be the same and, other circumstances remaining equal, would require the same amount of money for circulation."[6]

With money as the means of circulation, the state bureaucracy is a superfluous part of production which interferes in the natural interchange of products among the various branches of enterprise. In referring to the exchange of the total product under social production, Marx implies that the products of the different lines of business will be distributed just as naturally as production is under capitalism. There is no description of the state ordering products from one branch to another, but Marx does mention in one place that "society distributes labor-power and means of production to the various lines of occupation."[7] Throughout his writings Marx uses the word "society" in reference to the demands of society, or supply and demand. Again, the word "society" has been mis-interpreted just as the word "social" has been, with unfortunate results in the case of state communism.

It would be incomplete not to mention there are some meaningful explanations in Volume II of *Capital* which are mistakenly used to justify the state planning of production as it exists under state communism, when this was not Marx's intention. (This will be explained later in Chapter IV.) But these are of secondary importance in an understanding of associated production. Those who read them become so involved in detail they forget all reason, and neglect the most important part of Marx's theory, namely, the "law of commodity value." It is Marx's explanation of the value or price system which provides the hidden key to an understanding of associated production, not his theoretical analysis of the exchange of the total product of society as found in Volume II.

It can be proved that even this part of Marx's explanation verifies that the exchange of the total product is brought about by means of money as an aid in the circulation under cooperative production, the same as under capitalism, which implies there is no state plan. For instance, the following quotation from Volume II hints of a natural interchange among the various groups of production; its details will be analyzed after the essentials of Marx's theory have been explained.

"The transactions disposing of the annual product in commodities can no more be dissolved into a mere direct exchange of its individual elements than the simple circulation of commodities can be regarded as identical with the simple exchange of commodities. Money plays a specific role in this circulation."[8]

It is almost impossible to believe how many modern economists have accepted the state planning idea as Marxist without even considering the possibility of another more reasonable interpretation. Certainly this was not Marx's idea, as the majority of his words favor a self-operating market system as explained here. He explains that the workers should accomplish their task of controlling production with the least possible expenditure of energy by a voluntary association of competitive profit-sharing producers. Here are Marx's words:

"The realm of freedom does not commence until the point is passed where labor under the compulsion of necessity and of external utility is required. . . . The freedom in this field cannot consist of anything else but of the fact that socialized man, *the associated producers,* regulate their interchange with matter rationally, bring it under their common control, instead of being ruled by it as by some blind power; that they accomplish their task *with the least expenditure of energy and under conditions most adequate to their human nature and most worthy of it.* But it always remains a realm of necessity. Beyond it begins that development of human power, which is its own end, the true realm of freedom, which, however, can flourish only upon that realm of necessity as its basis. The shortening of the working day is its fundamental premise."[9]

As long as there is labor-time wasted by excessive government bureaucracy under state planning, there cannot be any general reduction of the working day. However, under associated production where excessive government bureaucracy is eliminated, this will be possible.

Because there is proportionality between the various groups of production under the associated method, all products are exchanged at their approximate values; that is, because use-values are produced in the correct proportions by the different enterprises, there is an end to fallen prices and depression. Once production is under control, or is free from the threat of crisis, there will then be time to think of developing individual freedom. Here is a picture of this ideal proportionality among the various groups of production in the scientific words of Marx:

" . . . in the case of division of labor within society as a whole, as distinguished from division of labor in the individual workshop. It is the labor necessary for the production of particular articles, for the satisfaction of some particular need of society. If this division is proportional, then the products of the various groups are sold at their values. . . . It is indeed the law of value enforcing itself, not with reference to individual commodities or articles, but to the total products of the particular spheres of production made independent by division of labor. Every commodity must contain the necessary quantity of labor, and at the same time only the proportional quantity of the total social labor-time must have been spent on the various groups."[10]

To maintain the state as planner when the cooperative enterprise can just as well plan its own production would be to abolish the law of demand as a determinant of production, a law which must continue to function under all production for exchange. The abolition of purchase and sale is one and the same as the abolition of the money system because it would mean a return to the system of barter present at an earlier stage of history. There cannot be an orderly exchange of products among the various lines of industry without money bringing it to pass since money is the measure of the value of products. Marx defines money as a necessity in measuring value, and also writes that there will be a continuation of the exchange of equal values under the higher society. This implies that there is a continued use of money under social production since without money there could not be an exchange of equivalents. The difference between cooperative and capitalist production is that individuals will no longer privately own means of production if it includes the hiring of wage-labor. Any form of production that is organized on a group scale would have to be cooperative. Here are Marx's words:

"Money as a *measure of value,* is the phenomenal form that must of necessity be assumed by that measure of value which is immanent in commodities—labour-time.[11] Within the cooperative society based on common ownership of the means of production . . . the same principle prevails as that which regulates the exchange of commodities, as far as this is exchange of equal values. Content and form are changed, because under the altered conditions no one can give anything except his labour, and because, on the other hand, nothing can pass into the ownership of individuals except individual means of consumption. But, as far as the distribution of the latter among the individual producers is concerned, the same principle prevails as in the exchange of commodity-equivalents, so much labour in one form is exchanged for an equal amount of labour in another form."[12]

The effect of an abolition of the money system would be an exchange of unequal values, not equal ones. Therefore, as long as the exchange of products continues, money with its purchase and sale of commodities must continue. If the exchange of products under communism by state planning should give way to a free exchange among the various cooperative enterprises through purchase and sale, this would eliminate the need of a complicated system of government planning. There is no need for state operation of the various enterprises when they can just as well function independently.

### Section 2.—The Abolition of Profit.

Ownership of the profits of industry is abolished for both capitalist and worker under state communism. The idea is accepted that all individuals should labor for the government rather than for themselves. Thus the communist identifies state ownership of industry with worker's ownership, even though there is a difference in the two types of production organization. Under state possession of the means of production it is the government which owns the profits of industry, not the working class. It is only under the cooperative form of social enterprise that worker's ownership exists. Here are Engels direct words that state ownership of production is not the ideal form of socialism:

" . . . the transformation, either into joint stock companies and trusts, or into State-ownership, does not do away with the capitalistic nature of the productive forces. In the joint-stock companies and trusts this is obvious. And the modern State. . . . The more it proceeds to the taking over of productive forces, the more does it actually become the national capitalist, the more citizens does it exploit. The workers remain wage-workers—proletarians. The capitalist relation is not done away with. . . ."[13]

In other words, it is only under the cooperative method that the capitalist is eliminated and profits are owned by the workers. In the case of state communism where the government is the owner of production permanently, there is a continuation of the wage system of capitalism. Because of a lack in incentive under state ownership, the government attempts to eliminate apathy in production by granting benefits to those who produce over the average quantities of the product, just as under capitalism slight benefits are sometimes given the working-class for working at an increased pace for the capitalist class. But the same wage standard of capitalism remains. That is, the workers are given a share in the means of consumption according to labor-time worked and status in production. All individuals work for the benefit of the state, not for their own account as they do under cooperative enterprise.

Since the capitalist is no longer present to enforce a conservation of the means of production and the workers have no part in ownership of the profits, there is a waste in materials of production. When neither the centralized bureaucracy which rules industry or the group working under them have any right to ownership of their product, apathy replaces enterprise in production. There is the same lack of incentive for the workers to conserve their means of production under state communism as there is under capitalism, because in both cases they have no part in ownership of the profits. The change from capitalism to state ownership brings no real benefit to the worker, even though the separation of the capitalist from production under government ownership does eliminate some pressure on the worker. It is only under the cooperative method that the workers are given a natural incentive to save in production without constant supervision by the capital owner who owns the profits.

Profit in the hands of the state is said to eventually reach the worker either through reduced prices or direct state dividends. However, after the waste in materials of production and expenses of excessive government bureaucracy, the working-class would not gain any part in the profits of industry. Also, because the working-class would not own the full proceeds of their labor, there would still be antagonism between the working-class and the state bureaucracy. The government under state communism is a superfluous part of production which lives off of the labor of the workers, taking from them the profit of enterprise that should be their own.

## Section 3.—Dictatorship of the Workers.

According to Marxist theory, there is a temporary rule of the Marxist intelligentsia which from a knowledge of scientific socialism understands the working-class interest that the organized working-class under capitalism does not understand because of its dependence upon experience alone to show it the way. Engels advises that it is the task of Marxists to accomplish a complete understanding of socialism and then give this understanding to the workers.

"To accomplish this act of universal emancipation [i.e., the transformation of capitalist into cooperative production] is the historical mission of the modern proletariat. To thoroughly comprehend the historical conditions and thus the very nature of this act, to impart to the now oppressed proletariat class a full knowledge of the conditions and of the *meaning* of the momentous act it is called upon to accomplish, this is the task of the theoretical expression of the proletarian movement, scientific Socialism."[14]

Once the Marxist intelligentsia thoroughly comprehends the nature of socialism, it places itself in opposition to the permanent working-class movement under capitalism, which maintains the class antagonism, and instead advocates the abolition of the capitalistic property relations. Here is how the matter is stated by Marx:

"Instead of the conservative motto, 'A fair day's wages for a fair day's work!' they [the working class] out to inscribe on their banner the revolutionary watchword, 'Abolition of the wages system!' "[15]

Those who understand scientific socialism lead the majority working-class as it exists under capitalism to eliminate capitalism, and working-class rule replaces capitalistic rule. There is a temporary dictatorship of the working-class during the period of transition; that is, they use the power of the state to enforce the elimination of capitalistic ownership of industry, and their rule is maintained until cooperative production is well established. Eventually there is a withering away of the state bureaucracy, and self-government of the workers, or the ideal of majority rule, is accomplished. Here are Marx's words on this:

"Between capitalist and communist society lies the period of the revolutionary transformation of the one into the other. There corresponds to this also a political transition period in which the state can be nothing but the revolutionary dictatorship of the proletariat."[16]

To be more exact, "the revolutionary dictatorship of the proletariat" means their rise to political rule by means of majority voting power: ". . . the proletariat must first of all acquire political supremacy, must rise to be the leading class of the nation, must constitute itself the nation."[17]

Communism is founded on the idea of a temporary dictatorship of the workers and a temporary rule of state bureaucracy. During the time of the abolition of capitalism there is a dictatorship of the workers, that is, it is the will of the working-class which ends capitalistic rule. However, after capitalism is destroyed, the rule of state bureaucracy cannot disappear because of the organization of state communism itself. The despotic government which exists under state ownership follows as a natural outcome of the bureaucratic planning of all lines of production. Also, under a method of production in which all phases of economic life are under the rule of the centralized bureaucracy, dictatorship rule cannot be temporary. It could not disappear and become working-class rule unless there was a change in the method of production organization. If the state as part of production should disappear so that each cooperative enterprise would operate independent of the government bureaucracy, this would be an accomplishment of the ideal, namely, a self-operating cooperative system. Engels' words that state interference in all branches of production will eventually become unnecessary would then be materialized:

"The first act by virtue of which the State really constitutes itself the representative of the whole of society—the taking possession of the means of production in the name of society—this is, at the same time, its last independent act as a State. State interference in social relations becomes, in one domain after another, superfluous, and then dies out of itself; the government of persons is replaced by the administration of things, and by the conduct of processes of production. The State is not 'abolished.' It dies out."[18]

There is no permanent dictatorship under associated production, but a temporary rule of the working-class during the period of transition. When the capitalist-class no longer exists and all production has become cooperative in form, there is no further need for the rule of one class over another, as there is just a union of free and independent individuals in the cooperative enterprise. Under state communism, on the other hand, the rule of bureaucracy is maintained indefinitely. While working-class rule exists under cooperative production, it is government bureaucracy which rules under nationalized industry.

### Section 4.—State Ownership of Land.

Private possession of land is eliminated along with all private ownership of buildings and other improvements on the land when communism is established. State enterprises are established on the land, and members of the organizations are ordered what and how much to produce by the government bureaucracy. It is the state which determines how the land shall be used, not those working on the land.

It will be proved later that this form of agriculture is not what Karl Marx advocated. But it is enough to say now that as long as the landlord with his collection of ground rent is eliminated, there is no other form of land ownership which is interfered with. The Russians, for example, made the mistake of interfering with ownership by the producers working on the land. The state became the only land owner and assumed the private landlord's place in collecting ground rent.

Associated production is less destructive of the rights of property than communism because those who inhabit the land continue to own it legally and are free to buy and sell it. They are not ordered by the state what they may possess since the freedom to purchase products by society is not interfered with, including the freedom to own buildings and other improvements on the land.

## Section 5.—A Forceful Establishment.

According to Marxist theory, capitalism is destroyed either by legal or forceful means. The more advanced the status of the working-class under capitalism, that is, the more benefits given it under capitalism, the less violent is the revolutionary change. In nations with the republican method of government it is established legally, while in the less advanced nations the forceful method is used. With reference to this, Marx states that it is to the interests of the ruling class to better the conditions of the working-class, so that when the time arrives for economic change it will come to pass legally:

"In England the progress of social distintegration is palpable. When it has reached a certain point, it must react on the continent. There it will take a form more brutal or more humane, according to the degree of the development of the working-class itself. Apart from higher motives, therefore, their own most important interests dictate to the classes that are for the nonce the ruling ones, the removal of all legally removable hindrances to the free development of the working-class itself."[19]

Even though original Marxist theory justifies both the legal and forceful method of establishment, the follower of communism usually advocates the use of forceful methods, because Russia, the first nation to destroy capitalism, accomplished it by forceful means. Government is taken over by the organized force of the working-class, not by their voting strength. Once the tools of central government are taken over by force, the means of production of the nation become owned by the government, without legal compensation to the former owners. Lack of property compensation is sometimes justified by the followers of communism in Marx's theory that the original value of the capitalist's investment has already been regained by taking value without payment from the working-class, once he has consumed a value equal to his capital. However, this was not Marx's intention and should not be advocated.

"When he [the capitalist] has consumed the equivalent of his original capital, the value of his present capital represents nothing but the total amount of the surplus-value appropriated by him without payment. Not a single atom of the value of his old capital continues to exist."[20]

After capitalism has been destroyed, great confusion reigns due to a lack in definite knowledge of the system that is to take the place of capitalism. The government aims at materializing the exact word of the *Communist Manifesto*—not *Capital*—because the book only hints at the exact form of communism through an explanation of capitalism. However, an understanding of associated production requires a complete study of Marx's writings, not an occasional quotation, and an explanation of associated production is no easy matter as can be seen from the length of this book, as well as the three volumes of *Capital* which it explains. Even the study of *Capital* must cover a period of years as its writing on Marx's part required a lifetime. It is possible that Marx wrote *Capital* in order to explain what he meant in the *Communist Manifesto*. This is especially true in the case of his explanation of "ground rent," as will be seen later in the chapter on capitalism. He did it with the hope that someone would be able to give new meaning to words as he did.

Of course, each student of Marx believes that his explanation of *Capital* is correct, and therefore he is one of the Marxist intelligentsia. There is one thing certain, however, and it is this. Those who believe in state communism are not the Marxist intelligentsia, because such communism does not materialize the ideal of a "stateless" economic system. But they do accomplish something equally important. They honor the words of Karl Marx and make his words generally known; and in the case of the Russians, it is proved through great hardship that state planning of all branches of production is impractical from the standpoint of freedom for the individual. They experiment with first one interpretation and then another, while the people live under hardship and confusion as the various experiments are materialized. Any deviation from communist accepted theories is prevented by the threat of retaliation from the government in power.

Control by forceful methods under communism is not an advancement over the rule by force that exists under capitalism. Even though under capitalism the workers are subject to control by the owners of production, their control under state ownership by a hierarchy of bureaucracy does not better the condition of the worker. While under capitalism the freedom of capital owners to own the worker's means of production does force submission on the part of the majority of society, under communism the power of state law is used to force the plans of the government bureaucracy on to society in general. Freedom for the worker does not exist under either system.

It is only when there are no longer two classes in production and the rule of bureaucracy under state communism will have given way to the self-government of the workers, that equality for all individuals can be accomplished. Here is how this same idea is stated by Marx: ". . . with the abolition of class differences all the social and political inequality arising from them would disappear of itself."[21]

### Section 6.—World Organization by Centralized Dictatorship.

In Marxist theory there is no definite plan for world organization after the destruction of capitalism is accomplished. The capitalist system is eliminated in each individual nation, and peace between nations is permanently accomplished.

The experience of the revolution in Russia has given rise to centralized control over all Marxist socialism. While this control has become diminished in recent years, the fundamental power remains. Because many socialists in all nations look upon Karl Marx as the intellectual leader of revolutionary change, and because the Russian nation idealizes the words of Marx, many go willingly under the will of this particular "Marxist intelligentsia." The Marxists in each individual nation are not independent but they are centrally controlled.

After capitalism would have been generally destroyed in all nations by means of centralized dictatorship, there would probably be a planning of world production, not just a planning of national production as under the associated method. Under such conditions there would be no definite barrier in the development of world government. With a lack in control of such international government, world despotism by a centralized bureaucracy can at least be imagined.* However, if the demise of capitalism should be accompanied by a federation of nations instead of a centralized dictatorship, freedom for all nations would be maintained. The abolition of capitalism would not mean a loss in the already established freedoms, but an enlargement of freedom.

Marxist theory claims that a world wide revolutionary change should come to pass through an independent destruction of capitalism in each country, not by the force of an outside nation:

". . . the struggle of the proletariat with the bourgeoisie is at first a national struggle. The proletariat of each country must, of course, settle matters with its own bourgeoisie.[22] The international activity of the working classes does not in any way depend on the existence of the International Workingmen's Association."[23]

In other words, there is no need for the control of one nation over others in order to accomplish a revolutionary change in individual countries. However, Marx and Engels do mention that the leading civilized nations should begin the world wide revolutionary change by establishing associated production without their boundaries, thereby forming a pattern which others can follow:

"United action, of the leading civilized countries at least, is one of the first conditions for the emancipation of the proletariat."[24]

The question is, why have not the leading civilized nations naturally taken the leadership in establishing socialism within their boundaries and brought about a world-wide revolutionary change as a result of it? The answer to this problem is found in the fact that the followers of socialism have not yet given a picture of socialism that is powerful enough to cause the leading nations to revolutionize production. When Russia accomplished the destruction of capitalism it did not have an ideal picture of socialism before it; therefore, it could not be expected that all other nations would follow naturally in its leadership. In other words, a knowledge of socialism must precede its universal accomplishment.

If we assume that the ideal form of socialism does find understanding—something which, according to Marx's theory of economic

---

* This is no longer possible in our time; in the past it could have existed, though, before the recently improved understanding of Marx.

necessity, must inevitably come to pass as a result of study once the time for world-wide socialism is at hand—then the Russian form of communism would give way to this ideal version. After a changed understanding of Marx within Russia itself, dictatorship in national production would disappear, along with dictatorship over other nations. Because the workers in each nation would take care of their own capitalist-class, there would then be no need for a centralized dictatorship and division among nations.

While there is no direct reference to a federation of nations in Marx's writings, yet his and Engels' words do describe the universal friendliness of peoples which a federation of nations would formally materialize:

"National differences and antagonism between peoples are daily more and more vanishing, owing to the development of the bourgeoisie, to freedom of commerce, to the world-market, to uniformity in the mode of production and in the conditions of life corresponding thereto." [25]

However, Marx states, in addition, that it is not the purpose of socialists to destroy the individuality of nations:

"The unity of the nation was not to be broken [under associated production] . . . that unity of great nations which, if originally brought about by political force, has now become a powerful coefficient of social production." [26]

If there should be a federation of nations, there would be world organization, but the maintenance of national individuality would keep government close to the people.

# Chapter III

# CAPITALISM

## Section 1.—A Competitive System.

Under capitalism each line of commodity production is divided into competitive enterprises, with their production under the control of the price system. The price system, in turn, is dependent on money as a measure of commodity value. Marx explains how, in the course of history, gold as one commodity among others assumes the money form. He calls gold "the pure form of value." [1]

Gold is the pure form of value because like all other commodities it requires a definite amount of labor-time for its production, which includes also the labor-time contained in its means of production. Later, token money assumes the place of gold, but this token money still represents the gold commodity which contains a given amount of labor-time. Thus, when money representing ¼ ounce gold is worth so much linen, then theoretically speaking, these two quantities of the commodities gold and linen contain equal quantities of labor-time. As the labor-time in either of these commodities falls, so does their relation to one another change. As the "pure form of value," gold not only measures the value of linen but also the value of all other commodities on the market.

Now when Marx states that commodities are sold at their values, it can also mean they are sold at modifications of their values. Under capitalism, for example, the price of a commodity is determined by its cost price in labor-power and means of production, plus the general rate of profit on the total capital invested. This "price of production" becomes the form of value production which exists under capitalism. It will be explained later in more detail how even under capitalism the prices of commodities are controlled by the law of value, or their price is determined by approximate quantities of labor-time contained in them. It is enough to say now that the

37

"price of production" of a commodity becomes the ideal market value of a commodity, around which the daily market prices oscillate according to changes in supply and demand.

Even when commodities are not sold at their values in the case of slight deviations between supply and demand, Marx considers them as sold at their values, since the deviations balance each other. As for the cause of deviations between price and value, they are caused by changes in the relation of supply and demand, or competition. Marx refers to the balancing of supply and demand as a cessation of the deviation of market price from the regulating average price or "the cessation of the influence of competition."[2]

Now all forms of commodity production include the determination of their values by labor-time, plus oscillations above and below their values caused by competition, or changes in supply and demand. For instance, even under the cooperative method these conditions exist, because as Marx writes, "the determination of value continues to prevail" under social production.[3]

The existence of competition between producers in an individual sphere is an important characteristic of commodity production. In reference to this, Marx writes that "competition can . . . make the producers within the same sphere of production sell their commodities at the same prices and make them sell their commodities in different spheres of production at prices which will give them the same profit."[4]

The mere fact that the law of value continues to function under the cooperative method implies the existence of competitive producers in the individual spheres, even though there is voluntary association for the purpose of regulating production and avoiding crisis. What distinguishes the cooperative method of commodity production from the capitalistic one is that it is understood by the common mind just what is causing a crisis; that is, it is caused by nothing more complicated than an over-supply of commodities which results in a fall in commodity prices or crisis. To avoid a crisis, then, it is only necessary to avoid overproduction in a particular sphere. If one sphere brings crisis under control, then so do all spheres.

Under capitalism, however, there is constant speculation as to an approaching crisis, with no exact understanding of what it is, or what will stop it. In this regard, Marx calls the law of value a blind law under capitalism: "Only as an internal law, and from the point of view of the individual agents *as a blind law*, does the law of value exert its influence here and maintain the social equilibrium of production in the turmoil of its accidental fluctuations."[5]

As Marx expresses the idea more directly, "the sphere of competition . . . considered in each individual case, is dominated by accident. In other words, the internal law, which enforces itself in these accidents and regulates them, does not become visible until large numbers of these accidents are grouped together [i.e., in the general economic crisis]. It remains invisible and unintelligible to the individual agents in production."[6]

But it is a generally known fact that capitalism is not always in the midst of a general economic crisis. There are periods of time when production is normal, or there is a social equilibrium of production, even though the producers themselves are unaware of how the law of value is holding the system in order, that is, even though it is a "blind law."

This, then, is the price system which is common to both capitalism and associated production, and which we shall now analyze further from the standpoint of competition. Marx explains that it is competition which determines the quantity of commodity production. He defines competition as "the sale or purchase of commodities above and below their values."[7] A rise in prices yields higher profits from enterprise and influences additional production, whereas a fall in prices brings less production. There is not only competition (a rise and fall in prices) in individual spheres which causes the producers to produce more or less, but there is a change from one sphere to another under the influence of competition, or a rise and fall in prices.

"If the prices of commodities in a certain sphere are below or above the price of production (leaving aside any oscillations, which are found in every business and are due to fluctuations of the industrial cycles), a balance is effected by an expansion or restriction of production. This signifies an expansion or restriction of the quantities of commodities thrown on the market by industrial capitalists, by means of an immigration or emigration of capital to and from particular spheres."[8]

There is another quotation from Marx which describes the operation of competition as a determinant of production but not value. He writes that supply and demand is brought into coordination by changes in market price. But competition (a change in supply and demand) ceases to act as a determinant of market price once supply and demand are in coordination. It should be noticed that Marx defines competition from two different points of view. In the above case, he defined competition as "the sale or purchase of commodities above and below their values" according to changes in supply and demand; then in the following quotation it is defined as competition between the producers in an individual sphere. However, neither of these is a determinant of value.

"We have . . . assumed that competition ceases to act as a determinant, that it abolishes its effects by the equilibrium of its two opposing forces [supply and demand]. . . . The average profit must be determined by an average rate of profit; how is this rate determined? By the competition between the capitalists? But this competition itself is conditioned upon the existence of profit. It presupposes the existence of different rates of profit, and thus of different profit, either in the same or in different spheres of production. Competition can influence the rate of profit only to the extent that it affects the prices of commodities. Competition can merely make the producers in the same sphere of production sell their commodities at the same prices, and make them sell their commodities in different spheres of production at prices which will give them the same profit. . . . Hence competition cannot balance anything but inequalities in the rate of profit. In order to balance unequal rates of profit, the profit as an element in the price of commodities must already exist. Competition does not create it. It lowers or raises its level [i.e., by changes in market price], but it does not create this level, which appears whenever the balance has been struck [i.e., the coordination of supply and demand, and the sale of commodities at their price of production]."[9]

In other words, the value of a commodity exists to begin with; it is not created by either changes in the relation between supply and demand or competition between the producers.

### a. *The Law of Commodity Value*

We shall now go into a detailed explanation of Marx's "law of commodity value." It is an important study because it proves once and for all what Marx means by "planned production."

Before we can analyze how an oversupply or undersupply of a commodity causes its price to fall or rise, it must first be known what the value of the commodity is. As Marx tells us, the value of a commodity is the important point of understanding:

" . . . the change in the relations of demand and supply [explains] in regard to the price of . . . commodities, nothing except its changes, i.e., the oscillations of the market price above or below a certain mean. If demand and supply balance, the oscillation of prices ceases, all other conditions remaining the same. But then demand and supply also cease to explain anything. The price of [a commodity], at the moment when demand and supply are in equilibrium, is its natural price, determined independently of the relation of demand and supply.[10] The exchange, or sale, of commodities at their value is the rational way, the natural law of their equilibrium. It must be the point of departure for the explanation of deviations from it, not vice versa the deviations the basis on which this law is explained."[11]

For the time being, then, we will leave aside the question of supply and demand in order to find what it is that determines the value of a commodity. According to Marx's theory, the value of a commodity is determined by the quantity of labor-time necessary to produce it, and the quantity of labor-time incorporated in a commodity includes the labor-time necessary in the production of the raw materials and instruments of production, as well as the new labor added during the productive process:

"A use-value, or useful article . . . has value only because human labour in the abstract has been embodied or materialized in it. How, then, is the magnitude of this value to be measured? Plainly, by the quantity of value-creating substance, the labour, contained in the article. The quantity of labour, however, is measured by its duration, and labour-time in its turn finds its standard in weeks, days, and hours."[12]

The total value of a commodity is equal to the value of the raw materials contained in it, the value of the auxiliary materials used up in its production, that portion of the value of the instruments of production which is lost by depreciation during the productive process, and the value newly added by the laborer to the product. Let us assume the value of the raw and auxiliary materials consumed for production of a particular commodity amounts to $11, and a $1 value in the instruments of production is lost by depreciation for its manufacture. Now suppose each $1 in value produced represents 1 hour of labor-time. There is then 12 hours of past materialized labor-time contained in the $12 value of the consumed means of production.

Let us imagine that 8 hours of new labor-time is required to transform the raw and auxiliary materials into a new product. Let us also suppose that the average daily expense for the worker's means of subsistence such as food, clothing, housing, etc., is $5. Since we have assumed that each $1 congealed value represents 1 hour of labor-time, then the worker's daily means of subsistence contain 5 hours of materialized labor-time. Under capitalism the private owner will pay the worker $5 in wages so that he can buy his $5 in means of subsistence and put him to work for 8 hours time. After 5 hours in time has elapsed the laborer has added a $5 value to the materials of production which replaces the $5 in wages paid him by the capitalist for his 8 hour day, since we have assumed that each hour of labor-time produces a value of $1. During the last 3 hours of the work day the worker produces $1 an hour just as he does in the first 5 hours of the work day. As the last 3 hours pass by, he produces $3 above and beyond his wages, and this $3 is surplus-value for the capitalist. Marx writes that it is the appropriation of surplus-value from the laborer that makes production **capitalistic**:

"The process of production, considered on the one hand as the unity of the labour-process and the process of creating value, is production of commodities; considered on the other hand as the unity of the labour-process and the process of producing surplus-value, it is the capitalist process of production, or capitalist production of commodities."[13]

The $3 value produced by the worker during the last 3 hours of his working day is surplus-value because the capitalist takes it without paying an equivalent value to the laborer who produced it. During his 8 hour working day the worker adds a total value of $8 to the $12 in raw and auxiliary materials, and machinery depreciation given up for the production of the commodity. The commodity produced has a total value of $20, and since each dollar of its value represents 1 hour of congealed labor-time, there are 20 hours of past materialized labor-time contained in it. When the capitalist sells his commodity at a price of $20, he is selling it at its value determined by the labor-time contained it it. Yet, at the same time, he is gaining $3 surplus-value from its sale.

Now that we have seen how surplus-value is appropriated from production, let us see how surplus-value is appropriated by means of the investment of surplus-value in production. Marx calls the investment of surplus-value in production, "the accumulation of capital."[14]

Let us suppose that a particular capitalist advanced $10,000 to production, of which 4/5 ($8,000) was invested in means of production, including raw materials, machinery, etc., and 1/5 ($2,000) in wages. We will imagine he produces 600 commodities annually, with a total value of $12,000. Of the $12,000 value produced, $8,000 of it, or 400 of the produced commodities, represents a reappearance of the value of the $8,000 in means of production contained in the 600 commodities, while $2,000 of it, or 100 commodities, represents the value invested in labor-power. And last of all, $2,000 of the $12,000 value produced, or 100 of the 600 commodities represents the surplus-value or surplus-product appropriated by the capitalist without payment. When the total 600 commodities are sold, the capitalist has regained his original capital of $10,000, and, in addition, he has gained $2,000 in surplus-value.

Now let us imagine that the $2,000 surplus-value is to be put back into production along with the original $10,000, making a total outlay of $12,000. Four fifths ($9,600) is invested in means of production and 1/5 ($2,400) in wages. Suppose that under these conditions, 720 commodities are produced annually, with a total value of $14,400. The capitalist has invested $12,000, and appropriated $14,400, which makes his surplus value $2,400. He has gained $2,400 in surplus-value annually instead of $2,000 because of the investment of surplus-value in production.

This continual investment of surplus-value in production on a progressive scale is an example of the accumulation of capital. The more surplus-value the capitalist invests in enterprise, the more surplus-value he appropriates. The following words of Marx expose the motives of capitalist production:

"By turning his money into commodities that serve as the material elements of a new product, and as factors in the labour-process, by incorporating living labour with their dead substance, the capitalist at the same time converts value, i.e., past, materialized, and dead labour into capital, into value big with value, a live monster that is fruitful and multiplies." [15]

The capitalist, then, does not produce to satisfy wants but in order to produce more and more surplus-value. In our illustration we assumed that the capitalist hired only one laborer. As a matter of fact, under normal conditions the capitalist hires a large number of laborers and therefore appropriates surplus-value from many individuals. He produces a certain number of products daily, depending upon the number of wage-laborers hired to produce them, and is one capitalist producer among others that produce the same kind of commodity. Capitalist production is carried on upon a large scale, with a large or small number of competitive capitalist producers in each branch of enterprise.

We will imagine that all of the competitive producers in a given line of industry bring—as cooperative products—a total of 10,000 commodities to the market as a whole, or a total value of $200,000, assuming that each commodity has a value of $20 determined by the labor-time contained in it. This total product of 10,000 commodities is the result of a collective process, or it is the effect of all producers of a particular commodity bringing their produce to market. In reference to this, Marx writes that the supply of a commodity is the cooperative product of independent producers in an entire line of production:

"If we look closer at the matter, we find that the conditions determining the value of some individual commodity become effective . . . as conditions determining the value of the total quantities of a certain kind. For, generally speaking, capitalist production is from the outset a mass-production. And even other, less developed, modes of production carry small quantities of products, the result of the work of many small producers, to market as co-operative products . . . concentrating and accumulating them for sale in the hands of relatively few merchants. Such commodities are regarded as *co-operative products of an entire line of production.*"[16]

Even though the total product brought to market by the various competitive producers is the result of a collective process, still there is no associated control over this co-operative product as there is under associated enterprise. Under the capitalist method, each competitive producer has a plan of his own for the production of a particular commodity. That the total supply of the commodity meet the total demand under such conditions is a matter of chance. Marx implies that a "social control over production" means a regulation of the total supply of commodities in each individual line, when he writes that the social character of production and consumption is manifested in (1) the total supply, and (2) the total demand for a given commodity. In other words, he does not mean that the total of all lines of production carried on simultaneously is a group process that needs government control; he means that there is no unified control over the total supply of the commodity as there is under the associated method.

"In a question of supply and demand . . . the supply means the sum of the sellers, or producers, of a certain kind of commodities, and the demand the sum of the buyers, or consumers, of the same kind of commodities (both productive and individual consumers). There two bodies react on one another as units, as aggregate forces. The individual counts here only as a part of a social power, as an atom of some mass, and it is in this form that *competition* enforces the *social character of production and consumption.*[17] In the effects of [over-production] the fact that *production as a social process is not subject to social control* is strikingly emphasized. . . ."[18]

We can assume, then, that social control of production means (for Marx) the control exerted by a voluntary association of the competitive producers. With this taken for granted, let us return to our illustration.

Let us imagine that while the total supply of a commodity on the market amounts to 10,000 pieces valued at $200,000, the total demand is for only 8,000. This means there are 2,000 pieces of the commodity on the market that is not demanded of it. There is $160,-000 in money ready to purchase 8,000 commodities, but there are 10,000 products with a value of $200,000 ready to be sold. While the 10,000 articles having a total value of $200,000 are worth $20 each, they would not be sold at a price of $20 under such conditions. Due to the 2,000 piece surplus of the commodity, the prices of all 10,000 would fall below their value of $20 each. For instance, the market demands 8,000 articles, and the exchange value of 8,000 pieces at $20 each is $160,000. The 10,000 commodities on the market would be sold at a total price of $160,000, or that figure which represents the exchange value of the 8,000 piece demanded quantity of the product. Each of the 10,000 articles would sell at a price of $16 instead of $20 because of a 2,000 piece oversupply. The labor-time devoted to the 2,000 surplus commodities would be wasted because it creates no new value, that is, 10,000 products would be sold at the value of 8,000 just as if the 2,000 extra ones had not been produced.

As Marx describes this, the total supply and total demand are represented by different factors. The use-value or commodity produced represents the supply, while the exchange-value, or money expressing the socially required quantity of labor-time contained in the commodity, represents the demand. While the exchange-value of an individual commodity is determined by the labor-time socially necessary to produce it, the value of the total supply is equal to the total labor-time that society requires of that particular line of production. If the supply exceeds the demand then the total supply is sold at the total value of the quantity demanded, since it is total demand which determines the exchange-value of commodities. Thus Marx writes:

"The proportion of supply and demand repeats, in the first place, the relation of the use-value and exchange-value of commodities, of commodity and money, of buyer and seller; in the second place the relation of producer and consumer. . . ."[19] Although both commodity and money represent units of exchange-value and use-value, we have already seen in volume I, chapter I, 3, that in buying and selling both of these functions are polarised at the two extremes, the commodity (seller) representing the use-value, and the money (buyer) the exchange-value. It was one of the first conditions for the sale of a commodity that it should have a use-value and satisfy some social need. The other essential condition was that the quantity of labor contained in a certain commodity should represent socially necessary labor, so that its individual value (and what amounts to the same under the present assumption, its selling price) should coincide with its social value. Now let us apply this to the mass of commodities on the market, which represent the product of a whole sphere of production. The matter will be most easily explained by regarding this whole mass of commodities, coming from one line of production, as one single commodity, and the sum of the prices of the many identical commodities as one price. In that case the statements made in regard to one individual commodity apply literally to the mass of commodities sent to the market by one entire line of production. The postulate that the individual value of a commodity should correspond to its social value has then the significance that the total quantity of commodities contains the quantity of social labor necessary for its production, and that the value of this mass is equal to its market-value.[20] "Consider . . . the supply . . . every individual article, or every definite quantity of any kind of commodities, contains, perhaps, only the social labor required for its production. . . . Nevertheless, if this commodity has been produced in excess of the temporary demand of society for it, so much of the social labor has been wasted, and in that case this mass of commodities represents a much smaller quantity of labor on the market than is actually incorporated in it.[21] ". . . take it that proportionally too much cotton goods have been produced, although only the labor-time necessary for this total product under the prevailing conditions is realised in it. But too much social labor has been expended in this particular line, in other words, a portion of this product is useless. *The whole of it is therefore sold only as though it had been produced in the necessary proportion.* This *quantitative limit* of the quota of social labor available for the various particular spheres is but a wider expression of the law of value, although the necessary labor-time assumes a different meaning here. Only just so much of it is required for the satisfaction of the social needs. The limitation is here due to the use-value. Society can use only so much of its total labor for this particular kind of products under the prevailing conditions of production.[22] ". . . it is in the form of the market price . . . that the nature of value asserts itself in commodities. It becomes evident, in this way, that it is not determined by the labor-time necessary in the case of any individual producer for the production of a certain quantity of commodities, or of some individual commodity, but by the *socially necessary labor-time. This is that quantity of labor-time, which is necessary for the production of the socially required total quantity of commodities of any kind on the market* under the existing average conditions of social production."[23]

When Marx uses the term "socially necessary labor-time" here he means the total work-time contained in the commodities demanded. In order to find this total labor-time, we multiply 20 hours times 8,000 pieces (assuming that each commodity contains 20 hours of necessary labor) and this gives 160,000 hours as the labor-time required to produce the 8,000 articles demanded. 160,000 hours is the socially required labor-time of whatever quantity of commodities is produced by the given line of production, that is, whether 8,000 or 10,000 commodities represent the total supply. Since we have assumed that each hour of labor-time represents a value produced of $1, then the monetary value of the total supply is $160,000.

It was our assumption that each commodity in our illustration had a value of $20 determined by the labor-time contained in it. However, there was an over production of 2,000 commodities which made the price fall to $16. From the $16 that the competitive capitalist appropriates from the sale of the product, he gains the $12 he paid out for materials of production, $4 of the $5 he paid out as wages, and no $3 profit. The commodity sale of the various competive enterprises has not given them a profit because of a discrepancy between supply and demand. As Marx writes:

"The minimum limit of the selling price of commodities is indicated by their cost-price [i.e., the value of the wages and means of production necessary in their production]. If they are sold below their cost-price, then the consumed elements of productive capital cannot be fully reproduced out of the selling price. If this sort of thing continues, then the value of the advanced capital disappears."[24]

Let us now suppose that there is an undersupply rather than an oversupply. Take it that the total demand for the commodities increases from 8,000 to 10,000, and there are only 8,000 brought to market. In this case the 8,000 commodities on the market with a value of $160,000 would be sold for $200,000, the value of the 10,-000 that are demanded, or that are socially necessary. In other words, each of the 8,000 commodities on the market would be sold at a price of $25 instead of at their $20 value because of the 2,000 piece undersupply.

We see, then, that the quantity of the total demand must be known, just as the number of products in the total supply must be known, if the two opposing forces are to be compared for the purpose of considering the effect of deviations between supply and demand on the market prices of commodities. Marx writes as follows:

". . . this question of the extent of a certain demand becomes essential, whenever the product of some entire line of production is placed on one side, and the social demand for it on the other. In that case it becomes necessary to consider the amount, the quantity, of this social demand."[25]

However, a comparison of the quantity of the total demand and total supply could not alone explain prices. All that could be explained by such a comparison would be that the prices of commodities fall above and below a particular natural price according to the conditions of supply and demand. Supply and demand cannot explain why price fluctuations remain around a certain value and no other. As Marx explains:

"Nothing is easier than to realise the inequalities of demand and supply and the resulting deviation of market-prices from market values. The real difficulty consists in determining what is meant by balancing supply and demand. . . . If demand and supply balance, then they cease to have any effect, and for this reason commodities are sold at their market values. If two forces exert themselves equally in opposite directions, they balance one another, they have no influence at all on the outside, and any phenomena taking place at the same time must be explained by other causes than the influence of these forces. If demand and supply balance one another, they cease to explain anything, they do not affect market values, and therefore leave us even more in the dark than before concerning the reasons for the expression of the market value in just a certain sum of money and no other."[26]

For instance, if 10,000 commodities are demanded and 10,000 of them with a value of $200,000 are brought to market, then each commodity is sold at a price of $20, as the supply is in direct coordination with the demand. Now suppose the value of the 10,000 commodities is reduced by ½ because of a decrease in labor-time, so that each of the 10,000 articles has a value of $10, with a total value of $100,000. If we imagine that the supply is in coordination with the demand, which we will assume as before is for 10,000 commodities, then each article is sold at a price of $10. The coordination of supply and demand is still represented by 10,000 commodities, yet the price of the product has changed.* And this proves that the

---

\* In the book, "On Economic Knowledge" (1965), written by Adolph Lowe, an outstanding economist who had read all of my above explanation of value before and after its publication in 1963, he gives an interesting comment on page 40: "In this terminal state of . . . 'equilibrium' . . . all quantities supplied are supposed to be equal to all quantities demanded, this

relations of supply and demand do not explain the natural value of commodities but only deviations from this natural value. According to Marx:

"It is admitted [by the ordinary economist] that with two different natural prices of the same commodity at different times demand and supply may balance one another and must balance one another, if the commodity is to be sold at its natural price in both instances. Since there is no difference in the proportion of supply and demand in either case, but only a difference in the magnitude of the natural price itself, it follows that this price is determined independently of demand and supply, and cannot very well be determined by them." [27]

In other words, it is not supply and demand which determines the natural value of commodities. Their value is determined by the quantity of labor-time necessary to produce them. To prove otherwise would be an impossibility at this stage of understanding.

Let us return to the question of changes in the natural value of commodities due to changes in necessary labor-time. We will assume that the price of the $20 commodity in our illustration falls because of a decrease in the labor-time necessary to produce it, not because of an oversupply of it on the market. Take it that one of the competitive capitalists uses an improved method of production so that two commodities are produced in 8 hours labor-time rather than just one. Each of the commodities has a $12 value in raw and auxiliary materials and machinery depreciation contained in it, and 4 hours of new labor-time, or $4 of newly produced value. The new total value of the product is $16, not $20. If two $16 commodities are produced daily by the laborer, then the daily product of his 8 hours in labor-time has a total value of $32. We know that $24 of this $32 value represents the materials used up in the manufacture of the two articles, and $8 is the new value produced in them during the 8 hours labor-time of the worker. If the capitalist

---

equality occurring at the lowest level of prices that is compatible with the technical conditions of production. . . . At long last we understand the full significance of the movements which the Law of Supply and Demand describes and as a consequence the central position which the law holds in the theory of the market." But shouldn't at least Karl Marx been given the credit?

sells each of his commodities for $18, he is selling them at a price $2 above their value of $16 each, or is gaining $2 extra profit on each commodity; however, he is selling them at a price $2 lower than the other capitalists in his line of industry who sell at a price of $20. The capitalist who introduces the new method of production is compelled to lower its price below the old $20 value in order to create an increased demand for the extra commodity that is produced in the 8 hours labor-time. The other capitalists are then forced to introduce the improved method of production in order to compete with the capitalist who has introduced the new method. In this way, the price of the commodity becomes generally reduced to its new social value.[28]

Under associated production, if this $20 product should be produced in one half the work-time, its market price would still have to be lowered to a new price by the cooperative enterprises because there would then be twice as many of the articles produced by so much labor-time, and they would lower their prices in order to create a demand for the increased quantity manufactured. Thus Marx explains that the law of value will continue to operate in determining the value of products under the associated method:

"Whatever may be the way in which the prices of the various commodities are first fixed or mutually regulated, *the law of value always dominates their movements.* If the labor time required for the production of these commodities is reduced, prices fall. . . ."[29] This reduction of the total quantity of labor incorporated in a certain commodity seems to be the essential mark of an increase in the productive power of labor, no matter under what sort of social conditions production is carried on. There is no doubt that the productivity of labor *would be measured by this standard* in a society, in which the producers would regulate their production according to a preconceived plan, or even under a simple production of commodities."[30]

This is in contradiction to the general idea that the abolition of capitalism constitutes an end to the constant improvement in factory methods. Here are Marx's words on this:

"Any employment of machinery, except by capital, is to him [the apologist of capitalism] an impossibility. Exploitation of the workman by the machine is therefore, with him, identical with exploitation of the machine by the workman. Whoever, therefore exposes the real state of things in the capitalistic employment of machinery, is against its employment in any way, and is an enemy of social progress!"[31]

Assuming, then, that there is a continuation of social progress under social enterprise, let us go on to a further analysis of the price system. With reference to its more detailed analysis, Marx has the following to say. He seems to be referring to the price system as it should exist under the cooperative method, and as it occasionally does exist under capitalism.

" In order that the prices at which commodities are exchanged with one another may correspond approximately to their values, no other conditions are required but the following: 1) The exchange of the various commodities must no longer be accidental or occasional, 2) So far as the direct exchange of commodities is concerned, these commodities must be produced on both sides in sufficient quantities to meet mutual requirements, a thing easily learned by experience in trading, and therefore a natural outgrowth of continued trading, 3) So far as selling is concerned, there must be no accidental or artificial monopoly which may enable either of the contracting sides to sell commodities above their value or compel others to sell below value. An accidental monopoly is one which a buyer or seller acquires by an accidental proportion of supply to demand."[32]

This, of course, implies that no monopolies should exist under associated production, although a voluntary association in the individual spheres for the purpose of regulating production would prevent the sale of commodities from being accidental or occasional. As for selling, the mercantile trade is competitive.

Let us see how the competition between buyers and sellers operates. Suppose, first of all, that the sellers of a particular type of product have an accidental undersupply, that is, suppose the total demand for a particular commodity changes so that the demand exceeds the supply. The buyers would begin to bid at a higher price because of the undersupply, and then all buyers would have to spend more for the commodity. At the same time, the sellers would seek to gain as high a price as possible. On the other hand, if there was an oversupply caused by a change in demand, the buyers would have the favorable position. Because of the oversupply the sellers would begin to sell their products at prices below value, while the buyers would aim at paying as low a price as possible. The following is Marx's explanation of the competition between buyers and sellers:

"That side of competition, which is momentarily weaker, is also that in which the individual acts independently of the mass of his competitors and often works against them, whereby the dependence of one upon the other is impressed upon them, while the stronger side always acts more or less unitedly against its antagonist. If the demand for this particular kind of commodities is larger than the supply, then one buyer out-bids another, within certain limits, and thereby raises the price of the commodity for all of them above the market-price, while on the other hand the sellers unite in trying to sell at a high price. If, vice versa, the supply exceeds the demand, some one begins to dispose of his goods at a cheaper rate and the others must follow, while the buyers unite in their efforts to depress the market-price as much as possible below the market-value. . . . If one side has the advantage, every one belonging to it gains. It is as though they had exerted their common monopoly."[33]

We have seen before that when a price changes as a result of changes in demand, this is actually the law of value operating, as the socially necessary labor-time is determined by the total demand. In what is to follow, Marx explains how commodities can be considered as sold at their values, even though from an actual standpoint they are sold at prices above or below their values.

For instance, take it that the value of a commodity is $10, and its price one day is $10.50 because of an undersupply on the market. Now suppose that production of the article is increased because of the rise in price above its value of $10. After the increased production the price of the product falls to $9.50 as a result of an oversupply. If we add these two prices together, $10.50 and $9.50, we find that the total price of the articles is $20, or a price that represents the total value of the two products. It is as if both articles had been sold at their values since the rise and fall in price of the particular kind of commodity balanced each other; that is, what was at first the gain of $.50 by the sale of the product above its value was later lost by its sale at $.50 below value. Thus the daily oscillations of market price cancel each other out and have the effect of the sale of products at their values. Or, to put it in another way, what was at first an undersupply later becomes an oversupply, which has the effect of bringing supply and demand into coordination. For instance, suppose 10,000 of a particular commodity are demanded and only 9,500 are brought to market. Then imagine 10,500 are brought to market because of the rise in price, and the demand is still for 10,000. The total demand amounts to 20,000, with first 9,500 and then 10,500 being brought to market, making a total of 20,000 articles, the total quantity demanded over a period of time. Supply and demand are thus brought into coordination through an alternating process of undersupply and oversupply; in other words, the balancing of supply and demand is made possible only by means of their deviations. Marx puts this idea in the following way:

"As a matter of fact supply and demand never balance, or, if they do, it is by mere accident. . . . Since supply and demand never balance each other in any given case, their differences follow one another in such a way that supply and demand are always balanced only when looking at them from the point of view of a greater or smaller period of time. For the result of a deviation in one direction is a deviation in the opposite direction. Such a balance is only an average of past movements, a result of a continual movement in contradictions. By this means the market-prices differing from the market-values reduce one another to the average of market-values and balance the different plus and minus in their divergencies. And this average figure has not merely a theoretical, but also a practical value for capital, since its investment is calculated on the fluctuations and compensations of more or less fixed periods of time."[34]

The actual everyday prices do not have to be identical with value under the new method of production. The point of the associated method as differentiated from the capitalist one is that there is an associated regulation of production, but this does not mean that slight deviations between total price and total value cease to exist. According to Marx, it is the daily oscillations of market price which maintains an equilibrium between the labor-time that is required of the various lines of production and the actual labor-time spent in them. The assumption that commodities are sold at their value means only that their value is the center of gravity around which the daily market prices fluctuate.

"In order that a commodity may be sold at its market-value, that is to say, in proportion to the necessary social labor contained in it, the total quantity of social labor devoted to the total mass of this kind of commodities must correspond to the quantity of the social demand for them, meaning the solvent social demand. Competition, the fluctuations of market-price which correspond to the fluctuations of demand and supply, tend continually to reduce the total quantity of labor devoted to each kind of commodities to this scale.[35] The assumption that the commodities of the various spheres of production are sold at their value implies, of course, only that their value is the center of gravity around which prices fluctuate, and around which their rise and fall tends to an equilibrium."[36]

Under large scale industry, the direct coordination of supply and demand would be an impossibility. It is only under the small scale enterprise of the past that a direct meeting of supply and demand was possible. For instance, in the case of small-scale production in former times, demand preceded the supply, or production was not for an unknown market as it is under large-scale factory methods. Here is Marx's explanation of this point:

"This true proportion between supply and demand which again begins to become the object of so many vows has long ceased to exist. It has died of old age. It was only possible in the epoch in which the means of production were limited, and in which the exchange only took place within very narrow limits. With the birth of great industry this just proportion disappeared. . . . What was it which maintained production in just proportion or nearly so? It was the demand which governed the supply which preceded it. Production followed consumption step by step. The great industry forced by the very instruments of which it is disposed to produce on an ever increasing scale could not wait for the demand. Production preceded consumption, the supply forced the demand.[37] The quantity of commodities produced by capitalist production depends on the scale of production and on the continual necessity for expansion following from this production. It does not depend on a predestined circle of supply and demand, nor on certain wants to be supplied. *Production on a large scale* can have no other buyer, apart from other industrial capitalists, than the wholesale merchant."[38]

Because slight deviations between total supply and total demand continue under associated production, there is also a continuation of the sale and purchase of commodities above and below their values, or competition, just as there is under capitalism when production is normal. Marx writes that when the inner connection of prices is understood, it will then be realized there is no need of continuing the capitalist system. Thus, after a complete analysis of the "law of value" it is now known what a control over production means; also, that Marx intended to perpetuate the operation of the "law of value" in production, not eliminate it.

When we illustrated that labor-time is a measure of value under associated production as well as capitalism by showing that a decrease in necessary labor-time causes prices to fall under both systems, we proved that value is independent of the capitalist system, or continues to exist after its abolition. But this was not the main point of understanding. The important thing was to understand how the law of value operates in production as a whole, in a particular line of business. We have already seen how it operates in production as a whole, that is, how the prices of commodities in a given branch of enterprise coincide with their value determined by the labor-time contained in them whenever the total labor-time devoted to that line of production coincides with the labor-time contained in that quantity of commodities which is demanded of that line, that is to say, whenever supply and demand are in balance. From this it follows, that in order to control production it is not necessary to control production as a whole, but only production in each individual sphere by means of a voluntary association of the competitive producers. The problem is to control the total supply that is put on the market by the various competitive producers as it is the supply's deviation from the demand which causes the price of commodities to deviate from that value which represents the socially required labor-time. As mentioned before, the socially required labor-time of a given branch of production is one and the same as the demand for commodities of that line.

Thus, the law of value continues to operate under associated production; the social demand is still a limited quantity determined naturally, and the supply must be brought into approximate co-ordination with it if prices are to coincide approximately with their value. However, as Marx expresses it, the law of value operates under changed circumstances in the case of associated enterprise. It is no longer the price system alone which directs production; there is also associated planning.

Marx observes that it is to the interest of the ruling classes to perpetuate confusion in an understanding of the law of value because as long as that law goes by mis-understood, the meaning of production control is also beyond understanding. The non-Marxist economist believes that the point of capitalism is its exchange of products above and below value, not its lack of production control. Once this confusion is eliminated, the idea of capitalist enterprise—justified as an economic theory—is theoretically conquered. Here are Marx's words:

"The mass of products corresponding to the different needs requires *different and quantitatively determined* masses of the total labour of society. That this necessity of distributing labour in definite proportions cannot be done away with by the particular form of social production, but can only change the form it assumes, is self evident. *No natural laws can be done away with.* What can change, in changing historical circumstances, is the form in which these laws operate. And the form in which this proportional division of labour operates, in a state of society where the interconnection of social labour is manifested in the private exchange of the individual products of labour, is precisely the exchange value of these products. *The science consists precisely in working out how the law of value operates. . . .*The vulgar economist has not the faintest idea that the actual everyday exchange relations need not be directly identical with the magnitudes of value. *The point of bourgeois society consists precisely in this, that a priori there is no conscious, social regulation of production.* The reasonable and the necessary in nature asserts itself only as a blindly working average. And then the vulgar economist thinks he has made a great discovery when, as against the disclosures of the inner connection, he proudly claims that in appearance things look different. In fact, he is boasting that he holds to the appearance and takes it for the last word. Why, then, any science at all? But the matter has also another background. *When the inner connection is grasped all theoretical belief in the permanent necessity of existing conditions breaks down before their practical collapse.* Here, therefore, it is in the interests of the ruling class to perpetuate this unthinking confusion. And for what other purpose are [the ideologists of capitalism] paid, who have no other scientific trump to play, save that in political economy one should not think at all?"[39]

It is obvious from this that Marx wanted to perpetuate the "law of commodity value." This means that capitalist economists no longer have a "monopoly ownership" of the price system since there is still a continued use of it under the cooperative method.

---

Before leaving this explanation of a normal operation of the "law of commodity value" there is one more point which needs mentioning because it also assumes a production carried on without economic crisis.

Aside from the social equilibrium of production brought about by competition, or the sale of commodities above and below their values within the various spheres, there is also a form of accumulation (that is not capital accumulation) which exists under both cooperative and capitalist production without crisis. This has to do with increases in demand caused by an increased population, and in colonies by continual immigration. According to Marx, this increased production is brought about by the formation of new independent capitals or enterprises within the individual spheres. In the following quotation, Marx describes this accumulation which exists without crisis. It should be noticed he mentions it as existing under different modes of production, which is one way of saying it will exist under the cooperative method. He calls it a "relative overproduction," but it is not overproduction of the kind which causes crisis because it has future demand as its basis:

". . . that relative overproduction, which is in itself identical with accumulation takes place even with average prices, whose stand has neither a paralysing nor an exceptionally stimulating effect upon production. This takes place in agriculture as well as in all other capitalistically managed lines of production. *Under different modes of production,* this relative overproduction is effected directly by the increase of population, and in colonies by continual immigration. The demand increases constantly, and in anticipation of this new capital is continually invested in new land, although the products of this land will vary according to circumstances. It is the formation of new capitals which in itself brings this about"[40]

### b. *The Periodic Crisis*

Under all conditions so far, we have assumed that production exists without crisis under capitalism. That is, we have analyzed the "law of commodity value" which is common to both capitalism and association, but we have neglected that contradiction which exists only under capitalism, namely, the periodic economic crisis. We did this because before a crisis can be understood it must first be known what the ideal situation is which differentiates it from crisis.

In the following words, Marx differentiates normal production from business that is interrupted by "natural and social accidents" or the periodic crisis:

"The market prices fall below or rise above (their regulating market value) but these fluctuations balance each other. If one studies price lists during a certain long period, and if one subtracts the cases, in which the real value of commodities is altered by a change in the productivity of labor, and likewise the cases in which the process of production has been previously disturbed by natural or social accidents, one will be surprised, in the first place, by the relatively narrow limits of the fluctuations, and, in the second place, by the regularity of their mutual compensation."[41]

At this point we will leave this normal operation of the price system in order to concentrate on the "natural or social accidents" which interrupt its harmonious operation.

From what has gone before, it is obvious that the greater the difference between the total supply and the total demand for a given product, the greater the difference there is between its value and its market price, that is, the greater the oversupply or undersupply of commodities, the greater the fall or rise in prices.[42] If the total supply far exceeds the total demand, it can bring a crisis in production. The prices of commodities may even fall below "that price which corresponded to the condition of the supply" because of the "complete stopping of sales and the panic" which comes at a time of crisis, "with its correspondingly high rate of interest" on loan capital which the capitalist needs to meet his obligations with.[43] Because he cannot borrow money, he must transform his commodities into money at any price in order to have money to pay his creditors. Without capital, the capitalist cannot continue production on the regular scale, and a number of laborers in that branch of industry are separated from employment. When all lines of production experience overproduction simultaneously, the entire operation of capitalism comes to a practical standstill. The owner of stock no longer gains a profit on his investment, and the value of his stock falls. The overproduction of commodities would have produced a crisis.

With reference to the cause of crisis in production as a whole, Marx observes that its cause is in the increase of capital values, or money wealth, as well as in the development of enormous productive powers under capitalism. When these two forces unite, or when this enormous wealth goes into production to an excess, there is a general crisis in production.

"The stupendous productive power developing under the capitalist mode of production relatively to population, and the increase, though not in the same proportion, of capital values (not their material substance), which grow much more rapidly than the population, contradict the basis, which, compared to the expanding wealth, is ever narrowing and for which this immense productive power works, and the conditions, under which capital augments its value. This is the cause of crisis."[44]

We have seen that anarchy in the individual lines of production is the cause of overproduction in them. But now let us analyze the cause of an absolute overproduction, or overproduction in all lines of production simultaneously. Marx's explanation for the cause of periodic crisis is connected with his explanation of capital accumulation. We have already seen how surplus-value originates from production and how the investment of surplus-value in production is the "accumulation of capital." Now as long as the accumulation of capital, and the steady increase in production which it involves, produces for a progressively steady and increasing demand, the productive process proceeds normally under capitalism. But at a certain point it cannot go on increasing indefinitely. Even the existing population forms a definite limit to the total demand. Needless to say, at a certain stage of development, there is an over-accumulation of capital in all spheres of production which means that capital has gone beyond its limits of demand, or there has been a general overproduction of commodities. Here are Marx's words regarding an absolute overproduction:

"An overproduction of capital, not of individual commodities, signifies . . . simply an over-accumulation of capital—although the overproduction of capital always includes an overproduction of commodities. In order to understand what this over-accumulation is . . . it is but necessary to assume it to be absolute. When would it be an over-production which would not affect merely a few important lines of production, but which would be so absolute as to extend to every field of production?"[45]

To illustrate this question of an absolute overproduction, let us look upon all lines of production as they exist at the beginning of a cycle, immediately after a crisis, when production is being carried on upon a reduced scale by the various enterprises. We see the total capital that is invested in the different businesses continually enlarge, as a result of the investment of surplus-value in production on a progressive scale, until practically the entire working class is absorbed to carry on production on an ever larger scale. The surplus-value that is appropriated from production is used either in the individual enterprise that produced it, or it separates from the old capital and functions as a new and independent capital. Marx calls this the means of production enlargement. He explains, further, that credit or borrowed capital is the means whereby the capitalist can enlarge his production with capital that has been accumulated outside of his own sphere of production:

"The different individual investments of capital within each of these lines of industry, according to age, that is to say, the space of time during which they have served . . . must be in different stages of the process of successive transformation from surplus-value into potential money-capital. It is immaterial whether this money-capital is to serve for the expansion of the active capital, or for the establishment of new industrial enterprises, which constitute the two forms of expansion of production.[46] Credit . . . is the means whereby accumulated capital is not used directly in the sphere where it is produced, but where it has the most chance of being turned to good account."[47]

We know that accumulation is not only an enlargement of production; it is also a constant increase in the employment of labor-power. The limit for the expansion of production would be dependent upon the demand for products under a full employment of labor power. Let us suppose, then, that production has increased to such an extent that practically the entire working class is absorbed, and wages are high because of the strong demand for labor-power. Because of the higher wages and increased employment of workers, the production of means of subsistence has steadily increased, along with the manufacture of means of production. There is everywhere an abundance of commodities, and yet a crisis approaches.

After capital has reached its limits of demand in one country, it reaches out to other nations. Marx explains that there can be surplus capital in one nation simultaneously with a superfluity of wage laborers. That is, there is still labor-power on the market but it is not hired because the high standard of wages does not make its employment profitable enough. In this case, capital is invested in foreign labor-power. Here are Marx's words:

"If capital is sent to foreign countries, it is not done because there is absolutely no employment to be had for it at home. It is done because it can be employed at a higher rate of profit in a foreign country. But such capital is absolute surplus-capital for the employed laboring population and for the home country in general. It exists as such together with the relative overpopulation, and this is an illustration of the way in which both of them exist side by side and are conditioned on one another."[48]

However, aside from this investment of capital in foreign labor-power for the purpose of increased profits, capitalist production does assume a universal character in that it moves from country to country in search of markets for its products. Assuming its limits of demand have been reached in its own country, it establishes enterprises elsewhere so that when the world limits of demand have finally been reached, it becomes a universal crisis. Marx writes that the crowning point of crisis is "the universal crisis," such as the one that happened in 1929, for example.

"That crisis is once again approaching, although as yet but in its preliminary stage; and by the *universality* of its theatre and the intensity of its action it will drum dialectics even into the heads of . . . [the leaders] of the new, holy Prusso-German empire."[49]

We will assume that capitalist enterprise as a whole at last reaches a point where its full productive powers are exerted as all opportunities for profitable investment in the various lines of production have been filled. There is a superfluity of money capital because there is no further outlet for investment under the existing demands of the market. In reference to the limits of demand under capitalism, Marx explains that these limits depend on the income of the various classes which exist under the system. He also writes that the fullest possible exertion of industrial capital means an increase in consumption by laborers and capitalists, as well as increased consumption of means of production:

"The 'social demand,' in other words, that which regulates the principle of demand, is essentially conditioned on the mutual relations of the different economic classes and their relative economic positions, that is to say, first, on the proportion of the total surplus-value to the wages, and secondly, on the proportion of the various parts into which surplus-value is divided (profit, interest, ground-rent, taxes, etc.) And this shows . . . that absolutely nothing can be explained by the relation of supply and demand, unless the basis has first been ascertained, on which this relation rests[50] . . . the fullest employment of industrial capital [is] the utmost exertion of its reproductive power without regard to the limits of consumption. These limits of consumption are extended by the exertions of the process of reproduction itself. On one hand this increases the consumption of revenue on the part of laborers and capitalists, on the other it is identical with an exertion of productive comsumption."[51]

Production can increase only up to a certain point because of the given demand for commodities under capitalism—a demand that is pre-determined by the relations of production—which means that capitalism has its own definite barriers. (This is not to say that since cooperative production has certain limits of demand, it will also overproduce when it reaches its limits. It should be remembered that associated enterprise is independent of "capital accumulation" and therefore could not have an overproduction of capital.) Because the superfluous capital cannot go into new enlargement of production, it competes with the already invested capital for a place in the system that cannot be enlarged because of the limits of demand. The superfluous capital must somehow be eliminated if capitalism is to continue normally; and it is eliminated when it goes into production and causes an oversupply of commodities that depreciates the value of all capital, with the loss shared differently by the individual capitals in an economic crisis. Here again are Marx's words:

"How would this conflict [of an absolute overproduction of capital] be settled and the 'healthy' movement of capitalist production resumed under normal conditions? The mode of settlement is already indicated by the mere statement of the conflict whose settlement is under discussion. It implies the necessity of making unproductive, or even partially destroying, some capital, amounting either to the complete value of the additional capital . . . or to a part of it. But a graphic presentation of this conflict shows that the loss is not equally distributed over all the individual capitals, but according to the fortunes of the competitive struggle, which assigns the loss in very different proportions and in various shapes by grace of previously captured advantages or positions, so that one capital is rendered unproductive, another destroyed, a third but relatively injured or but momentarily depreciated, etc. But under all circumstances the equilibrium is restored by making more or less capital unproductive or destroying it."[52]

For instance, take it that the total demand for all commodities on the market is equal to 800 billion dollars, but a total product valued at 850 billion dollars is produced by all lines of production together. Under such conditions there would be a general depreciation in commodity values, that is, commodities valued at 850 billion dollars would depreciate to a price of 800 billion, or the value of the product demanded. Since it is overproduction which causes the returns on capital to fall, there would be a general depreciation of capital values, as well as an overproduction of commodities.

We can now understand Marx's statement that crisis is not caused by the worker's lack of purchasing power, but by certain tendencies within capital itself:

"It is purely a tautology to say that crises are caused by the scarcity of solvent consumers, or of a paying consumption. The capitalist system does not know any other modes of consumption but a paying one, except that of the pauper or of the 'thief.' If any commodities are unsaleable, it means that no solvent purchasers have been found for them, in other words, consumers (whether commodities are bought in the last instance for productive or individual consumption). But if one were to attempt to clothe this tautology with a semblance of a profounder justification by saying that the working class receive too small a portion of their own product, and the evil would be remedied by giving them a larger share of it, or raising their wages, we should reply that crises are precisely always preceded by a period in which wages rise generally and the working class actually get a larger share of the annual product intended for consumption. . . . It seems, then, that capitalist production comprises certain conditions which are independent of good or bad will and permit the working class to enjoy that relative prosperity only momentarily and at that always as a harbinger of a coming crisis."[53]

In times of crisis, more capital has been invested in production and more commodity values have been produced, but capitalism has produced the same monetary value as before the enlargement of production, which means that individual capitals have a smaller part in the total monetary value produced. In other words, because there is more capital to share the surplus-value than is required, the individual capitalist's share in the surplus-value falls. As Marx puts it, while before it was a question of each individual capital sharing profits, it is now a question of their sharing losses. Some of the capital is made temporarily unproductive, while other portions are destroyed. There is a sudden and general depreciation in the value of capitals:

"As soon as it is no longer a question of sharing profits, but of sharing losses, every one tries to reduce his own share to a minimum and load as much as possible upon the shoulders of some other competitor. However, the class must inevitably lose. How much the individual capitalist must bear of the loss, to what extent he must share in it at all, is decided by power and craftiness, and competition then transforms itself into a fight of hostile brothers. . . . The principal work of destruction would show its most dire effects in a slaughtering of the value of capitals. That portion of the value of capital which exists only in the form of claims on future shares of surplus-value or profit . . . would be immediately depreciated by the reduction of the receipts on which it is calculated. . . . Then there is the added complication that the process of reproduction is based on definite assumptions as to prices, so that a general fall in prices checks and disturbs the process of reproduction. This interference and stagnation paralyses the function of money as a means of payment, which is conditioned on the development of capital and the resulting price relations. The chain of payments due at certain times is broken in a hundred places. . . . Thus violent and acute crisis are brought about, sudden and forcible depreciations, an actual stagnation and collapse of the process of reproduction and finally a real falling off in reproduction."[54]

There was a given demand for commodities both before and after the superfluous capital went into production. Just as we saw before than any production beyond the demand has the effect of creating no new value but only depreciating the value of each individual commodity, so here the investment of surplus-value, or a further enlargement of production, has created the same value as was created before the accumulation. A larger capital invested in production has created no more value than a smaller one, which means that capitalism as a whole has overproduced.

Thus the overproduction of capital would have caused an overproduction of commodities, a fall in prices, and finally a general depreciation in capital values. However, according to Marx, this is not the end of the process. Capital gradually gains strength after a crisis, and again the cycle of moderate activity, prosperity, and crisis comes to pass, each time bringing a greater depreciation in commodity values because of an ever increased development of the powers of production. Here is Marx's explanation of how the cycle of capital accumulation begins once more:

"At the same time [in times of crisis] still other agencies would have been at work. The stagnation of production would have laid off a part of the laboring class and thereby placed the employed part in a condition in which they would have to submit to a reduction of wages. . . . The depreciation of the elements of constant capital [means of production] would be another factor tending to raise the rate of profit. . . . The present stagnation of production would have prepared an expansion of production later on, within capitalistic limits. . . . And in this way the cycle would be run once more. One portion of the capital which would have been depreciated by the stagnation of its function would recover its old value. For the rest, the same vicious circle would be described once more under expanded conditions of production, in an expanded market, and with increased productive forces."[55]

According to Marx, there is no way to correct the contradictions inherent in private money capital, but it must be completely eliminated under social production. He rejects the idea that a control over the credit system can abolish the periodic crisis because it is the capital owner's desire to accumulate more and more profit which causes crisis, not his use of borrowed capital. It is a generally known fact that capitalism as a system constantly boasts of the steady increase in its production, and it registers alarm if growth does not continue. Its motives of continual growth must inevitably reach their limit. Marx does admit, however, that stability of the credit or banking system, with an extension of loans in depression, will prevent a panic:

"The superficilaity of Political Economy shows itself in the fact that it looks upon the expansion and contraction of credit, which is a mere symptom of the periodic changes of the industrial cycle, as their cause. As the heavenly bodies, once thrown into a certain definite motion, always repeats this, so it is with social production as soon as it is once thrown into this movement of alternate expansion and contraction. Effects, in their turn, become causes, and the varying accidents of the whole process, which always reproduces its own conditions, take on the form of periodicity.[56] . . . no manner of bank legislation can abolish a crisis.[57] On the other hand, it is obvious that so long as the credit of a bank is not shaken, it will alleviate the panic in such cases by increasing the credit money, and intensify it by contracting this money."[58]

In Marx's opinion, the assumption that production is brought under control brings with it the necessity of eliminating the private money capitalist. There is no need for associated enterprise to control the use of private capital in production as private money capital is eliminated. It should be remembered that "private money capital"

means the investment of money in labor-power and means of production. Credit or borrowed capital is not one and the same as
private capital, even though credit can be used under capitalism.
The following words of Marx summarize the idea that when capital
accumulation takes over as a determinant of production instead of
the demands of the market, this results in crisis:

"With the development of capitalist production, the scale of
production becomes less and less dependent on the immediate demand
for the product and falls more and more under the determining
influence of the amount of capital available in the hands of the individual capitalist, of the instinct for the creation of more value
inherent in capital, of the need for the continuity and expansion of
its processes of production.[59] But if this new accumulation meets
with difficulties in its employment, through a lack of spheres for
investment, due to the overcrowding of the lines of production and
an oversupply of loan capital, then such a plethora of loanable
money-capital proves merely that *capitalist production has its limits.*
The subsequent swindle with credit proves, that no positive obstacle
stands in the way of the employment of this superfluous capital.
The obstacle is merely one immanent in its laws of self-expansion,
namely the limits in which capital can expand itself as such. A
plethora of money-capital [i.e., loan capital] does not necessarily
indicate an overproduction, nor even a lack of spheres of investment
for capital. The accumulation of loan-capital consists simply in the
fact that money is precipitated as loanable money. This process is
very different from an actual transformation into capital . . . there
must be a plethora of money-capital in definite phases of the cycle
. . . and this plethora must develop with the organisation of credit.
And simultaneously with it must also develop the necessity of driv-
ing the process of production beyond its capitalistic limits, by overproduction, excessive commerce, extreme credit. And this must
take place in forms that call forth a reaction."[60]

It should be emphasized again that it is capital accumulation
which is the basic weakness of capitalism; it is capital that causes
the periodic crisis, not the credit system. It is the freedom of the
capital owner to invest his money in labor-power and means of

production for the gain of profit—and especially his motive to ac-
cummulate more and more—which results in crisis. That capitalism
should be morally wrong to begin with, and periodically insufficient
from the profit standpoint, gives an excuse to destroy two evils
simultaneously with the establishment of cooperative production.
According to Marx, capital is destroyed by its own inherent tendencies, that is, even as it enlarges itself it goes down in crisis:

"It is clear that capitalist production can only exist and endure,
in spite of the revolutions of capital-value, so long as this value
creates more value, that is to say, so long as it goes through its
cycles as a self-developing value, or so long as the revolutions in
value can be overcome and balanced in some way. . . . If social
capital-value experiences a revolution in value, it may happen, that
the capital of the individual capitalist succumbs and fails, because
it cannot adapt itself to the conditions of this conversion of values.
To the extent that such revolutions in value become acute and frequent, the *automatic nature of self-developing value* makes itself
felt with the force of elementary powers against the foresight and
calculations of the individual capitalist, the course of normal production becomes subject to abnormal speculation, and the existence
of individual capitals is endangered. These periodical revolutions
in value . . . prove . . . the independent nature of value in the form
of capital, and its increasing independence in the course of its development."[61]

That Marx should have named his book "Capital" was exactly appropriate, because it is precisely private capital which he attempts to
destroy. (He has been falsely accused of attempting to destroy the
market system, private ownership of land, and certain other permanent freedoms which go by untouched with an abolition of capitalism.) When it is realized that capital has been free to engage in
untold of evils during the course of its growth to this stage in history,
there should be no regret at its demise—only satisfaction to see it
gone at last. Here is another of Marx's criticisms of capital:

"The real barrier of capitalist production is capital itself. It is
the fact that capital and its self-expansion appear as the starting
and closing point, as the motive and aim of production; that pro-

duction is merely production for capital, and not vice versa, the means of production mere means for an ever expanding system of the life process for the benefit of the society of producers. The barriers, within which the preservation and self-expansion of the value of capital . . . can alone move, these barriers come continually in collision with the methods of production, which capital must employ for its purposes, and which steer straight toward an unrestricted extension of production, toward production for its own self, toward an unconditional development of the productive forces of society. The means, this unconditional development of the productive forces of society, comes continually into conflict with the limited end, the self-expansion of the existing capital. Thus, while the capitalist mode of production is one of the historical means by which the material forces of production are developed and the world-market required for them created, it is at the same time in continual conflict with this historical task and the conditions of social production corresponding to it."[62]

It is Marx's idea that unless capital accumulation is eliminated, there can not be a collective regulation of production. If there is to be a control over the enormous productive forces that have been developed under capitalism, the competitive profit-sharing producers must join in voluntary association for the purpose of planning production. The producers of a particular commodity would then bring the demanded quantity of it to market, and the product would be sold at its approximate value. Under the cooperative system the producers would enjoy continual gain from enterprise, while the capitalist method is fated to endure periodic overproduction and depression. Here are Marx's words:

"Only when production will be under the conscious and prearranged control of society, will society establish a direct relation between the quantity of social labor time employed in the production of definite articles and the quantity of the demand of society for them . . . if the quantity of social labor spent in the production of a certain article corresponds to the social demand for it, so that the quantity produced is that which is the ordinary on that scale of production and for that same demand, then the article is sold at its market-value."[63]

Before ending this explanation of the periodic crisis, it would seem appropriate to give Marx's summary of the antagonisms of capitalist production and his solution to the antagonisms. It should be noticed that he refers to disproportion between all lines of production as one and the same as disproportion between supply and demand in individual branches. This implies that the proportionality of supply and demand in each individual line of business by means of its associated planning brings proportionality between the different branches of enterprise, or an abolition of the general economic crisis.

"Since the aim of capital is not to minister to certain wants, but to produce profits, and since it accomplishes this purpose by methods which adapt the mass of production to the scale of production, not vice versa, conflict must continually ensue between the limited conditions of consumption on a capitalist basis and a production which forever tends to exceed its immanent barriers. Moreover, capital consists of commodities, and therefore the overproduction of capital implies an over-production of commodities. Hence, we meet with the peculiar phenomenon that the same economists who deny the overproduction of commodities, admit that of capital. If it is said that there is no general overproduction, but that a disproportion grows up between various lines of production, then this is tantamount to saying that within capitalist production the proportionality of the individual lines of production [i.e., the coordination of supply and demand in an individual line of production] is brought about through a continual process of disproportionality, that is, the interrelations of production as a whole enforce themselves as a blind law upon the agents of production instead of having brought the productive process under their common control [i.e., the common control  of the supply in each individual line of production], *as a law understood by the social mind. . . .* But the contradiction of this capitalist mode of production consists precisely in its tendency to an absolute development of productive forces, a development, which comes continually in conflict with the specific conditions of produc-

tion in which capital moves and alone can move. . . . It is not a
fact that too much wealth is produced. But it is true that there is
periodical overproduction of wealth in its capitalistic and self-con-
tradictory form."[64]

## Section 2.—Private Ownership of Profit.

Marx defines capitalism as the investment of capital in labor-power
and means of production for the gain of profit. The product that
emerges as a result of the productive process is the property of the
money capitalist because he is the owner of the means of production,
even though the product is produced by the group carrying on production. If the manager of enterprise is a wage-laborer, then all
members of production labor for the benefit of the capitalist, not
themselves.

Under the capitalist corporation the capital owner no longer performs an active part in production but yet draws from his stock both
the general rate of interest on capital and the profit of enterprise.
While the money lender draws interest alone, the stockholder—who
is separate from production just as the banker is—owns interest on
his money plus the profit of enterprise. He owns the total profit in
the form of dividends flowing automatically from his capital investment. Here is Marx's explanation of this:

"[By means of the formation of stock companies] Transformation
of the actually functioning capitalist into a mere manager, an admin-
istrator of other people's capital, and of the owners of capital into
mere owners, mere money-capitalists. Even if the dividends which
they receive include the interest and profits of enterprise, that is, the
total profit . . . this total profit, is henceforth received only in the form
of interest, that is, in the form of a mere compensation of the ownership of capital, which is now seperated from its function in the actual
process of reproduction in the same way in which this function, in the
person of the manager, is separated from the ownership of capital.
The profit now presents itself . . . as a mere appropriation of the
surplus-labor of others, arising from the transformation of means of
production into capital, that is, from its alienation from its actual pro-

ducer, from its antagonism as another's property opposed to the individuals actually at work in production, from the manager down to the last day laborer."[65]

The capitalist stockholder is unnecessary in the case of cooperative enterprise since borrowed capital (in its various forms) replaces private investment. Marx writes that once the capitalist has been separated from industry under the corporation, production is then similar to the cooperative method, that is, no members of production are private owners, including the manager. And, in addition, capital has assumed a social form by becoming concentrated in banks, so that the capitalist is no longer needed either for the advancement of money capital or as a functionary in production. He also writes that cooperative production, or group ownership of the profits, is the new form of production. What else could he mean but that borrowed capital replaces the capitalist investor under cooperative enterprise? Marx would not mention that capital has assumed a social form by being concentrated in banks and then emphasize the lack of private ownership by the group working in production under the corporation, if he was not advocating this method of business organization under the cooperative method. This must be what he means by the forms developed under capitalist production, that is to say, the forms of (1) cooperative factories owned by workers, and (2) capitalist corporations, separated and freed from their antagonistic private capital character. For instance, corporations imply a loaning of money without activity in production; likewise, bonds provide money but do not include private ownership of production. Bonds would therefore replace stock under cooperative enterprise, or ownership of profits by the workers. If all of these ideas are reasoned together, that is, the use of bonds and bank loans, it can be imagined just what the organization of cooperative production involves.

"Stock companies in general, developed with the credit system, have a tendency to separate [the] labor of management as a function more and more from the ownership of capital, whether it be self-owned or borrowed. . . . Since the mere owner of capital, the money-capitalist, has to face the investing capitalist, while *money-capital itself assumes a social character with the advance of credit,* being concentrated in banks and loaned by them instead of its original owners, and since, on the other hand, the mere manager, who has no title whatever to the capital, whether by borrowing or otherwise, performs all *real* functions pertaining to the investing capitalist as such, only the functionary remains and the *capitalist disappears from the process of production as a superfluous person.*[66] To the extent that the labor of the capitalist is not the purely capitalistic one arising from the process of production and ceasing with capital itself, to the extent that it is not limited to the function of exploiting the labor of others, to the extent that it rather arises from the social form of the labor-process as a combination and co-operation of many for the purpose of bringing about a common result, to that extent, *it is just as independent of capital as that form itself, as soon as it has burst its capitalistic shell.* To say that this labor [labor of superintendence] as a capitalistic one, as a function of the capitalist is necessary, amounts merely to saying that the vulgar economist cannot conceive of the *forms* developed in the womb of capitalist production *separated and freed from their antagonistic capitalist character."* [67]

The stockholder is already separated from activity in production under the capitalist corporation; therefore, he is no longer needed in the productive enterprise any more than the owner of bonds or bank loans is needed in production under the cooperative method. Management is performed by hired employees, showing that the leader of production does not have to be a private owner, that is to say, a capitalist. When all active members of production, from the manager down to the last day laborer, are separated from capital ownership, business is ready to be separated in actuality from the owner of capital; that is, it should be owned as well as operated by the group working in it. Production is then no longer owned by a capitalist investor and carried on by non-owners, but ownership and labor in enterprise became at one with each other. Marx writes that the cooperative factories of the workers under capitalism, as well as stock companies, furnish the proof that the capitalist is no longer needed as a functionary in production:

"  . . . separated from capital, the process of production is simply a labor-process.[68] The capitalist mode of production itself has brought matters to such a point, that the labor of superintendence, entirely separated from the ownership of capital, walks the streets. It is, therefore, no longer necessary for the capitalist [to perform] the labor of superintendence himself. A director of an orchestra need not be the owner of the instruments of its members, nor is it a part of his function as a director, that he should have anything to do with the wages of the other musicians. The cooperative factories furnish the proof that the capitalist has become . . . superfluous as a functionary in production."[69]

The capitalist under the corporation is not only separated from performing any active function in production; he also no longer owns business privately. Ownership of industry under the capitalist corporation has assumed the form of shares of stock, mere titles of ownership. Production is owned collectively by a group of capitalists, not by a private owner. It is the group profit enterprise of capitalists, just as the associated method is the group profit production of associated laborers. Thus Marx refers to stock companies as social enterprise, and he also calls the higher method of production social enterprise— as distinguished from private enterprise. However, he mentions several antagonisms in the case of social enterprise under capitalism:

"[By means of the formation of stock companies] Capital, which rests on a *socialised* mode of production and presupposes a social concentration of means of production and labor-powers, is here directly endowed with the form of social capital (a capital directly associated individuals) as distinguished from private capital, and its enterprises assume the form of social enterprises as distinguished from individual enterprises. It is the abolition of capital as private property within the boundaries of capitalist production itself.[70] This is . . . a self-destructive contradiction, which represents on its face a mere phase of transition to a new form of production. It manifests its contradictory nature by its effects. It establishes a *monopoly* in certain spheres and thereby challenges the interference of the state. It reproduces a new aristocracy of finance, a new sort of parasite in the shape of promoters, speculators and merely nominal directors; a whole system of swindling and cheating by means of corporation juggling, stock jobbing, and stock speculation. It is private production without the control of private property." [71]

It should be noticed, again, that Marx refers to stock companies as "socialized" enterprises, and stock companies are not state enterprises but profit sharing ones. As a further enlargement of this idea, Marx writes that when the capitalist class as a whole, share equally in the profits on a given total investment (as in the case of the general rate of profit), they practice "capitalist communism." [72] This implies that when the workers share equally in the total profits of industry, it is no longer capitalist communism, but communism.

Another point which should be noticed in the above quotation is that Marx refers to "monopoly" as a contradiction that "challenges the interference of the state." This is another proof that he did not advocate monopoly in the individual spheres since he refers to it directly as a contradiction; that is, its opposition to the law of value "challenges" state interference.

Still another contradiction mentioned by Marx in connection with the corporations under capitalism is their uncontrolled management. Under cooperative production, management is brought under control by the people working in business, and the "swindling and cheating" which now exists under the corporation form is eliminated.

But regardless of their contradictions, the capitalist corporations and the cooperative factories of the workers which grow up under capitalism may be considered examples of group enterprise within the boundaries of the old system. They constitute a transition to the group method of business enterprise, or to a higher method of production. Group profit ownership under the capitalist corporation does not abolish the labor-capital antagonism because it is still the capitalist who owns the profit of enterprise. However, under the cooperative method of industry there is an abolition of class antagonism, because it is the group working which owns the profits. In the case of cooperative production under capitalism, however, the workers invest their own private capital in enterprise and share in the profits indefinitely according to how much capital they invest; in other words, they become their own money capitalists.

It is not that there is anything contradictory in the workers supplying their own money for an enterprise, but it is a contradiction from the
standpoint of cooperative production that their loan should guarantee
ownership of the profits indefinitely. Their right to interest on money
would have to end once the loan is repaid; otherwise, their loan would
mean a continuation of capitalism and prevent an equal sharing in
the profits by all workers in the business. Here are Marx's words on
this:

"The co-operative factories of the laborers themselves represent
within the old form the first beginnings of the new, although they
naturally reproduce, and must reproduce, everywhere in their *actual
organization* all the shortcomings of the prevailing system. But the
antagonism between capital and labor is overcome within them, although only in the form of making the *associated laborers* their own
capitalists, that is, enabling them to use the means of production for
the employment of their own labor. They show the way, in which a
new mode of production may naturally grow out of an old one, when
the development of the material forces of production and of the corresponding forms of social production has reached a certain stage.
Without the factory system arising out of the capitalist mode of production the co-operative factories could not develop, nor without the
credit system arising out of the same mode of production. The credit
system is not only the principal basis for the gradual transformation
of capitalist private enterprises into capitalist stock companies, but
also a means for the gradual extension of cooperative factories on a
more or less natural scale. The capitalist stock companies as well as
the co-operative factories may be considered as forms of transition
from the capitalist mode of production to the associated one, with
this distinction, that the antagonism is met negatively in the one, posi-
tively in the other." [73]

Again, Marx refers to stock companies as the outcome, or one form
of the credit system. He requires some imagination on the part of
his fellow economists here, as who would think to say that private
ownership of bonds is maintained but not the investment of capital
in labor-power and means of production? Bonds appear to be private
money-capital, but yet they are not under Marx's definition.

In one place, Marx mentions that cooperative production is his ideal, along with associated planning by the various competitive enterprises, and then he admits that some of the ruling classes also realize that cooperative factories owned by the workers is the ideal solution. Even though these capitalists have no idea what Marx advocates, they know that state communism is impossible and that cooperative production is possible, that is, a realistic economic solution.

"From the public accounts of the co-operative factories in England, it is manifest, that the profit, after the deduction of the wages of the superintendent, which form a part of the invested capital the same as the wages of the other laborers, was higher than the average profit, although they paid occasionally a much higher interest than the *private factories*. The cause of the greater profit was in all these cases a greater economy in the use of constant capital.[74] [The socialists] wanted to make individual property a truth by transforming the means of production, land and capital, now chiefly the means of enslaving and exploiting labour, into mere instruments of free and associated labour. But this is Communism, *'impossible'* Communism! Why, those members of the ruling classes who are intelligent enough to perceive the impossibility of continuing the present system—and they are many—have become the obtrusive and full-mouthed apostles of co-operative production. If *co-operative production is not to remain a sham and a snare; if it is to supersede the capitalist system; if united co-operative societies are to regulate national production upon a common plan*, thus taking it under their own control and putting an end to the constant anarchy and periodical convulsions which are the fatality of capitalist production—what else, gentlemen, would it be but Communism, *'possible'* Communism." [75]

Marx writes directly here that an association of cooperative producers for the purpose of regulating production is communism. We have already shown why this means an association of enterprises within each individual sphere, not government planning. Also, he does not advocate monopoly in individual branches; only a voluntary association of competitive producers. The maintenance of competition implies the system would be self-operating and allow new branches of enterprise to grow up naturally.

When production is cooperative, money capital is no longer an alien power in the hands of the private money capitalist. It becomes a mere instrument of the workers, not a means of controlling the labor-power of individuals. According to Marx's prophecy, it is inevitable that capital will go down because it prepares the conditions for its own elimination:

" . . . the growing accumulation of capital implies its growing concentration. Thus the power of capital, the personification of the conditions of social production in the capitalist, grows over the heads of the real producers. Capital shows itself more and more as a social power, whose agent the capitalist is, and which stands no longer in any possible relation to the things which the labor of any single individual can create. Capital becomes a strange, independent, social power, which stands opposed to society as a thing, and as the power of capitalists by means of this thing. The contradiction between capital as a general social power and as a power of private capitalists over the social conditions of production develops into an ever more irreconcilable clash, which implies the dissolution of these relations and the elaboration of the conditions of production into universal, common, social conditions. This elaboration is performed by the development of the productive powers under capitalist production, and by the course which this development pursues." [76]

It is interesting to dissolve the mystery which surrounds Marx's explanation of cooperative production. He gives hints throughout *Capital* in the hope that someone will see them, but for almost one hundred years these hints have gone by unnoticed, perhaps because the belief in state communism has been an overpowering obstacle. It has been such a barrier that even when Marx writes in direct words that cooperative production is his ideal, his words go by unnoticed. Also, in another place he refers to those who idealize the credit system as prophets of the future society—which is one way of saying that the credit system continues under the cooperative method—but even this goes by unnoticed because "interest" is considered one and the same as capitalism. Marx explains, however, that capital used as credit is the opposite of competition between capitals. While credit (the banking system) distributes capital in proportion to productive needs in the individual spheres, under competition the capitals are independent, and controlled by the general rate of profit. He thus implies that under associated production, borrowed capital is distributed naturally without the need of government planning in the individual lines.

"Two natures . . . are immanent in the credit system. On one side, it develops the incentive of capitalist production, the accumulation of wealth by the appropriation and exploitation of the labor of others, to the purest and most colossal form of gambling and swindling, and reduces more and more the number of those, who exploit the social wealth. On the other side, it constitutes a *transition to a new mode of production.* It is this ambiguous nature, which endows the principal spokesmen of credit from Law to Isaac Pereire with the pleasant character of swindlers and prophets.[77] It is . . . credit through which the capital of the whole capitalist class is placed at the disposal of each sphere of production, not in proportion to the capital possessed by the capitalists of this sphere, but *in proportion to its productive needs*—whereas in competition the individual capitals seem to be independent of each other. This is as much the consequence as the condition of capitalist production, and it makes a convenient *transition for us from competition between capitals to capital as credit.*" [78]

Marx is hinting by this that credit or loan capital (including bonds and bank loans) is the money-capital of the future, or of the new method of production. At the present time, stocks and bonds are a part of the gambling, but the majority of gambling will disappear with the abolition of stock ownership.

## Section 3.—Despotism in Production.

Under capitalism the owner of the means of production is the supreme ruler over all individuals working in business. When capitalist enterprise becomes large scale, there are large numbers of hired workers laboring together in enterprise, which means that many individuals thereby come under the control of single productive or commercial organizations. There is no self-government afforded this majority of society, but they still remain under the will of the owners

of production. While leadership is required under any group productive process, leadership under capitalism is despotic because it is
the control over human beings who do not own their own labor-power
and who therefore are not free. When an individual worker sells his
ability to work, he sells himself as a commodity; that is, once he has
sold his labor-power, he is no longer a free individual but one who has
gone under the will of his purchaser. Capitalism is not based on a
union of free and independent individuals—it is the purchase of the
labor-power of one individual by another for the purpose of gaining
a profit from production.

The moment the laborer sells himself as a wage-laborer to the
capitalist, a class relation is established between individuals. The
capitalist uses the money form of the product that the laborer produces to purchase his wage-labor anew, and consumption of his
means of subsistence forces the laborer to return to the capitalist again
to sell himself. Because he has no right to ownership of his product,
he is held down indefinitely as a worker, and the continual gain of
profit from him by the capitalist maintains the capital owner as the
ruler of production. According to Marx, the worker is in economical
bondage to capital even before he has sold himself to the capitalist.

"Capitalist production . . . of itself reproduces the separation between labour-power and the means of labor. It thereby reproduces
and perpetuates the condition for exploiting the labourer. It incessantly forces him, to sell his labour-power in order to live, and enables
the capitalist to purchase labour-power in order that he may enrich
himself. It is no longer a mere accident that capitalist and labourer
confront each other in the market as buyer and seller. It is the process
itself that incessantly hurls back the labourer on to the market as a
vendor of his labour-power, and that incessantly converts his own
product into a means by which another man can purchase him. In
reality, the labourer belongs to capital before he has sold himself to
capital. His economical bondage is both brought about and concealed
by the periodic sale of himself, by his change of masters, and by the
oscillations in the market price of labour-power." [79]

The fact that the value produced by capitalist enterprise is divided
into wages for labor-power and profit for capital implies a conflict

of classes. If we look upon the profit of enterprise as value taken from the laborer that should be his own because he created it, then if the capitalist is to gain a maximum of profit he must exploit the laborer to the greatest possible extent, that is, he must take the greatest possible quantity of profit from the worker. As production increases and wages are high because of the increased demand for labor-power, there is more abundance for the working-class; but this circumstance does not abolish the submission of one class to another any more than better food, clothing, and lodging for the slave does away with exploitation of the slave. It only means that there is a temporary relaxation of the pressure on the working-class and that more workers have gone under the control of the large-scale capitalist organizations. Exploitation is carried on, but it is done on a more extensive scale; that is, profit is gained from more laborers than previously. Here is Marx's version of this:

"Instead of becoming more intensive with the growth of capital, this relation of dependence only becomes more extensive, i.e., the sphere of capital's exploitation and rule merely extends with its own dimensions and the number of its subjects. A larger part of their own surplus-product, always increasing and continually transformed into additional capital, comes back to him in the shape of means of payment, so that they can extend the circle of their enjoyments. . . . But just as little as better clothing, food, and treatment, and a larger peculium, do away with the exploitation of the slave, so little do they set aside that of the wage-worker. A rise in the price of labour, as a consequence of accumulation of capital, only means, in fact, that the length and weight of the golden chain the wage-worker has already forged for himself, allow of a relaxation of the tension of it." [80]

While in times of prosperity more individuals are employed by capital, in periods of crisis many are separated from their employment and there is an increased exploitation of those individuals still working in enterprise. Because there is an oversupply of labor-power on the market and wages are low, the capitalist gains increased profit from their labor. The employed segment of society must be more submissive to the capitalist than under more prosperous conditions; otherwise, they are threatened with a loss in their means of subsistence. When the capitalist owners of industry are free to control the means of subsistence of the majority of society and force them to submission because of an oversupply of labor-power, it is not liberty for those individuals who must endure such submission. Speaking of this, Marx states that when one portion of the working-class is in enforced idleness while the other portion is overworked, this completes the despotism of capital:

"The condemnation of one part of the working-class to enforced idleness by the over-work of the other part, and the converse, becomes a means of enriching the individual capitalist. [81] If its [capital's] accumulation, on the one hand, increases the demand for labor, it increases on the other the supply of labourers by the setting free of them [because of the introduction of labor saving machinery that renders the worker superfluous], whilst at the same time the pressure of the unemployed compels those that are employed to furnish more labour, and therefore makes the supply of labour, to a certain extent, independent of the supply of labourers. The action of the law of supply and demand of labour on this basis completes the despotism of capital." [82]

There is an antagonism which develops under large scale capitalism that should be mentioned here. When enterprise becomes large scale, the workers join together in trade unions to resist the power of capital over them, and the capitalists then use pressure to overpower their resistance. Once antagonism between organized wage-labor and the capital owner becomes a permanent part of capitalist production, it is ready to be transformed into the cooperative method. The following words of Marx show that the development of class conflicts under capitalism is inevitable, and that it is the development of such antagonisms — along with the periodic crisis — which will eventually bring about the complete abolition of capitalism:

"The directing motive, the end and aim of capitalist production, is to extract the greatest possible amount of surplus-value, and consequently to exploit labour-power to the greatest possible extent. As the number of co-operating labourers increases, so too does their resistance to the domination of capital, and with it, the necessity for capital to overcome this resistance by counter-pressure.[83] . . . the historical development of the antagonisms, immanent in a given form of production, is the only way in which that form of production can be dissolved and a new form established."[84]

It is interesting to note in regard to this, that class antagonisms in America are less pronounced than in other nations. Its system of free land ownership, as distinguished from the old feudal system in Europe, seems to have diminished its class conflict. If the individual remains unfree in the productive enterprise, his freedom to own land gives him the idea that he is independent, nevertheless. This, of course, is an error in understanding which will eventually be corrected, as whatever is lacking in freedom must inevitably go down. It is not that land ownership will go down, but private ownership of capital must give way to something better. The capitalist class may attempt to harmonize an unfree relation between capital and labor, but an unseen antagonism must always be there, at least for those members of the working class who recognize inequality when it exists.

The class antagonism of capitalism (seen or unseen) is not in harmony with the ideal of brotherhood. The establishment of the classless society of cooperative production would materialize the ideal of "liberty, equality, and fraternity" by abolishing the purchase and sale of wage-labor. Under the cooperative method there is a more equitable distribution of profit and an abolition of class antagonisms. The value produced by the enterprise is no longer divided into wages for the working-class and profit for the capitalist, but both wages and profit of enterprise are owned by the group working in business. But most important of all, the workers have control over management and are not maintained submissive as a class. There is freedom of speech; they are no longer silent before the will of capital.

Because of the abolition of capital accumulation under the cooperative method, production is no longer pushed periodically beyond the demands of the market, and there is an end to recurring unemployment. Also, the worker is no longer forced into submission because of an oversupply of labor on the market. Marx emphasizes that capital accumulation is not a law of nature, but it is a law which automatically maintains the continual exploitation of labor-power by capital. He writes that once the accumulation of capital has been eliminated, material wealth will exist to satisfy the needs of the worker; the laborer will not exist merely to satisfy the needs of the self-expansion of capital:

"The law of capitalistic accumulation, metamorphosed by economists into a pretended law of nature, in reality merely states that the very nature of accumulation excludes every diminution in the degree of exploitation of labour, and every rise in the price of labour, which could seriously imperil the continual reproduction, on an ever enlarging scale, of the capitalistic relation. It cannot be otherwise in a mode of production in which the labourer exists to satisfy the needs of self-expansion of existing values, instead of on the contrary, material wealth existing to satisfy the needs of development on the part of the labourer."[85]

While capitalism is a society of classes, cooperative enterprise materializes the ideal of a classless society. It abolishes the capitalist class as the ruling one, and at the same time abolishes the existence of classes. Production is so organized under the cooperative method that there is no further opportunity for separate class rule. Since the word "class" implies separate classes, associated production is a classless society of the workers. There is still leadership in the case of cooperative enterprise, but management is a part of the group which owns the means of production and profits.

### Section 4.—Ground Rent.

When Marx refers to the "abolition of private property in land" he does not mean the abolition of all land ownership but only the capitalist form of it. He defines *the capitalist form* of private property as the landlord's absentee ownership of land, or "title to the rent." Since it is only by means of Marx's analysis of ground rent that this point can be understood, we must therefore study this part of his theory in detail. If the explanations appear trivial and overly detailed, it should be remembered that such details are

important if they become the means of preserving private ownership of land as we understand it.

To preserve this particular freedom would be an honor for any-
one; in fact, it is an honor even to attempt it when one considers
the bulwark of economic theory lodged against its preservation.
For instance, it involves the overthrow of one of the most time
honored of classical economic theories, namely, the theory of
ground rent. And along with this, there is also the demise of an
even more time honored theory—that is, the general rate of profit
on capital. An understanding of this latter theory must precede an
undersanding of ground rent. Marx writes that these theories—
ground rent and the general rate of profit on capital (including
also a third theory of wage-labor)—form the theoretical basis of
the capitalist system of production. Thus, when the capitalist
method of enterprise is dissolved, so does its method of distribution go down as expressed in the following trinitarian formula:
(1) land—rent, (2) labor—wages, and (3) capital—profit.

The fact that the "abolition of private property in land" involves
only the abolition of landlordism in the form of ground rent is at
least implied in the above formula of "rent, wages and profit," but
further proof and understanding is necessary through an analysis
of ground rent. We can be confident that Marx is with us in this
disputed point, because without his explanations the point in
question could not be proved. In other words, the quotations
from Marx are present in *Capital* to preserve private ownership,
but there are certain distractions to be found in Marx's writings
which have prevented an understanding of land ownership up
until now. It is these distractions, unintended on Marx's part,
which become an almost insurmountable obstacle in proving the
point, even though the idea of landlordism as only one form of
private property in land is obvious to begin with. It is especially
in this part of Marx's writings that his meaning is hidden under
detail, and there is no way out but to study this detail.

However, at least an attempt will be made to render the subject
of ground rent easy to understand by beginning its explanation with
Marx's ideas on the general rate of profit. He seems to advocate

this method of explanation when he writes that "the entire difficulty in the analysis of rent consists in the explanation of the excess of agricultural profit over the average profit."[86] So far in this explanation of capitalism, we have not analyzed the theory of the general rate of profit in its details, but this is essential for an understanding of ground rent.

### a. *The General Rate of Profit*

Marx explains that "the entire process of capitalist production is regulated by the prices of products. But the regulating prices of production are in their turn regulated by the equalization of the rate of profit and by the distribution of capital among the various social spheres of production in correspondence with this equalization. Profit, then, appears here as the main factor, not of the distribution of products, *but of their production itself,* as a part in the distribution of capitals and of labor among the various spheres of production."[87]

In *Section 1-Competition* it was mentioned that the value of a commodity under capitalism is represented in the form of its "price of production." We shall now study this question in more detail. The existence of a "price of production" presupposes, first of all, the historical establishment of a general rate of profit on capital. Marx has the following explanation for its establishment:

Let us imagine that a particular capitalist advanced $10,000 to business enterprise, with $9,000 of this representing means of production, including raw materials, machinery, etc., and $1,000 taking the form of wages. We will suppose that of the $9,000 advanced for means of production, $6,200 of it is paid out for fixed capital, including machinery, buildings, etc., and $2,800 of it is spent for raw materials necessary in the production. It is also assumed that the capitalist produces a certain number of products annually which have a total value of $5,000. This total value in commodities is made up of the value which the capitalist gives up for their production, plus the surplus-value contained in them. The capitalist pays out $1,000 in wages, $2,800 in raw materials, and loses $200 in wear and tear on his fixed capital. The cost-price of the $5,000 value in commodities is therefore $4,000, while the surplus-value contained in them is equal to $1,000.

Now in the explanation here, the $1,000 surplus-value is compared to the $4,000 consumed in the production of the $5,000 commodity value. But as a matter of fact, that $1,000 surplus-value is not just an addition to the $4,000 capital actually consumed in the production of the commodity. It is also an addition to the total $10,000 invested in the enterprise, including that portion of the fixed capital, which is not actually consumed in production.

When we look upon the $1,000 yearly surplus-value as an addition to the total $10,000 advanced, "surplus-value assumes the change of form known as profit. . . . The value of a commodity is equal to its cost price plus the profit." If a product is sold at its value then a profit is gained which is equal to the surplus-value contained in the commodity.[88]

Marx calls surplus-value measured by the advance of wages "rate of surplus-value." On the other hand, he calls surplus-value measured by the total capital advanced "rate of profit."[89] For instance, in our illustration, the rate of surplus-value is

$$\frac{1{,}000 \text{ (surplus-value)}}{1{,}000 \text{ (wages)}}$$

or 100% and the rate of profit is

$$\frac{1{,}000 \text{ (surplus-value)}}{10{,}000 \text{ (advanced capital)}}$$ or 10%.

Thus, when we say that the capitalist gains $1,000 annually and compare it to the total capital advanced of $10,000, we then say that he gains a 10% annual rate of profit. He still appropriates the same quantity of surplus-value from his investment in labor-power, but it appears in this case as an addition to the total capital, not just an addition to the capital invested in wages. At this point, profit and surplus-value are one and the same thing in the price of the commodity, as commodities are assumed to be sold at their values.[90]

Now that we have defined the individual rate of profit, let us go on to see how profit is transformed into a general rate of profit. So far we have considered the rate of profit for one capital, but we shall now compare the rates of profit of different capitals.

To begin with, we will assume each capital in the various lines of production has the same rate of surplus-value, or the ratio of the surplus-value to the wages is the same. But for a given quantity of capital investment, say $100, one capital will differ from another as to its investment in labor-power and means of production. For instance, capital A might pay $20 out of the $100 for labor-power and $80 for means of production, while capital B might pay out $80 for labor and $20 for materials of production. The proportion of labor-power as compared to means of production differs because of the difference between the various lines of production. A definite quantity of labor-power is required to work up a definite quantity of means of production for the daily product required of an individual line of production, and therefore a definite value in wages and another definite value in means of production must be advanced by the capitalist for the manufacture of the given commodities. The proportion of value advanced for labor-power and means of production ( $80 + $20, etc.) is what Marx calls the "organic composition of capital."[91]

In our illustration, if we assume the rate of surplus-value is 100%, then capital A which pays $20 for wages and $80 for means of production out of a $100 advanced capital will appropriate $20 surplus-value, and the rate of profit will be 20/100 or 20%. On the other hand, capital B which pays out $80 for wages and $20 for means of production will appropriate $80 surplus-value, and its rate of profit will be 80/100 or 80%. The difference in rates of profit exist because, according to the quantities of labor-power employed, the surplus-value differs. It is a question of which part of the $100 is composed of wages and which of means of production. Because capitals of equal quantities in different lines of production are divided differently into means of production and labor-power and produce different amounts of surplus-value and profit, this means that the rate of profit must differ also.[92]

As long as the commodities are sold at their values, there is no general rate of profit, that is, a $100 investment does not produce the same profit in all lines of production. Let us go on to see how a general rate of profit is established by means of the transformation of commodity values into prices which are either above or below their individual values. Here is Marx's explanation:

"Capital withdraws from spheres with low rates of profit and invades others which yield a higher rate. By means of this incessant emigration and immigration, in one word, by its distribution among the various spheres in accord with a rise in the rate of profit here and its fall there, it brings about *such a proportion of supply to demand* that the average profit in the various spheres of production become the same, so that values are converted into prices of production.[93] Competition shows . . . the fluctuations of market prices, which reduce the average market price of commodities in a given period of time, not to the market value but to a market price of production differing considerably from this market value."[94]

Thus Marx explains that competition, or the influence of supply and demand on prices, equalizes the different rates of profit. Let us consider exactly how this process of transformation of values into prices of production would be accomplished. The attraction of high profits, or surplus-value, in branches of industry which produce commodities requiring a large proportion of labor-power, draws much capital into them until the profit is reduced for each individual capital because of the oversupply of the commodity and its sale below its value. The sale of a product below its value means that less surplus-value is appropriated from it than is actually contained in it. At the same time, there is not enough attraction for capital to invest in those lines which produce with small quantities of labor-power because they give less surplus-value. This causes an undersupply of commodities in that line, and therefore the sale of commodities above their value. The sale of products above value means an appropriation of profit above the actual surplus-value contained in the commodities, and thus the riddle is solved how the law of supply and demand, or the deviations of price from value, equalizes profit in the various lines of production. As long as one kind of commodities produces more, and another less surplus-value, the attraction or lack of attraction of profit will cause more or less production and therefore a fall or rise in prices until profits are equalized. In other words, because capital withdraws from those spheres which produce at a low rate of profit into those which produce at a higher rate of profit, they cause all prices to rise or fall to the point where all lines of production attract capital equally, or surplus-value is equalized in all lines of production through deviations of price from value.

Now that we have a general idea of how commodity values are transformed into prices of production, we must analyze the question in more detail in order to show how prices of production are "merely changed forms of value" as determined by labor-time.[95] Marx explains that the transformation of commodity values into prices of production does not abolish the law of value as determined by labor-time, but perpetuates it in a different form. In order to understand how the law is perpetuated, we must necessarily go into more detail.

We will begin by calling the money invested in wages variable capital (v) and the the money invested in means of production constant capital (c). The money invested in labor-power is variable capital because the laborer produces more than his own value in the product, while the value invested in means of production is constant capital because it transfers only its given value to the product. The surplus-value (s) is the value which the laborer produces over his wages.

In our former illustration we assumed that capital A pays out $20 for labor-power and $80 for means of production, while capital B pays out $80 for labor-power and $20 for means of production. Since the rate of surplus-value is 100%, the value of commodity A is composed of 80c plus 20v plus 20s or a total value of 120. On the other hand, the value of commodity B is composed of 20c plus 80v plus 80s or a total value of 180. If the two commodities are sold at their values, then the first product is sold at a price of 120, of which 20 is surplus-value, and the second is sold at a price of 180, of which 80 is surplus-value. The surplus-value of the two commodities differ, but their cost prices are the same; that is, A pays out 20v plus 80c and B pays out 80v plus 20c, or each pay out 100. Thus, the cost prices are the same for the products of the different lines of production in which equal quantities of capital have been invested, regardless of their organic composition. As Marx writes, "the equality of cost prices is the basis for the competition of the invested capitals, by which an average rate of profit is brought about."[96]

We shall now compare five different spheres of production in the following table of Marx's, and let the capital in each one of them have a different organic composition. We will assume the rate of surplus-value is 100% for all lines of production and that the complete value of the constant capital (means of production) is transferred to the product, including the fixed capital composed of machinery, buildings, etc.

TABLE I.

*Capital,* III, p. 183.

| | Capitals | Rate of Surplus Value | Surplus Value | Value of Product | Rate of Profit | |
|---|---|---|---|---|---|---|
| I. | 80c plus 20v | 100% | 20 | 120 | 20% | |
| II. | 70c plus 30v | 100% | 30 | 130 | 30% | |
| III. | 60c plus 40v | 100% | 40 | 140 | 40% | |
| IV. | 85c plus 15v | 100% | 15 | 115 | 15% | |
| V. | 95c plus 5v | 100% | 5 | 105 | 5% | |
| | 390c plus 110v | | 110 | 610 | 100% | Total |
| | 78c plus 22v | | 22 | 122 | 22% | Average |

The sum total of the capitals advanced to these five branches of production is 500 and the sum total of the surplus-value is 110. The total value of all the commodities is 610. Now let us look upon the 500 total of the five capitals as one single capital, and let capitals I to V be its various parts. That is, if we add the constant capital advanced we get 390c, and the variable capital added is 110v. In other words, the composition of this capital is 390c plus 110v. Now if we regard each of the 100 advanced as 1/5 of the total capital, we can find the average composition of capital by dividing 390c and 110v by 5. This gives us 78c plus 22v as the average composition of capital. Every 100 would make a surplus-value of 22s with a rate of surplus-value of 100%.

The average profit for each capital would be 22%, and the price of every fifth of the product would be 122, as we assumed that each capital had a cost price of 100 and 22 surplus-value. Each product of 100 capital would have to be sold at a price of 122 if the rate of profit is to be identical in the various lines of production.

Now we must leave our assumption that the cost prices for commodities are the same in all lines of production. A part of the capital is invested in fixed capital, such as machinery, which transfers only a portion of its value through depreciation to the product. In comparing the values produced by each 100 of the different capitals, they will differ as to whether their fixed capital wears out more or less rapidly, with the result that each will transfer unequal quantities of value to the product in equal periods of time. But this is immaterial as far as the rate of profit is concerned, as the profit is still compared to the total capital advanced, not to that portion of it which is actually consumed in production.[97] In order to make this clear, Marx gives the following table in which he transfers a portion of the constant capital value of each of the five capitals to the value of their product:

TABLE II

III, p. 185, Ibid.

| Capitals | | | Rate of Surplus Value | Surplus Value | Rate of Profit | Used Up C | Value of Commodities | Cost Price |
|---|---|---|---|---|---|---|---|---|
| I. | 80c plus | 20v | 100% | 20 | 20% | 50 | 90 | 70 |
| II. | 70c plus | 30v | 100% | 30 | 30% | 51 | 111 | 81 |
| III. | 60c plus | 40v | 100% | 40 | 40% | 51 | 131 | 91 |
| IV. | 85c plus | 15v | 100% | 15 | 15% | 40 | 70 | 55 |
| V. | 95c plus | 5v | 100% | 5 | 5% | 10 | 20 | 15 |
| 390c plus 110v | | | | 110 | 100% | | | Total |
| 78c plus | 22v | | | 22 | 22% | | | Average |

Now let us look again upon capitals I to V as one single capital. The composition of this 500 capital is 390c plus 110v plus 110s, or an average composition of 78c plus 22v, and the average-surplus value is 22s. If we distribute this 22 surplus-value equally from capital I to V, the following prices are arrived at in another table of Marx's:

TABLE III

III, p. 185, Ibid.

| Capitals | | Surplus Value | Value | Cost Price of Com- modities | Price of Commod- ities | Rate of Profit | Deviation of Price from Value |
|---|---|---|---|---|---|---|---|
| I. | 80c plus 20v | 20 | 90 | 70 | 92 | 22% | +2 |
| II. | 70c plus 30v | 30 | 111 | 81 | 103 | 22% | −8 |
| III. | 60c plus 40v | 40 | 131 | 91 | 113 | 22% | −18 |
| IV. | 85c plus 15v | 15 | 70 | 55 | 77 | 22% | +7 |
| V. | 95c plus 5v | 5 | 20 | 15 | 37 | 22% | +17 |
| [Total] | | | [422] | | [422] | | |

The prices which come into existence as a result of drawing the average of the different rates of profit in the various branches of production and adding this average to the cost prices of the commodities, Marx calls the "prices of production."

We now see that the commodities of capitals I, IV, and V are sold at 2, 7, and 17 above their values, or a total of 26 above value, while capitals II and III are sold at 8 and 18 below their values, or a total of 26 below value. Because the commodities as a whole are sold at 26 above and 26 below their values, it is the same effect as if they had been sold at their values, as in the same proportion that some commodities are sold above their values, others are sold below it.[98] Thus Marx writes:

"This always amounts in the end to saying that one commodity receives too little of the surplus-value while another receives too much, so that the deviations from value shown by the prices of production mutually compensate one another."[99]

If we suppose capitals I to V belong to the same man, then the quantity of variable and constant capital used up for each 100 of the invested capitals in the production of commodities would be known, and these parts of the value of commodities I to V would make up a part of their price, because at least this cost price is required to recover the consumed portions of the advanced capitals. These cost prices would vary for each class of the commodities from I to V, and the capitalist would identify them differently. However, the different quantities of surplus-value or profit could easily be looked upon as profits of his total capital, so that every 100 of the total capital would get its proportional quota. The commodities produced in the five depart-

ments would have different cost prices, but that part of their
selling price which results from the addition of profit for every
100 capital advanced would be the same for all of these commodities.[100] And as Marx explains, their total price would be
equal to their total value:

"The aggregate price of the commodities I to V would be
equal to their aggregate value, that is to say it would be equal
to the sum of the cost prices I to V plus the sum of the surplus
values, or profits produced in I to V. It would actually be the
*money expression* of the total quantity of past and present labor
incorporated in the commodities of I to V. And in the same way
the sum of all the prices of production of all commodities in
society comprising the totality of all lines of production is equal
to the sum of all their values."[101]

Thus, if we add the total value of the commodities in the table
and consider this the total commodity production of society, we
get 422; likewise, if we add the total prices at which the commodities are actually sold we also get 422, so that the commodities as a whole are purchased at their values. A given quantity
of money 422 is exchanged for a certain number of commodities
of the same value, that is to say, with a value which represents
the same quantity of labor-time. The fundamentals of the law of
value remain unchanged as commodities and money representing equal quantities of value as determined by labor-time are
equated to each other.

The capitalists in the different branches of production recover
the value of their consumed capital, but they do not receive the
surplus-value and therefore the profit created in their own line
of production. They only receive that surplus-value or profit
which is proportionate to the part which their capitals represent
in the total social capital of society. One branch of production
contributes more than its actual production of surplus-value to
the price of its product, while another contributes less, but these
differences balance each other, so that capitalist production as
a whole contributes the surplus-value actually produced by it
according to its total employment of labor power. The total

surplus-value is equal to the total profit, and each capital, according to its size, shares equally in this total surplus-value or profit. Here is how Marx expresses the idea:

"The average profit cannot be anything else but the total mass of surplus-value allotted to the various masses of capital in the different spheres of production in proportion to their magnitudes."[102]

Even in connection with his explanation of the general rate of profit, Marx gives an idea on associated production. It is only a hint, but it is a thought which Marx had considered carefully as we shall see later when an analysis of profit under cooperative production is considered in more detail. Here are Marx's words:

"What competition is striving to attain between the various masses of capital—differently constituted and invested in different spheres of production—is *capitalist communism*, namely that the mass of capital belonging to each sphere of production should snatch an aliquot part of the total surplus value proportionate to the part of the total social capital that it constitutes."[103]

---

We have seen in the above explanation, that the transformation of values into prices of production did not alter the operation of the law of value, that is, the prices of commodities as a whole are still sold at their approximate total values. Marx gives a similar argument in connection with his explanation of ground rent, but in the case of prices of production under ground rent, there is deviation away from their individual prices of production in the direction toward their individual values. In either case the law of value continues to operate. The following words of Marx mention ground rent in connection with the general rate of profit:

"Neither is the law of value changed by the fact that the equalization of profit, that is, the distribution of the total value among the various capitals, and the obstacles, which private land to some extent puts in the way of this equalization (in absolute rent), makes the regulating average prices different from the individual values of the commodities."[104]

With an understanding of the general rate of profit, we are now ready to begin Marx's explanation of ground rent.

### b. *The Transformation of Surplus Profit into Ground Rent*

## (1.) Differential Rent.

Marx begins his explanation of differential rent with the example of waterpower in the form of a waterfall which exists on one piece of land, but not on others. He explains how the capitalist producer who uses this natural power is able to acquire profit over the general rate of profit because of his favorable position in regard to land with a waterfall.

However, according to Marx, it is not the capitalist who owns this surplus profit; the absentee land owner takes it over from the capitalist by collecting ground rent.

After mentioning surplus profit from the waterfall as an example of rent, Marx goes on to distinguish this form of differential rent from agricultural differential rent. He emphasizes that agricultural rent is but one form of differential rent that gives surplus profit from the land:

"Differential rent appears every time and follows the same laws as the agricultural differential rent . . . wherever natural forces can be monopolized and thereby guarantee a surplus profit to the industrial capitalist using these forces, whether it be waterfalls, or rich mines, or waters with fish, or a favorably located building lot, there the person who by his or her title to a portion of the globe has been privileged to own these things will capture a part of the surplus profit of the active capital by means of rent."[105]

We will disregard for now all forms of differential rent except that of agricultural differential rent, as this is what Marx does in his explanation. The two general causes of agricultural rent, or surplus profit, are: (1) fertility, and (2) location of lands.[106] One piece of land may be more or less fertile than another, and, also, one piece of land may be more or less favorably located than another. But according to Marx, the "progress of social production has . . . the general effect of leveling the differences arising from location as a cause of ground rent."[107] This leaves only fertility as a cause of differential rent; soil fertility is what we shall concentrate on now.

Marx explains agricultural differential rent as the difference between the produce gained by the employment of two equal quantities of capital on the same quantity of land with unequal results:

"Surplus profit . . . is always produced as a difference between the products of two equal quantities of capital and labor. This surplus profit is transformed into ground rent, when two equal quantities of capital and labor are employed on equal quantities of land with unequal results."[108]

Marx further defines surplus profit as "the excess of the individual profit over the average profit,"[109] and it is the landowner who catches this difference between the individual and average profit in the form of ground rent.[110]

Marx defines agricultural rent as it exists under capitalism as follows:

"The premises for a capitalist production in agriculture are these: the actual tillers of the soil are wage-laborers, employed by a capitalist, the capitalist farmer, who carries on agriculture merely as a special field of exploitation for his capital, an investment of his capital in a special sphere of production. This renting capitalist pays to the land owner, the owner of the soil exploited by him, a sum of money at definte periods fixed by contract, for instance annually . . . for the permission to invest his capital in this particular sphere of production. This sum of money is called ground rent. . . ."[111]

The amount of ground rent the capitalist farmer must pay is dependent on the high or low quantity of profit gained from producing on the particular piece of land. Any profit from the land that is over the average profit on capital investment is paid to the landlord in the form of rent.

Marx explains the theory of differential rent by assuming the existence of four kinds of soil, A, B, C, D, with A representing the worst soil and D the most fertile soil. Now assuming a given demand for an agricultural commodity, say wheat, it is soils A through D which must produce for the given demand, at a particular time.

Marx gives the following table which shows different fertilities with the same investment of capital on the same quantity of land:

TABLE I.

III, p. 764, Ibid.

| Class of Soil | Product | | Capital Advanced | Profit | | Rent | |
|---|---|---|---|---|---|---|---|
| | Quarters | Shillings | | Quarters | Shillings | Quarters | Shillings |
| A | 1 | 60 | 50 | 1/6 | 10 | — | — |
| B | 2 | 120 | 50 | 1-1/6 | 70 | 1 | 60 |
| C | 3 | 180 | 50 | 2-1/6 | 130 | 2 | 120 |
| D | 4 | 240 | 50 | 3-1/6 | 190 | 3 | 180 |
| Totals | 10 | 600 | | | | 6 | 360 |

Assuming the prevailing market price for wheat is 60 shillings per quarter, then soil A for 50 shillings investment on a given quantity of land produces 1 quarter of wheat at a price of production of 60 shillings, that is, a price which includes the wages of labor-power and means of production used in the production of the wheat, or 50 shillings advanced capital plus 10 shillings average profit. We must assume that this capitalist is producing on land he owns privately, as he gains no surplus profit from his production, and because ground rent is surplus profit there is no basis for the payment of ground rent. He only gains 10 shillings profit, which is the general rate of profit on 50 shillings.

Soil B, on the other hand, for 50 shillings advanced capital on a piece of more fertile land of the same quantity produces 2 quarters of wheat, which when sold at the prevailing market price of 60 shillings a quarter, gives a total price of 120 shillings. If we subtract the 50 shillings advanced capital and the 10 shillings average profit from the 120 shillings that the capitalist gains from selling the 2 quarters of wheat, we have 60 shillings left which is surplus profit. This 60 shillings is the ground rent he pays to the landowner for the use of the land.

The next fertile soil C, for 50 shillings advanced capital, produces 3 quarters of wheat. When these 3 quarters of wheat are sold at a price of 60 shillings per quarter, the capitalist gains 180 shillings. If we subtract the 50 shillings advanced and the 10 shillings average profit which is the price of production, we have 120 shillings surplus profit, or 120 shillings in ground rent.

And, finally, soil D for an investment of 50 shillings produces 4 quarters of wheat, which when sold at a price of 60 shillings per quarter, gives 240 shillings. When the price of production of 60 shillings is subtracted from the 240 shillings, the surplus profit and ground rent is 180 shillings.

Now let us suppose, for the sake of illustration, that the 1 quarter of wheat of soil A, the 2 quarters of wheat of soil B, the 3 quarters of wheat of soil C, and the 4 quarters of soil D represent the total wheat production of a nation, or that these 10 quarters of wheat comprise the total product of the separate capitals invested in wheat production. The 10 quarters of wheat are sold at a total price of 600 shillings, even though their value (if it is assumed here that the price of production of a commodity and its value are one and the same thing) is only equal to 240 shillings altogether. That is, all four capitals invested in soils A through D have a price of production of 60 shillings, which gives a total of 240 shillings. However, the total product is sold at a price of 600 shillings.

Marx gives this same explanation in *Capital*. He writes that the prices of agricultural products under associated production would differ because of the abolition of ground rent. This is the most direct of Marx's explanations of price under social production. It proves in direct words that he did not advocate the end of all value production, as he writes of the prices of products under association. It also shows that when Marx refers to associated production as "society organized as a conscious and systematic association" he means associated planning in the individual lines of production, as he explains prices in an individual branch of agriculture. And finally, Marx explains away the idea of state ownership of ground rent when he writes that this would not mean any change over what already exists in the form of private ownership of ground rent.

"The actual price of production of these 10 quarters is 240 shillings. But they are sold at 600 shillings, 250% too dear. . . . If we imagine that the capitalistic form of society is abolished and society is organized as a conscious and systematic association, then those 10 quarters represent a quantity of independent labor, which is equal to that contained in 240 shillings. In that case society would not buy this product of the soil at two and a half times the labor time contained in it. The basis of a class of land owners would thus be destroyed. This would have the same effect as a cheapening of the products to the same amount by foreign imports. While it is correct to say that, by retaining the present mode of production but paying the differential rent to the state, the prices of the products of the soil would remain the same, other circumstances remaining unchanged, it is wrong to say that the value of the products would remain the same, if capitalist production were superceded by association. . . . What society in its capacity as a consumer pays too much for the products of the soil, what constitutes a minus for the realisation of its labor time in agricultural production, is now a plus for a portion of society, for the landlords."[112]

Marx thus compares the reduction of prices through the abolition of ground rent to the circumstance that prices might be reduced from 600 shillings to 240 shillings for the home products in a certain line of production through foreign imports. That is, the price of 600 shillings for the total supply of a given commodity in a country would still be 600 shillings but it would be spread over more products, including foreign imports, and the prices of the individual products would fall. According to Marx, the result would be the same in the case of the abolition of ground rent where the 360 shillings which had heretofore gone to the landlord disappears from the total price of the product, and only 240 shillings remain as the total price of the commodities in the particular sphere. In the case of foreign imports, the price of the same home product is reduced from 600 to 240 shillings, and 360 shillings disappears from the total price of the home product in exactly the same way.

As this important part of Marx's theory is explained, an additional comment is necessary in case the explanation should be taken literally. It would be a mistake to imagine more into Marx's words than he directly advocates throughout his writings. In other words, what he advocates is the abolition of ground rent, and here he mentions the reduction of prices which would result. It should be remembered that the idea of differential rent is a theory, just as the idea that prices fall through foreign imports to a certain point of 240 shillings is a theory. That is, it cannot be known beforehand what the exact effect the import of foreign goods will have on prices, and the same holds true with the abolition of ground rent. It is enough to say that, generally speaking, prices will fall.*

It is at least hinted at this point in the explanation that Marx advocates the abolition of landlordism with its collection of ground rent, not the abolition of land ownership in general. Another quotation from Marx will further clarify the idea. He writes that if the capitalist method of value production should be abolished, there should also be an alteration in the form of land ownership which accompanies it. His words indicate that it is "title to the rent," not land ownership by the producers, which should be eliminated.

" . . . title to the rent . . . was created in the first place by the conditions of production. As soon as these have arrived at a point, where they must shed their skin, the material source of the title, justified economically and historically and arising from the process which creates the material requirements of life, falls to the ground, and with it all transactions based upon it. From the point of view of a higher economic form of society, the private ownership of the globe [i.e., title to the rent] on the part of some individuals will appear quite as absurd as the private ownership of one man by another. Even a whole society, a nation, or even all societies together, are not the owners of the globe. They are only its possessors, its users, and they have to hand it down to the coming generations in an improved condition, like good fathers of families." [113]

With this interpretation of land ownership taken for granted, let us return to our analysis of ground rent. We will now present an-

---

* In regard to the lowering of prices through a reduction of ground rent, Marx mentions this point in another place. (See *The American Journalism of Marx and Engels*, pp. 146-147.) He mentions an agricultural distress in England as "confined to the discrepancy between the prices which the tenant farmer paid to the landlord for the land leased and the price at which he sold his agricultural produce. It [the agricultural distress] could therefore be abolished by the simple process of lowering ground rents, the source of income of the landed aristocracy. The latter naturally preferred to lower grain prices by legislative means [by Corn Laws] . . . . if thus the price of grain was maintained above the natural level under certain circumstances, the price of ground rent was kept above that level no matter what the circumstance."

other table of Marx's, which is essentially the same as Table I, but with different figures as its basis.

TABLE II

III, p. 801, Ibid.

| Class of Soil | Acres | Capital P/st | Profit P/st | Cost of Prod. P/st | Product Qrs. | Selling Price P/st | Yield | Rent Qrs. | Rent P/st | Rate of Surplus Profit |
|---|---|---|---|---|---|---|---|---|---|---|
| A | 1 | 2½ | ½ | 3 | 1 | 3 | 3 | | | 0% |
| B | 1 | 2½ | ½ | 3 | 2 | 3 | 6 | 1 | 3 | 12% |
| C | 1 | 2½ | ½ | 3 | 3 | 3 | 9 | 2 | 6 | 24% |
| D | 1 | 2½ | ½ | 3 | 4 | 3 | 12 | 3 | 9 | 36% |
| Totals | 4 | 10 | | 12 | 10 | | 30 | 6 | 18 | |

Marx explains that in studying rent, the point of departure will always be the soil producing the maximum of rent (D), and the closing point the soil yielding no rent (A).

As before, in the above table, there is a total product of 10 quarters—assuming this is the total demand for wheat at a given time—and the market price is 3 pounds sterling per quarter.

Now the question arises, why is the price 3 pounds sterling per quarter, as only class A of soil produces 1 quarter at a price of production of 3 pounds sterling? Because it is a part of the reasoning of the theory of ground rent that the price of production of the worst soil which yields no rent always has the regulating market price.[114]

According to Marx, at a price of production of 3 pounds sterling, the farmers with class A of soil would be prevented from going into production because of the "barrier of private ownership of land." By the barrier of private ownership of land he means the landlord. The capitalist farmer could not usurp a surplus profit from his land with that particular price of the product, which means he could pay no rent. And with no surplus profit or rent, the land would not be rented by the landlord to the capitalist.

"Private property in land is . . . the barrier which does not permit any new investment of capital upon hitherto uncultivated or unrented land without levying a tax, in other words, without demanding a rent, although the land to be taken under new cultivation may belong to a class which does not produce any differential rent, and which, were it not for the intervention of private property in land, might have been cultivated at a small increase in the market price, so that the regulating market price would have netted to the cultivator of this worst soil nothing but his price of production. But on account of the barrier raised by private property in land, the market price must rise to a point, where the land can pay a surplus over the price of production, in other words, where it can pay a rent."[115]

Now in the above table for differential rent, the total product is 10 quarters, assuming this is the quantity of the total demand for wheat at a particular time. Under the law of supply and demand, the demand for wheat might rise or fall, which means that the price would rise if the demand was for more than 10 quarters of wheat and the price would fall, at least temporarily, if the demand should decrease to less than 10. The demand and price might fall to a point where soil B could not produce a surplus profit, and therefore its individual price of production would assume A's place as the regulating market price of production. In turn, this would change the surplus profit and ground rent produced in C and D.

On the other hand, if we consider the growth of rent in a rising scale, the demand might have been for somewhat less than 10 quarters and gradually risen to that amount. The individual price of production found in C, for example, might have been the regulating market price of production, so that only soil D paid a ground rent. As the demand increased, so did the price increase. Soil C entered into the rent paying category at one point, and eventually B if the demand for wheat continued to increase. But when the demand for wheat reached 10, then even soil A went into production with its regulating market price of 3 pounds sterling.

Marx calls this last process a descending succession "from very fertile to less fertile soil." He writes that as soon as the 4 quarters produced by D did not suffice any more, the price of wheat rose to a point where the "missing supply" could be supplied by C.[116] In turn, as soon as the 3 quarters produced by C did not fill the total demand, the price would rise to a point where the missing supply would be filled by the 2 quarters of B and so on up to where the total demand was for 10 quarters, and therefore soil A would produce its 1 quarter at 3 pounds sterling.

There is one question that has not been solved at this point in the explanation. It is the question of how A enters into the production of wheat, assuming a demand for its production does exist, when it does not produce any surplus profit or ground rent. Marx gives the following answer:

"Since the real estate does not net any income until it is rented, a small rise of the market price above the price of production will suffice to bring the new land of the worst class upon the market." [117]

In other words, the market price has to rise to a point higher than the price of production of A, so that it can pay at least a small rent and therefore go into production. A then produces its additional supply, that is, 1 quarter. But "as soon as the additional supply has been created, the relation between supply and demand has been altered. Formerly the supply was insufficient, now it is sufficient. So the price must fall. In order to fall it must have been higher than the price of production of A. But the lesser fertility of the newly added soils of class A brings it about that the price does not fall quite as low as it was at the time when the price of production of the class B regulated the market. The price of production of A forms the limit, not for the temporary, but for the relatively permanent rise of the market price." [118]

The above explanation of rent is a brief summary of what Marx calls differential rent No. I. The complete details of the theory need not be presented here as these can be found from an analysis of *Capital.* We shall now go into an explanation of differential rent No. II.

Marx explains differential rent II as follows: We saw in Table II in the case of the first form of ground rent that different tenants invested 2½ pounds sterling each, on 1 acre of soils A, B, C, D respectively, with 10 quarters of wheat supplied by the four groups. Under differential rent II, on the other hand, it is imagined that the same total investment of 10 pounds sterling is invested successively four times at 2½ pounds sterling each on one and the same acre D, and it is assumed as before that the price of production is 3 pounds sterling. Its first investment of 2½ pounds sterling yields 4 quarters, the second 3 quarters, the third 2 quarters, and the fourth 1 quarter, with the last quarter produced by the least productive capital. At the price of 3 pounds sterling the least productive capital would not pay any rent but it would produce at its price of production, just as long as the supply of wheat with a price of 3 pounds sterling was needed. Thus the four capitals (in D) of 2½ pounds sterling each will make surplus profits according to the difference of their products. The formation of the surplus profit would then be the same as in differential rent I.[119]

But with a price of 3 pounds sterling, soils C and B would also come in, and even soil A might produce if the demand required it. For example, soil C could go into production with a total capital of 7½ pounds sterling, or 2½ pounds sterling invested successively three times. With its first capital of 2½ pounds sterling it could produce 3 quarters, with its second 2 quarters, and its last 2½ pounds sterling would produce 1 quarter at a price production of 3 pounds sterling that would not pay any rent. The capitalist using soil B might invest a total of 5 pounds sterling, with 2½ pounds sterling invested successively two times, that is, with the first capital of 2½ pounds sterling producing 2 quarters, and the second 2½ pounds sterling producing 1 quarter at a price of production of 3 pounds sterling which would pay no rent. And finally, if soil A should go into production, its capital of 2½ pounds sterling would produce 1 quarter and pay no rent.

Marx gives the following table for differential rent II. He explains differential rent II by comparing it with Table II which represents the first form of differential rent.

TABLE III

III, p. 803, Ibid.

| Class of Soil | Acres | Capital P. st. | Profit P. st. | Cost of Prd. P. st. | Product | Sell. Price P. st. | Yield P. st. | Rent Qrs. | Rent P. st. | Rate of S'rpls Profit |
|---|---|---|---|---|---|---|---|---|---|---|
| A | 1 | 2½ | ½ | 3 | 1 | 3 | 3 | 0 | 0 | 0% |
| B | 1 | 2½+2½= 5 | 1 | 6 | 2+1½= 3½ | 3 | 10½ | 1½ | 4½ | 90% |
| C | 1 | 2½+2½= 5 | 1 | 6 | 3+2 = 5 | 3 | 15 | 3 | 9 | 180% |
| D | 1 | 2½+2½= 5 | 1 | 6 | 4+3½= 7½ | 3 | 22½ | 5½ | 16½ | 330% |
| | | 17½ | 3½ | 21 | 17 | | 51 | 10 | 30 | |

In the above table the capital advanced has doubled in each case, but the total product has only increased from 10 to 17 quarters; that is, the total product produced has not doubled. Each of the capitalist farmers has gained 1 pound sterling profit instead of ½ pound sterling because of his doubled investment on the same quantity of land (except on soil A where a doubled investment is unprofitable).

Thus Marx writes of differential rent II:

"It it still the soil which shows different fertilities with the same investment of capitals, only that in this case the same soil does for a capital successively invested in different portions what different kinds of soil do in the case of differential rent No. I for various equally large portions of social capital invested in them." [120]

In the above table, the total rent paid has increased because of an increased intensity of capital on soils B, C, and D. That is, because the surplus profit has increased with each additional investment of capital, so has the total rent as it is surplus profit. It is the land-owner, not the capitalist, who usurps this surplus profit, however; the capital owner continues to gain only the general rate of profit on each successive investment.

Marx explains that additional investments do not have to be uniformly distributed over each class of soil as in the above table, but the point is that when capital is invested successively on the same piece of land, the total product increases, even though in a decreasing amount with each additional capital invested. He writes that it is "immaterial whether the additional second investments of capital are uniformly distributed over the various classes of soil or not; whether the decreasing production of surplus profit proceeds in equal or un-equal proportions; whether the additional investments of capital fall all of them upon the same rent paying class of soil, or whether they are distributed equally or unequally over soils of different quantity paying rent. . . . The only premise is that additional investments of capital must yield a surplus profit on any one of the rent paying soils, but in a decreasing ratio to the amount of the increase of the capital." [121]

Marx writes that as long as the additional capitals are invested in a given soil which yields a surplus profit, the absolute rent in grain and money increases. However, " . . . the limit is here formed by that additional capital which yields only the average profit or the price of production. . . . The price of production remains the same under these circumstances, unless the production upon the lesser soils become superfluous through an increased supply." [122]

According to Marx, the increased investment of capital on the same piece of land does not necessarily bring a decrease in its productivity (as in the case of differential rent II). It can be equally productive, less productive, or it might even increase in productivity. But there is always a rise in the rent calculated per acre.

"The magnitude of the rent calculated per acre increases . . . simply in consequence of the increase of the capital invested in the soil. This takes place when the prices of production remain the same no matter whether the productivity of the additional capital stays unaltered, or decreases or increases. These last named circumstances modify the value, in which the level of the rent per acre rises, but not the fact of this increase itself." [123]

But Marx does mention the fact "that the successive investment of capital upon the same land . . . reaches its limit [i. e., the point where it produces no surplus profit or rent] far more rapidly when the rate of productivity of the capital decreases and the regulating price remains the same, so that in fact a more or less artificial barrier is erected as a consequence of the mere formal transformation of surplus profit into ground rent, which is the result of private property in land [i.e., ownership by the landlord]." [124]

Again, in the above quotation Marx gives his original definition for private ownership of land, that is, he defines it as land ownership which draws ground rent. His explanation of differential rent II also emphasizes the point that with the development of capitalism there is an ever increased concentration of capital on a given piece of land, simultaneously with increased profits for the landlord.

". . . the more the capitalist mode of production develops, the more develops also the concentration of capital upon the same area of land, and the higher rises the rent calculated per acre." [125]

Before leaving this brief explanation of differential rent I and II, there is one additional point which should be mentioned. It might appear obvious, but yet it is important for an understanding of what Marx means by private ownership of land. In reference to his explanation of differential rent II, Marx writes that the successive investments of capital on the same land do not meet the "barrier of private ownership of land"; that is, the land is already in the hands of the producer after the first investment, whereas in the case of ground rent I, the land goes into the possession of the tenant only if it produces a surplus profit and therefore gives the landlord a reason for leasing it.

". . . successive investments of capital, when invested upon different pieces of land, meet the barrier of private ownership of land, which is not the case with successive investments of capital upon the same piece of land." [126]

### (2.) Absolute Rent

Marx's explanation of absolute rent differs somewhat from his explanation of differential rent. In the case of differential rent it was assumed that commodities were sold above their values because of the payment of ground rent. That is, we showed how all but the least productive soil A sold their commodities at a price that was above their individual price of production. And even A had to sell its commodity at its price of production plus "r" so that it could pay a rent. Thus, according to Marx:

"The general rule in differential rent is that the market value always stands above the total price of production of the mass of products." [127]

Now the above idea appears obvious from the standpoint of differential rent, but not under Marx's explanation of absolute rent. We must now leave this particular explanation of agricultural prices and go on to a more advanced one. That is to say, at a certain point Marx admits that while it would appear according to classical economics that the products of agriculture are sold above their values, in actual practice they are not. He explains just why he implied in his explanation of differential rent that agricultural products are sold above their values. It was because up until his explanation of the transformation of commodity values into prices of production (under the general rate of profit), economists did not understand the difference between the value of a commodity and its price of production.

Therefore, Marx does not consider it a contradiction to explain in
the chapter on Absolute Rent that the products of the soil are not
sold at prices above their values.

With an understanding of the labor theory of value, the truth of
his contention is obvious. For instance, in the field of agriculture,
labor is more intensive than in other fields. Products of agriculture
actually contain more surplus-value than is the general case, and
their prices of production stand below their individual values. When
these products are sold at prices which appear to be above their
value, they are actually reaching up toward their real value determined by their individual labor-time content, that is, their value as
distinguished from their price of production, which includes only
the general rate of profit in the price, not the actual value produced
in individual cases. Here is how Marx explains this:

". . . does it follow . . . that the price of the products of the soil
is necessarily a monopoly price in the ordinary meaning of the term,
or a price, into which the rent enters like a tax, only with the distinction that the landlord levies the tax instead of the state? . . . The
point is whether the rent paid by the worst soil passes into the price
of its products . . . whether this rent enters into the price as an element independent of its value. *This does not necessarily follow by
any means,* and the contention that it does has been made only
because the distinction between the value of commodities and their
price of production had not been understood up to the present."[128]

Since an understanding of Marx's explanation of absolute rent depends on an understanding of the transformation of values into prices
of production, we shall refer again to Marx's table on this as it will
make the explanation easier.

III, p. 185, Ibid.

| | Capitals | Surplus Value | Value | Cost Price of Com- modities | Price of Com- modities | Rate of Profit | Deviation of Price from Value |
|---|---|---|---|---|---|---|---|
| I. | 80c plus 20v | 20 | 90 | 70 | 92 | 22% | +2 |
| II. | 70c plus 30v | 30 | 111 | 81 | 103 | 22% | −8 |
| III. | 60c plus 40v | 40 | 131 | 91 | 113 | 22% | −18 |
| IV. | 85c plus 15v | 15 | 70 | 55 | 77 | 22% | +7 |
| V. | 95c plus 5v | 5 | 20 | 15 | 37 | 22% | +17 |

Here in this table it is shown "that the price of production of a
commodity may stand above or below its value, and coincides but

rarely with its value. Hence the fact that the products of the soil are sold above their prices of production does not prove by any means that they are sold above their values. . . . It is possible that the products of agriculture are sold above their price of production and below their value, while many products of industry bring the price of production only because they are sold above their values."[129]

Thus, in the above table capitals II and III sell commodities at prices of production below their individual values determined by their labor-time content, which in this particular case we will assume to be capitals invested in the field of agriculture. Now capital II sells its commodity at minus 8 below its value, and capital III sells its product at minus 18 below its value; these theoretical figures "minus 8" and "minus 18" enter into what Marx calls absolute rent.

For instance, let us concentrate on capital III as one particular type of agricultural production. The individual price of production of the commodity produced by capital III is 113, whereas the real value of the commodity is 131. As we have assumed that this capital is invested in the field of agriculture, then the capitalist pays ground rent, and all types of soil (A-D) must sell their products at prices which exceed the individual price of production of 113, with any increase of the price from 114 to 131 paid as absolute rent to the landlord.

We will suppose, for the sake of illustration, that the market price for the commodity in this particular line of agriculture stands at 130. Now the difference between 113 (its price of production) and 130 is 17. Actually, the commodity could have been sold at any price from 114 to 131 before it would be sold at a price above its value, that is, the difference between its price of production and selling price could be any figure from 1 to 18. At a price of 130 the product is still sold at a price of "minus 1" below its value of 131, determined by the relation of its constant to variable capital, but the price is "plus 17" above its price of production.

Under capitalism, the landlord usurps this 17 (or 1 to 18, as the case may be) in the form of absolute rent because his ownership of land gives him the right to ownership of the results of any addition to the market price of a commodity which exceeds its price of production. But most important of all, this 17 is what Marx calls absolute rent because it is actual value which exists in the commodity.

Marx does admit, though, that "the progress of agriculture expresses itself steadily in a relative increase of the constant over the variable capital"[130] the same as in other branches of industry. But the existence of absolute rent is conditioned on the fact that agricultural capitals use more variable capital, or employ more laborers, than do the capitals of average composition. Here are Marx's words on this:

". . . the value of the agricultural products cannot be higher than their prices of production unless this condition obtains. In other words, a capital of a certain size in agriculture produces more surplus-value, or what amounts to the same, sets in motion and commands more surplus labor (and with it employs more living labor) than a capital of the same size in industry of social average composition.[131] If the average composition of the agricultural capital were the same, or higher than that of social average capital, then absolute rent, in the sense in which we use this term, would disappear."[132]

Thus absolute rent exists so long as the capital invested in agriculture employs more living labor than the capital of average composition. And Marx assumes throughout his explanation of absolute rent that this condition does exist, so that the individual prices of production of the products of agriculture stand below their actual value.

Because the products of agriculture are sold above their individual prices of production, or are not "leveled to the plane of the price of production" like other products of industry, Marx writes that the products of agriculture are sold at monopoly prices and that "private property in land" (ground rent) creates these monopoly prices:

". . . on account of the barrier raised by private property in land, the market price must rise to a point where the land can pay a surplus over the price of production, in other words, where it can pay a rent. . . . So long as the rent is not equal to the excess of the value of agriculture products over their price of production, a portion of this excess would always enter into the general equalization

and proportional distribution of all surplus-value among the various
individual capitals. As soon as the rent is equal to the excess of the
value over the price of production, this entire portion of the surplus-
value over and above the average profit would be withdrawn from
the equalization. But whether this *absolute rent* is equal to the
whole surplus of value over the price of production, or only equal
to a part of it, the agricultural products would always be sold at a
monopoly price, not because their prices would exceed their value,
but because their price would be equal to their value or because
their price would be lower than their value but higher than their
price of production. Their monopoly would consist in the fact that
they are not, like other products of industry whose value is higher
than the general price of production, leveled to the  plane of the
price of production."[133]

In the foregoing illustration it was shown that the price of the
product produced by capital III could rise from 114 to 131 before
the commodity would be sold above its value of 131, and that these
figures of 114 to 131 are 1 to 18 over its price of production of 113.
Marx writes that in actual practice the price of the commodity
could rise gradually up to its value, according to the conditions of
the market. Thus, even though it is land ownership which causes
prices to deviate from their individual prices of production in agriculture, Marx explains that it depends upon the conditions of the
market to what degree the market price of a commodity will exceed
its price of production and approach its value:

"It follows . . . that the price of agricultural products may stand
higher than their price of production without reaching up to their
value. It follows, furthermore, that up to a certain point, a permanent increase in the price of agricultural products may take place,
before their price reaches their value. It follows also that the excess
in the value of agricultural products over their price of production
can become a determining element of their general market price
only because there is a monopoly in private ownership of land[i.e.,
the payment of ground rent]. It follows, finally, that in this case
the increase in the price of the product is not the cause of the rent,
but rather the rent is the cause of the increase in the price of the

product. If the price of the product of the unit of the worst soil is equal to P [price of production] plus r, then all differential rents will rise by the corresponding multiples of r, since the assumption is that P plus r becomes the regulating market price.[134]

"Although the private ownership of land may drive the price of the products of the soil above their price of production, it does not depend upon this ownership but upon the general conditions of the market to what extent the market price shall exceed the price of production and approach the value, and to what extent the surplus-value created in agriculture over and above the average profit shall either be converted into rent or enter into the general equalization of the surplus-value to an average profit. At any rate, this *absolute rent*, which arises out of the excess of value over the price of production, is but a portion of the agricultural surplus-value, a conversion of this surplus-value into rent, its appropriation by the landlord; so does the differential rent arise out of the conversion of surplus profit into rent, its appropriation by the landlord, under an average price of production which acts as a regulator. These two forms of rent [i.e., differential and absolute rent] are the only normal ones. Outside of them the rent can rest only upon an actual monopoly price, which is determined neither by the price of production nor by the value of commodities, but by the needs and the solvency of the buyers."[135]

Marx brings the question of monopoly prices in here, and it should be noticed he considers these an exception to the rule of commodity value. However, when he mentions monopoly prices in the above quotation he does not mean that monopoly price which is created by ground rent. He is referring to another kind of monopoly price which will be discussed later. Marx does not consider either differential rent or absolute rent as outside of the control of the law of supply and demand, and value, as the conditions of the market determine to what extent the price of an agricultural commodity may approach its value. But he calls land ownership a barrier which creates a monopoly price of P plus r, whereas without the payment of ground rent the price would be only P, the price of production of the least productive soil A.

It is interesting to note that Marx's explanation of absolute rent becomes a means to justify private ownership of land (aside from ownership by the landlord) in the form of forests, mines, etc. It becomes his way of combating the idea that private possession of land includes monopoly prices, once there is an abolition of ground rent.

For instance, in the case of enterprise in the forestry industry, he explains that these are labor intensive businesses, as the raw material is timber—a product of nature. This holds true, also, in the case of extractive industries such as mining, etc. Because of the payment of excessive ground rents to the landlords who are owners of the timber, coal, etc., with the higher prices which follow, it would appear that monopoly prices exist. However, Marx disagrees. He writes that these prices include absolute rent, or they represent prices which reflect the real value of the commodities involved. In other words, if commodities are not sold above their values, where is the monopoly price? Here are Marx's words on this:

"The absolute rent explains some phenomena, which seem to make a mere monopoly price responsible for the rent, at first sight. Take, for instance, the owner of some forest, which exists without any human assistance, say in Norway. . . . If this owner of the forest receives a rent from some capitalist, who has timber cut . . . or if this owner has the timber cut in his own capacity as a capitalist, then a greater or smaller rent will accrue to him in the timber, aside from the profit on the invested capital. This looks like a pure increment from monopoly in the case of this product of nature. But as a matter of fact the capital consists here almost exclusively of variable elements invested in labor-power, and therefore it sets more surplus labor in motion than another capital of the same size. The value of the timber contains a greater surplus of unpaid labor, or of surplus-value, than that of a product of some capital of higher organic composition. For this reason the average profit can be drawn from this timber, and a considerable surplus in the form of rent can fall into the hands of the owner of the forest. On the other hand it may be assumed that, owing to the ease with which the felling of timber as a line of production may be extended, the demand must rise very considerably in order that the price of timber should equal its value, so that the entire surplus of unpaid labor (over and above that portion which falls into the capitalist's hands as an average profit) may accrue to the landlord in the form of rent."[136]

Marx also mentions this absolute rent in the case of extractive industries as follows: First, the capitalist usurps surplus-value from the laborers in his line of industry, and then the landlord takes surplus-value from the capitalist in the form of absolute rent. (It has already been emphasized that surplus-value is value taken from the workers originally.) In other words, the surplus-value contained in commodities is shared by capitalist and landlord.

". . . the nature of absolute rent . . . consists in this. . . . The rent forms a portion of the value, or more specifically of the surplus-value, of commodities and instead of falling into the hands of the capitalists, who extract it from their laborers, it is captured by the landlords who extract it from the capitalists. . . . This absolute rent plays an even more important role in the extractive industry, properly so-called, where one element of constant capital, the raw material, is wholly missing, and where, with the exception of those lines, in which the capital consisting of machinery and other fixed capital is very considerable, by far the lowest composition of capital exists. Precisely here, where the rent seems wholly due to a monopoly price, extraordinarily favorable market conditions are necessary in order that commodities may be sold at their value, or that rent may become equal to the entire excess of surplus-value in a commodity over its price of production. This applies for instance to rent in fishing waters, stone quarries, naturally grown forests\*, etc."[137]

At this stage of the explanation Marx approaches a point where prices are practically re-transformed from prices of production

---

\* In one place Marx hints at the need for preservation and production of forests as follows: "The development of civilization and of industry in general has ever shown itself so active in the destruction of forests, that everything done by it for their preservation and production, compared to its destructive effect, appears infinitesimal." *Capital*, vol. II, p. 279.

into values—at least this holds true in the case of agricultural production, with its payment of absolute rent. We shall therefore repeat Marx's table which explains commodities sold at their values before the establishment of a general rate of profit.

III, p. 185, Ibid.

| | Capitals | | Rate of Sur. Value | Surplus Value | Rate of Profit | Used Up Capital | Value of Product | Cost Price |
|---|---|---|---|---|---|---|---|---|
| I. | 80c plus | 20v | 100% | 20 | 20% | 50 | 90 | 70 |
| II. | 70c plus | 30v | 100% | 30 | 30% | 51 | 111 | 81 |
| III. | 60c plus | 40v | 100% | 40 | 40% | 51 | 131 | 91 |
| IV. | 85c plus | 15v | 100% | 15 | 15% | 40 | 70 | 55 |
| V. | 95c plus | 5v | 100% | 5 | 5% | 10 | 20 | 15 |
| | 390c plus 110v | | | 110 | 100% | | | Total |
| | 78c plus 22v | | | 22 | 22% | | | Average |

Now in the case of absolute rent, we assumed that capital III might sell its commodity at 131, which is its value. We assumed that 18 of the 40 surplus-value might go to the landlord in the form of absolute rent, and 22 of the total price would go to the capitalist as the general rate of profit on capital.

Let us suppose, for the sake of illustration, that both the general rate of profit as personified by the capitalist, and ground rent as personified by the landlord were gone, but that the same organic composition of capital continues to exist in the various spheres, or the relation of constant to variable capital is the same as in the above table. Under these conditions the 40 surplus-value would reflect the number of workers or individuals in the particular sphere (including labor and management), not the general rate of profit on capital. Since it would no longer be a question of the capitalists sharing equally in the profits but the workers in all spheres sharing equally, there would no longer be any contradiction in the fact that commodities would be sold at their values in the particular spheres. In other words, in the case of cooperative production it is assumed that all commodities would eventually be re-transformed naturally back into their values, just as they already are in the case of absolute rent in agriculture. The landlord would no longer gain his 18 in absolute rent, and neither would the capitalist own his 22, but it would all go to those actually at work in production.

The difference in theory is that while under capitalism it is the general rate of profit which directs production, in the case of co-operative production it is the general rate of surplus-value which directs production. Thus, the law of value would go on without the general rate of profit on capital and ground rent. In other words, if the rate of surplus-value in a particular sphere should rise above 100% (as the rate of surplus-value is assumed to be in the above table) production would be increased in that sphere, while if the rate of surplus-value should fall below 100% there would be less production, according to the conditions of supply and demand.

It was mentioned before that Marx hints at this situation of the workers sharing equally in the profits when he writes that the capitalists practice *capitalist communism* when they share equally in the profits in the form of the general rate of profit on capital.

But to return to Marx's explanation of absolute rent. His contention that those who utilize the soil do not gain monopoly prices under absolute rent justifies the ownership of surplus-value by those who use the land. However, the details of land ownership still remain unclear at this point which means that further explanation is necessary.

Marx also mentions absolute rent in connection with small peasants' property, and he does it in a way which adds to the understanding of what he means by land ownership. He writes that when the farmer is the free owner of his land, there is differential rent, or a surplus portion of the prices of commodities goes to the producer with the superior or more favorably located lands, the same as under capitalism. But he writes that under this form, no absolute rent exists. It does not exist because there is no average profit or a landlord. This means that the worst land does not pay rent, and therefore "r" does not enter into the prices of products. The fact that the farmer might gain increased profits from his superior land is compensated for by the price of land which enters into his cost price. Marx gives the following explanation of small peasants property:

"Here the farmer is the free owner of his land. . . . Whatever may be the manner, in which the average market price of the products of the soil is regulated in this case, the differential rent, a surplus portion of the price of commodities from the superior or more favorably located lands, must evidently exist in this case just as it does under the capitalist mode of production. . . . Only it flows into the pocket of the farmer, whose labor realises itself under favorable natural conditions. It is precisely under this form that the assumption is correct, as a rule, that no absolute rent exists, so that the worst soil does not pay any rent. For under this form the price of land enters as an element into the actual cost of production for the farmer. . . . Absolute rent is conditioned either upon the realised surplus of the value of the product above its price of production, or a monopoly price exceeding the value of the product. But since agriculture is carried on here largely . . . for direct subsistence, so that the land is an indispensable field of employment for the labor and capital of the majority of the population . . . the regulating market price of the product will come up to its value only under extraordinary circumstances." [138]

It should be noticed that there is a similiarity between this form of private agriculture and the cooperative form that we have just described. That is, under both forms, the general rate of profit as personified by the capitalist and absolute rent as personified by the landlord do not exist. Now in our illustration it was shown that absolute rent consists of the 18 in money difference between the price of production of the commodity (122) and its value of 131. Just as in the case of the cooperative producers, the private farmer pockets this instead of the landlord. But what happens to the 22 as heretofore pocketed by the capitalist? It is here that a difference arises between the small farmer and the cooperative producers. The small farmer suffers from the lack of development of capitalism in the following way. He becomes an independent wage worker, that is, he only works sufficient time to create his means of subsistence, and there is little or no surplus-value as under capitalism. On the other hand, cooperative production is established on the basis of capitalism where surplus-value is created, and it is therefore shared by those who create it.

As Marx expresses this idea, under the small farmers' method "the regulating market price of the product will come up to its value only under extraordinary circumstances," and a certain amount of poverty exists. However, under capitalism and the cooperative method, the prices of commodities can reach up to their value. Under capitalism this is the result of the existence of ground rent, whereas under the cooperative method, it continues on the basis of what has already been established under capitalism.

But to return to the similarities between cooperative enterprise and the private farmer in agriculture. Absolute rent does not exist under either system, and this is the important point of understanding. The omission of absolute rent includes free ownership of land by the producer in the case of the private farmer, and this implies free ownership of land by the cooperative producers also. In other words, since it is the payment of ground rent which goes down with an abolition of landlordism and since independent farmers' production is an example of a society without ground rent, then the free land holding farmer gives some insight into what follows after capitalism with its abolition of the private landlord.

-----

Before leaving this explanation of ground rent, including differential and absolute rent, there is one more point which should be mentioned in connection with the cultivation of the soil after the abolition of capitalism. For instance, the question arises as to how the movement will be made from superior to inferior soils when the payment of ground rent no longer exists. Marx writes that this will come about naturally as a result of rising prices under the cooperative method the same as under those methods of production which precede it in history:

"The advance in the extension of the cultivated soil in general takes place either toward inferior soil, or upon the various existing soils in different proportions according to the way in which they present themselves. The step toward inferior soil naturally is never made voluntarily, but cannot be due to anything but to rising prices (assuming the capitalist mode of production to be a fact) and *under any mode of production* it will be a result of necessity. However, this is not absolutely so. An inferior soil is preferred to a relatively better soil on account of its location, which decides the point during all extension of cultivation in new countries; furthermore for the reason that, while the formation of the soil in a certain region may belong to the superior ones, the better will neverthless be relieved here and there by inferior soil, so that the inferior soil must be cultivated along with the superior on account of its location." [139]

### c. *The Price of Land*

Marx begins his explanation of the price of land by leaving out of consideration (1) all fluctuations of competition, or variations in supply and demand, (2) land speculation, and (3) small landed property. This latter form of property, or property of the small farmer, has a price system of its own since the land, in this case, is a primary instrument of production for the farmer, and he purchases it at any price in order to produce his means of subsistence. [140]

Marx writes the following in regard to the price of land, aside from the theory of it which exists under ground rent.

". . . the price of things . . . such as the land, or which at least cannot be reproduced by labor, such as antiquities, works of art of certain masters, etc., may be determined by many accidental combinations." [141]

We will disregard this explanation of the price of land, however, as Marx gives a further explanation for its price. He defines the price of land as "nothing but the capitalized and therefore anticipated rent" [142] and explains what he means as follows:

"If the surplus profit [i.e., rent] realised . . . amounts to 10 pounds sterling per year, and the average interest is 5% then these 10 pounds sterling annually represent the interest on a capital of 200 pounds sterling; and this capitalization of the annual 10 pounds sterling . . . appears as the capital value of the waterfall [or land]." [143]

This is Marx's definition of the price of land as it exists under capitalism. He goes on to explain that the 200 pounds sterling represents the surplus profit of 10 pounds sterling for 20 years. In other

words, in 20 years the land owner will receive back the 200 pounds
sterling paid out for the purchase of land, assuming he gains 10
pounds sterling each year from his appropriation of ground rent
from the capitalist. However, that same land ownership will enable
the landlord to usurp ground rent for 30, or 100, or an indefinite
number of years.[144]

Thus the price of land, although it appears to be a logical justification for ground rent and the landlord, has the hidden result of a
perpetual separation of the producers from ownership of the land,
or it contains a hidden despotism of the same kind which exists
under capitalism with its separation of the producers from ownership of their means of production.

But it is not the fact that land has a price which is the object of
criticism. It is the landlord's right to economic existence in the first
place, or his right to ground rent. Again, amidst all of the criticisms,
it should be remembered that the abolition of capitalism involves
only certain defined changes.

The question of rent on buildings, etc., is sometimes confused
with the subject of ground rent. Marx does away with this confusion
in the following words:

"Capital may be fixed in the soil, may be incorporated in it,
either in a transient manner, as it is by improvements of a chemical
nature, fertilization, etc., or more permanently, as in drainage canals,
irrigation works, leveling, farm buildings, etc. . . .The interest on
the capital thus incorporated in the soil . . . may form a part of the
rent paid by the capitalist farmer to the land owner, but it does not
constitute that ground rent." [145]

In the case of building rents, Marx only criticizes the building speculator mildly in comparison with the land owner, who in the mean-
time charges for ground rent. He writes that the builder who
charges rent does not gain anything on the rent of buildings; these
only yield him interest. It is the land owner and his ground rent
at the base of it all which causes the speculation. Here is a quotation from Marx on this:

"That it is the ground-rent, and not the house, which forms the
actual object of building speculation in rapidly growing cities, espe-

cially when building is carried on as an industry, as it is in London, we have already shown in Volume II . . . where we quoted from the testimony of a large . . . building speculator, Edward Capps . . . the same man said: . . . for the contractor makes very little profit out of the buildings themselves, he makes his principal profits out of the rise of ground-rents. He takes up, for instance, a piece of land and pays 300 pounds sterling annually for it. If he erects the right class of houses upon it after a careful building plan, he may succeed in making 400 or 500 pounds sterling out of it, and his profit would consist much more of the increased ground-rent of 100 or 150 pounds sterling annually than of the profit from the buidings, which in many cases he does not consider at all. And it should not be forgotten that after the lapse of the lease, at the end of 99 years, as a rule, the land with all the buildings upon it and with the ground-rent, generally increased to twice or thrice its original amount, reverts from the building speculator or from his legal successor to the original landlord who was the last to rent it." [146]

Such a criticism of landlordism or ground rent could mistakenly be considered an argument against building rent. But not if ground rent is understood as different from house and building rent. House and building rent reflect simple interest on capital and are not interfered with in the case of cooperative production. Again, it is the payment of ground rent which is the main object of Marx's criticism here, not land ownership or other forms of rent.

Marx writes that "the building of houses meets a barrier in the private ownership of the land upon which the houses are to be built by people who do not own this land. . . . But after this land has once been leased for the purpose of building houses on it, it depends upon the tenant whether he wants to build a large or a small house." [147]

In other words, if the landlord is a barrier to the building of houses on land, then when the landlord is gone and the land is purchased by those who would build on the land, there is no barrier to the building of houses.

Marx differentiates between ground rent and building rent in another place when he mentions these as both entering into the cost prices of individual capitalists, just as interest does in the case of borrowed capital:

". . . interest . . . enters into the cost price of the commodities produced by any individual capitalist. So does also the ground rent in the form of lease money fixed by contract in the case of the agricultural capitalist, and in the form of rent for business rooms in the case of other business men."[148]

What Marx advocates, and what others might advocate as a result of a pre-occupation with the subject of building rents, differ. For instance, there is Henry George (the well known American economist) who would have replaced the landlord's ownership of ground rent with state ownership of it. He would maintain private possession of the land but abolish the purchase and sale of land as a commodity, or ownership of land as we understand it. While this might appear on the surface to be acceptable, it is not Marx's idea. This was proved heretofore in the quotation from Marx which showed how state ownership of ground rent would not be any improvement over what already exists under capitalism.

There is a certain similarity between Henry George's and Marx's explanation, however, which proves that Henry George had good intentions. In other words, he would have maintained private possession of land just as Marx would, but he was deficient in his understanding of ground rent, a theory which only Marx has explained in its entirety.

Thus, while Marx also uses the term "private possession of land" and advocates its existence after the end of landlordism, in his case he means private ownership in the modern sense as it is understood in America. He would re-establish ownership of the land by the producers, not perpetuate a separation of the producers from ownership as in the case of state ownership of ground rent. (According to Marx's explanation, state ownership existed in times past under various forms of despotism.) For instance, here are Marx's words which praise the free holding of land as it exists in America, as differentiated from the landlordism of Europe. When he comments on the evils of slavery as it existed before the American Civil War, it should be noticed that he praises America's freedom of land ownership with as much enthusiasm as he praises our republican form of government:

". . . the true people of England, of France, of Europe, consider the cause of the United States [Northern side of Civil War] as their own cause, as the cause of liberty, and that, despite all paid sophistry, they consider *the soil of the United States as the free soil of the landless millions of Europe,* as their land of promise, now to be defended sword in hand from the sordid grasp of the slaveholders. . . . The first grand war of contemporaneous history is the American war. . . . The people of Europe know that a fight for the continuance of the Union is a fight against the continuation of the slavocracy—that in this contest the *highest form of popular self-government till now realized* is giving battle to the meanest and most shameless enslaving recorded in the annals of history."[149]

With such glowing words of praise for America, including its land ownership as distinguished from rented possession of land as it exists in Europe, there can be little doubt as to Marx's real motives. But at this point the theory of ground rent would still seem to argue against ownership of land by individuals, which means that further explanation is required.

With our purpose more clear in this study of ground rent, let us return to the question of the price of land. Now according to Marx, the price of land under capitalism is connected with ground rent, so that the more ground rent a particular piece of land draws each year, the higher would be its price on the market. We have seen that there are two causes for the high or low quantity of rent gained from a given piece of land. These are: (1) differences in fertility and (2) location.

In reference to the first cause of rent, Marx writes that "difference in natural fertility is one of the chemical compositions of the top soil, that is, of its different contents in plant nourishment. . . . Fertility, although an objective quality of the soil, always implies economic relations, a relation to the existing chemical and mechanical development in agriculture, of course it changes with such development. By dint of chemical applications . . . or of mechanical appliances (such as special plows for heavy soils) the obstacles may be removed, which made a soil of the same fertility as some other actually less fertile."[150]

The implication here is that the development of means of soil improvement and scientific agriculture will gradually lessen by artificial means the differences in soil fertility.

Location is mentioned as the second cause for differences in agricultural rent. However, it has already been explained in the section on differential rent that Marx discards even this factor as eventually unimportant because as civilization develops, all land becomes easily accessible. "The progress of social production has . . . the general effect of leveling the differences arising from location as a cause of ground rent, by creating local markets and improving locations by means of facilities for communication and transportation."[151]

It would be premature at this stage of history to predict that the ever increasing advance of civilization will eventually dissolve the theory of differential rent, even though Marx's explanation seems to hint at it. But regardless of his constant criticism of ground rent and the land owner, Marx always assumes the existence of differences in soil fertility.

His main argument against tenant agriculture is that its methods are a drawback to the improvement of the soil. As he puts it, the absentee ownership of the landlord is an obstacle to the rational development of agriculture. That is to say, because the landlord, not the tenant, owns any improvements made on the land, the tenant farmer lacks the necessary incentive to improve the soil. Here are Marx's words:

". . . as soon as the time stipulated by contract has expired . . . the improvements embodied in the soil become the property of the land owner as an inseparable part of the land. In the new contract, which the land owner makes, he adds the interest for the capital incorporated in the soil to the real ground rent. And he does this whether he leases the land to the same capitalist who made these improvements or to some other capitalist farmer. His rent is thus increased or, if he wishes to sell his land . . . its value has risen. He sells not merely the soil, but the improved soil, the capital incorporated in the soil for which he did not pay anything. . . . Thus they pocket a result of social development brought about without their help. . . . But this is at the same time one of the greatest obstacles to a rational development of agriculture, because the capitalist renter avoids all improvements and expenses, for which he cannot expect any returns during the time of his lease."[152]

Once the producers own their own soil, along with the improvments they make, there will be a more rational development of the soil because the necessary incentive will be present. Thus according to Marx, ". . . the soil if properly treated, improves all the time. The advantage of the soil is that successive investments of capital may bring gains without losing the older ones, and this implies the possibility of differences in the yields of these successive investments of capital."[153]

In one place Marx gives an example of deterioration of the soil— not because of landlordism but government interference. This might be considered one more argument against the idea of state owner- ship of land. Marx begins his argument by explaining that artificial irrigation by canals and water works was the basis of Oriental agri- culture. He then writes: "This prime necessity of an economical and common use of water, which in the Occident drove *private enterprise to voluntary association,* as in Flanders and Italy, neces- sitated in the Orient, where civilization was too low and the terri- torial extent too vast to call into life voluntary association, the *interference of the centralizing* power of the government. This artificial fertilization of the soil, dependent on a central government, and immediately decaying with the neglect of irrigation and drain- age, explains the otherwise strange fact that we now find whole ter- ritories barren and desert that were once brilliantly cultivated."[154]

In passing, it should be noted here that Marx again brings in the question of voluntary association as the ideal situation, aside from government planning.

Assuming there is a continuation of private ownership of land, along with improvements embodied in it, after the abolition of land- lordism (ground rent), the question of the price of land under such conditions still remains. It might be sufficient to say, as Marx does,

that the price of land may be determined "by many accidental combinations" such as competition, or supply and demand, etc. But the
fact remains that the price of land as it now exists is the result of
capitalist development. The question is, can the buying and selling
of land remain without ground rent, because according to the theory,
price is capitalized ground rent? Obviously, the answer is yes, as it
exists in America, for example, without ground rent. However,
experience alone is not sufficient here; there must be something in
Marx's theory to substantiate this idea in order for the point to be
proved once and for all. Let us continue then in our analysis of
the price of land.

There are quotations to be found in *Capital* which can be used
to justify the "price of land" after capitalism, and there are also
criticisms of it in connection with small peasants property. For
instance, in one place he refers to the circulation of land as a commodity, as existing both before and after capitalism. He writes that
it exists when capitalism "no longer" exists or when capitalism is
"not yet" in existence:

"The fact that the price of land plays such a role, that the sale
and purchase of land, the circulation of land as a commodity, develops to this degree, is a practical result of capitalist development,
since a commodity is here the form generally assumed by all products and all instruments of production. On the other hand, this
development takes place only wherever capitalist production develops but to a limited extent and does not bring forth all its pecu-
liarities. For this condition rests precisely on the fact that agriculture *is no longer, or not yet, subject to the capitalist* mode of
production."[155]

There is one other quotation in *Capital* which hints at the continued buying and selling of land as a commodity after capitalism.
He explains how the condition comes about that land develops a
price which seems to be independent of differential rent, even
though it is still indirectly connected with it. This substantiates our
idea that a price of land can exist without ground rent itself in
existence. It is in connection with small peasants' property that he
mentions this important point. It should be remembered again that

we noticed a similarity between this kind of ownership and that form which exists after capitalism. These are Marx's words:

"For under this form the price of land enters as an element into the actual cost of production for the farmer, since in the course of the further development of this form the price of land may have been figured, for instance in the case of a division of an estate, at a certain money value, or, in view of the continuous change in the ownership of the whole property, or of its parts, the land may have been bought by the tiller himself, largely by taking up money on a mortgage. In this way, the price of land, which is nothing else but a capitalized rent, is a pre-existing condition and rent seems to exist independently of any differentiation in the fertility and location of the land."[156]

It is interesting to see that Marx writes further on, in connection with this same independent farmers' kind of landed property, that ". . . the barrier of property is eliminated in his case." By the barrier of property he, of course, means a landlord to whom the farmer would otherwise have to pay ground rent if he did not own his own land. But Marx goes on to say that interest on the price of land then appears as a barrier. He writes that ". . . this interest can be paid out of that portion of the surplus labor, which would form the profit under capitalist conditions."[157]

At this point Marx goes on to criticize the price of land as a part of the cost price for the small farmer. He explains that ". . . the price of land is regulated by the rate of interest, if the ground rent is a given magnitude. If the rate of interest is low, then the price of land is high, and vice versa. Normally, then, a high price of land and a low rate of interest would have to go hand in hand, so that if the farmer paid a high price for the land in consequence of a low rate of interest, the same low rate of interest should also secure for him his running capital on easy terms of credit. But in reality things turn out differently under small peasants' property, as the prevailing form. In the first place the general laws of credit do not apply to the farmer, since these laws rest upon the capitalist as a producer. In the second place, where small peasants' property predominates . . . the price of land rises . . . while the rate of interest is relatively high."[158]

Now as one considers carefully these particular words of Marx, with a look to the future, even they become a means to justify the price of land after capitalism. Assuming, as Marx does, that a high price of land is compensated for by a low rate of interest, then under capitalism in which the laws of credit apply, no problem exists in the purchase of land. And since the laws of credit apply under capitalism they would also apply under the profit sharing method which follows, as it is also a scientific method of production.

If it is assumed that differences in fertility of the soil exist after the abolition of ground rent, then the high price paid for land of high fertility compensates for the rent that is not paid by these producers with the more fertile soil. There is like compensation with land of lower fertility. That is, in the case of land of the worst soil, its price is low, or practically no money is paid out for the land in purchase.

The above description of ownership without the payment of ground rent is, of course, only a restatement of what already exists under capitalism when the land is owned by the capitalist himself. It is included in the argument in order to alleviate the fear that all will be chaos and inequality with an end to the payment of differential rent.

It should be mentioned here that, according to Marx, capitalist ownership of land—and therefore its purchase by the capitalist producer who owns the land—is a deviation from the normal, or it exists under rare circumstances. That is why Marx writes that the purchase of land and its ownership by those who use it exists only after caplitalism, or before it in the case of the independent farmer.

That the price paid for land compensates for the non-payment of ground rent is reflected in the following words of Marx. He refers to the price paid for land as rent for land paid in advance:

"The price of the uncultivated soil of various classes (assuming differential rent to exist) is determined by the price of the cultivated lands of the same quality and equivalent location . . . even in the case of cultivated lands *their price pays only future rents,* as for instance, when the regulating rate of interest is 5% and the rent for 20 years is paid in advance at one time."[159]

Marx differentiates between the purchase of land by the producers and its purchase by a prospective landlord for the purpose of charging ground rent. In fact, in his definition of the purchase of land he assumes it to be purchased not for use but for "title to the rent." In one place, Marx rejects the idea that the purchase of land by the landlord is first or running capital, any more than the purchase of bonds is an investment in a productive line of industry. The landlord is separate from production in the same way that bonds are; that is, bonds are interest-bearing papers and form no ownership of industry.

". . . capital invested in the purchase of land [by the prospective landlord] . . . is neither first nor running capital, any more than the capital, which some one may invest at the Stock Exchange in the purchase of consols or state bonds, and which represent a personal investment of capital for him, is "invested" in any productive line of industry; it merely secures for the buyer a *title to the annual rent,* but has nothing to do with production of the rent itself."[160]

Marx expresses the same idea in another way when he writes:

"The price of the land is nothing but the capitalized, and therefore anticipated rent. If agriculture is carried on by capitalist methods, so that the landlord receives only the rent, and the tenant pays nothing for the land except his annual rent, then it is evident that the capital invested by the owner of the land himself in the purchase of the land constitutes an interest-bearing investment of capital for him, but that it has nothing to do with the capital invested in agriculture itself. If forms neither a part of the fixed nor of the circulating capital employed here."[161]

From the above, it can be seen again that when Marx refers to ownership of land he means "title to the rent" by the landlord as it exists under capitalism, not land ownership by those who use it.

Now under capitalism where the capitalist tenant pays ground rent to a landlord separate from production, the price of land does not enter into the cost price of commodities, but ground rent does.

It has already been shown, in the case of absolute rent, how the rent passes over into the market prices of products, so that agricultural prices rise in the direction toward their value. Further on, Marx goes so far as to say that the price of land passes over in the same way into the prices of products, because it is capitalized rent. Thus he writes:

". . . the rent, and with it capitalized rent, or the price of land, can pass into the prices of the products of the soil in two cases only. The first case is that in which the value of the products of the soil stands higher than their price of production and the market conditions enable the landlord to realize this difference [i.e., in the case of absolute rent]; this condition of values and prices of production obtains, when the composition of the agricultural capital raises the value above the price of production. This agricultural capital has nothing to do with the capital invested in the purchase of land. The second case is that in which a monopoly price exists. And both cases occur less under small peasants' property and small landownership *than under any other form,* because production largely satisfies the producers' own wants in their case and is carried on independently of the regulation by the average rate of profit." [162]

What Marx is explaining here, when he writes of the price of land passing over into the value of products, is capitalist farming where land is either owned by the capitalist or a landlord separate from the land. Let us consider, first, ownership by the landlord. When rent is paid to the landlord, it is at the same time a payment back to him of the price of the land. Thus, looked at from one point of view, the entrance of differential rent into prices is also a portion of the price of land passing into the price of the product. And it is the same way with the capitalist who owns his own land, that is, his profit from the land is a return of the price paid out for the purchase of land.

When Marx writes that the two economic categories (1) rent and (2) capitalized rent, or the price of land, have the same effect when they pass over into the prices of agricultural products, he is in fact stating that the system of differential rent continues after the abolition of ground rent, with the difference that the money spent for the purchase of land replaces the payment of ground rent. For example, the price paid for land depends on the surplus profits produced annually from the land; and as the land is used these surplus profits come back to the producers who use it, with the profits repaying (over a period of years) the original outlay of capital for land purchase. There is a difference, of course, in the total market price of the product after the abolition of ground rent. That is, the market price of a particular agricultural product will be lower than it is with the payment of rent to a landlord by the amount "r." It will still be the price of production of the least productive soil A which will be the regulating market price, but since there will be no ground rent paid, the regulating price of the worst soil A will be P, not P plus r.

It should be noticed, also, in the above quotation that Marx refers to capitalized rent, or the price of land, as entering into the prices of products "less under small peasants' property and small land ownership than under any other form." Now the only other forms of landed property which purchase land are (1) ownership by the landlord, (2) ownership by the capitalist, and (3) ownership by the producers under the cooperative method. Marx is thus implying that the price of land in the price of products continues after the abolition of capitalism. The words "any other form" imply a kind of land ownership other than that which exists under either capitalism or small peasants' property, but the price of land and independent ownership exist under all three forms.

Aside from these hints of the future implied in the above quotation, Marx brings in the question of monopoly prices. He mentions a second case where the price of land enters into the prices of products, that is, when there is a monopoly price. Marx goes so far as to give an example of what he means by a monopoly price here. Again, as in other cases, he considers the existence of a monopoly price as a deviation from the rule, so that there is no problem in the fundamental theory. The deviation from the rule exists in the fact that a particular commodity cannot be reproduced to an unlimited extent, according to the demand, as other commodities can be. Here are Marx's words:

"A vineyard producing wine of very extraordinary quality, a wine which *can be produced only in a relatively small quantity, carries a monopoly price.* The winegrower would realize a considerable surplus profit from this monopoly price, the excess of which over the value of the product would be wholly determined by the wealth and the fine appetite of the rich wine drinkers. This surplus profit, which flows from a monopoly price, is converted into rent and in this form falls into the hands of the landlord. . . . Here, then, the monopoly price creates the rent."[163]

---

There is one more point which should be mentioned before leaving this battle with words to preserve the buying and selling of land. As mentioned heretofore, Marx is in constant disagreement with small peasants' property. It is not that he would destroy this kind of land ownership, because it is the payment of ground rent or landlordism which goes down with an abolition of capitalism. However, as a side comment, he does consider it fortunate that the development of capitalism reduces this small peasants' type of land ownership. He is against it because it works against the group form of agriculture which exists under capitalism. He refers to the capitalist kind of agriculture as a rational, social utilization of the soil. Of course the profit sharing method is the same group form of agriculture that exists under capitalism, but the land is owned by the group in the enterprise, not an individual producer as in the case of small peasants' property. Thus, it is the type of land ownership which changes, not land ownership itself. But the individual producer, because his land ownership is within the boundaries of ownership separate from the landlord, is left untouched by the abolition of capitalism and ground rent. Here are Marx's words on this:

"Private ownership of the land [i.e., landlordism], and with it the expropriation of the direct producers from the land—the private property of some which implies lack of private property on the part of others—is the basis of the capitalist mode of production . . . in agriculture on a small scale, *the price of the land a form and result* of private ownership of land [i.e., the payment of ground rent], appears as a barrier of production itself. In agriculture on a large scale, and in the case of large estates resting upon a capitalist mode of production, private ownership [landlordism] likewise acts as a barrier because it limits the tenant in his investment of productive capital, which in the last analysis benefits, not him, but the land-lord. In both forms the exploitation and devastation of the powers of the soil takes the place of a consciously rational treatment of the soil in its role of an eternal social property, of an indispensable condition of existence and reproduction for successive generations of human beings. . . . in the case of small property this happens from lack of means and science, by which the social productivity of labor-power might be utilized. In the case of large property, it is done by the exploitation of such means for the purposes of the most rapid accumulation of wealth for the tenant and proprietor."[164]

Again, it should be noticed that Marx refers to the price of land as a "form and result" of the payment of ground rent or landlordism. If it is a form of ground rent, this means that even though the land-lord class is eliminated from economic society, the payment of ground rent continues to exist in the purchase price of land, because differences in soil fertility continue to exist.

Also, if both the capitalist and the landlord with his collection of ground rent should disappear, then the cooperative producers would purchase and own the land, and there would be an incentive in their case for an improvement of the soil. This incentive does not exist under capitalism because of landlordism.

### d. *The Historical Nature of Ground Rent*

*(In addition to Wage Labor and the General Rate of Profit)*

From what has gone before in this explanation of ground rent, a relatively clear picture is present as to what exists after its abolition, and even what exists before it in the form of small peasants' property has been explained. In other words, it is obvious that ground rent exists only at a definite period of history, or it exists simultaneously with capitalism. Still, there are more ideas from Marx on this point which should destroy once and for all those ideas which he did not advocate and make clear what he did.

According to Marx, the theory of ground rent is the fundamental theory of classical economics, and it holds the hidden key to an understanding of capitalism and all that it involves. By classical economics he means that theory which justifies capitalism. Consequently, as capitalism begins to manifest contradictions in its operations, its economic theory also begins to become inapplicable. Hence the attempt to imagine what comes after capitalism, or new versions of economic theory begin, as for instance in the section on absolute rent an attempt was made to picture a market controlled system without the general rate of profit on capital, and ground rent.

Marx refers to modern economists who imagine new theories of capital, wage-labor, and ground rent based on old economic conditions as unreasonable because classic economy is in its declining years:

"The physiocrates are . . . correct in stating that the production of surplus-value, and with it all development of capital, has for its natural basis the productivity of agricultural labor. . . . But what are we to say of more recent writers on economics . . . who repeat the most primitive conceptions concerning the natural requirements of surplus labor and surplus-value in general, at a time when *classic economy is in its declining years, or even on its deathbed,* and who imagine that they are thus saying something new and convincing on ground rent, after this ground rent has long developed a peculiar form and has become a specific part of surplus value? It is precisely characteristic of vulgar economy that it repeats things which were new, original, deep and justified during a certain outgrown stage of development, at a time when they become platitudinous, stale, false."[165]

Just as Marx says, at a certain point in history the theory of ground rent was new, and he explains in his writing just when it was new. That is, he goes back to the time when ground rent was not surplus profit in the modern sense of the word, but surplus labor for the feudal owner of the soil. It was not surplus labor-time in the form of surplus-value as we understand it in money, but simple unpaid labor-time for the feudal lord. The farmer under feudalism spent a part of his time producing his owns means of subsistence, with the rest of his time given as labor-time for the feudal lord. Marx calls this labor rent "the simplest and most primitive form of rent," and he describes it as follows:

"The rent is here the original form of surplus-value and coincides with it. Furthermore, the identity of surplus-value with unpaid labor of others does not need to be demonstrated by any analysis in this case, because it still exists in its visible, palpable form, for the labor of the direct producer for himself is still separated by space and time from his labor for the landlord, and this last labor appears clearly in the brutal form of forced labor for another." [166]

Now, according to Marx's explanation, as years passed this labor rent was transformed into rent in kind. In this case "the landlord does not get this surplus labor any more in its natural form, but rather in the natural form of the product in which it is realized." [167] In other words, the feudal peasants begin to give rent to the landlord in the form of a surplus product they have produced, above their own means of subsistence. But "the transformation of labor rent into rent in kind does not change anything in the nature of rent, economically speaking. This nature, in the forms of rent considered here is such that rent is the sole prevailing and normal form of surplus labor, or surplus-value." [168]

Marx explains further that when rent in kind exists there is usually a continuation of labor rent, and it is interesting to see that he mentions labor rent for the state as existing during those primitive times. This is government ownership of rent under an antiquated mode of production, which proves that the idea of state ownership of rent is not new:

"To the extent that rent in kind is the prevailing and dominant form of ground rent, it is always more or less in the company of survivals of the preceding form, that is of rent paid directly by labor, forced labor, no matter whether the landlord be a private person or the state." [169]

Marx gives an example of labor rent for the state. In some ways it resembles what has gone on under the Russian interpretation of Marx, with government ownership of land and ground rent. For the Russian peasant, a misunderstanding of Marx resulted in a backward step in history.

"A remainder of the old community in land, which had been preserved after the transition to independent peasant economy, for instance in Poland and Roumania, served there as a subterfuge for accomplishing a transition to the lower forms of ground rent. A portion of the land belongs to the individual farmers and is tilled independently by them. Another portion is tilled collectively and creates a surplus product, which serves either for the payment of community expenses, or as a reserve in case of crop failures, etc. These last two parts of the surplus product, and finally the whole surplus product together with the land, upon which it has been grown, are gradually usurped by state officials and private individuals, and by this means the originally free peasant proprietors, whose obligation to till this land collectively is maintained, are transformed into vassals, who are compelled to perform forced labor or pay rent in kind, while the usurpers are transformed into owners, not only of the stolen community lands, but of the lands of the peasants themselves."[170]

Now under labor rent and rent in kind, the forced laborers or serfs do acquire property or independent wealth even though they are not owners but only possessors of the land. Here is how Marx explains this historical fact:

"Some historians have expressed astonishment that it should be possible for the forced laborers, or serfs, to acquire any independent property, or relatively speaking, wealth, under such circumstances, since the direct producer is not an owner, but only a possessor, and since all his surplus labor belongs legally to the landlord. However, it is evident that tradition must play a very powerful role in the primitive and undeveloped circumstances, upon which this relation in social production and the corresponding mode of production are based. It is furthermore clear that here as everywhere else it is in the interest of the ruling section of society to sanction the existing order as a law and to perpetuate its habitually and traditionally fixed limits as legal ones. Aside from all other matters, this comes about of itself in proportion as the continuous reproduction of the foundation of the existing order and of the relations corresponding to it gradually assume a regulated and orderly form. And such regulation and order are themselves indispensable elements of any mode of production, provided that it is to assume social firmness and independence from mere accident and arbitrariness."[171]

This is another of Marx's hints in connection with cooperative production. For example, even the cooperative method must have a theory to justify it, and it will eventually have a regular and orderly form as it develops and reproduces itself after the abolition of capitalism. That even feudalism should have had a theory to justify it, along with a regular and orderly form, would seem unusual at this stage in history. It is hard to believe that a system of labor rent and rent in kind based entirely on forced labor should have had a theory to praise its existence. Yet capitalism, which is also grounded on surplus labor, has a theory which proves that wrong is right, even though the wrong is always there, nevertheless.

But to return to the question of labor rent and rent in kind. Marx explains that this labor rent and rent in kind gradually develop into money rent, and the old feudal system eventually begins to change into the modern form of ground rent as it exists under capitalism. Here is how Marx describes money rent:

"Under money rent, the direct producer no longer turns over the product, but its price to the landlord (who may be either the state or a private individual). . . . Although the direct producer still continues to produce at least the greater part of his means of subsistence himself, a certain portion of this product must now be converted into commodities, must be produced as commodities. . . . The direct producer still is the possessor of the land, either by inheritance or by some other traditional right, and he has to perform for his landlord, who is the owner of the land, of his most essential instrument of production, forced surplus labor, that is, unpaid labor for which no equivalent is returned, and this forced surplus labor is now paid in money obtained by the sale of the surplus product. . . . In its pure form, this rent, like labor rent and rent in kind, does not represent any surplus above the profit. It absorbs the profit, as it is understood. . . . In its further development money rent must lead . . .

either to the transformation of land into independent peasants' property, or into the form corresponding to the capitalist mode of production, that is, to rent paid by the capitalist tenant."[172]

Let us return to the subject of independent peasants' property, which develops out of money rent. Marx explains that this form of property exists under both ancient and modern times:

"This form of free farmers' property managing their own affairs, as the prevailing, normal, form constitutes on the one hand the economic foundation of society during the best times of classical antiquity, on the other hand it is found among modern nations as one of the forms arising from the dissolution of feudal landlordism. In this way we meet the yeomanry in England, the peasantry in Sweden, the farmers in France and Western Germany. We do not mention the colonies here, since the independent farmer there develops under different conditions."[173]

Now, according to Marx, as money rent develops it is accompanied by the formation of a class of propertyless day laborers, and the wealthier farmers begin to hire these individuals as wage workers:

"The transformation of rent in kind into money rent is not only necessarily accompanied, but even anticipated by the formation of a class of propertyless day laborers, who hire themselves out for wages. During the period of their rise, when this new class appears but sporadically, the custom necessarily develops among the better situated tributary farmers of exploiting agricultural laborers for their own account. . . . This class grows very rapidly."[174]

Further, in regard to the beginnings of the capitalist method in agriculture, or the group method of production on which it is based, Marx writes as follows:

"So far as the capitalist mode of production asserts itself . . . in a typical manner, it does so at first mainly in sheep pastures and cattle raising; after that it does not assert itself by a concentration of capital upon a relatively small area of land, but in production on a larger scale . . . so that . . . costs of production may be saved."[175]

Marx explains that when the worker is separate from the soil, as in the case of the propertyless wage workers who no longer possess the land owned by a landlord, and when the capitalist tenant takes over as the possessor of the soil, then the old feudal system of forced surplus labor is ended. Both the capitalist and landlord then own the surplus labor of the producers.

"When the capitalist tenant steps between the landlord and the actually working tiller of the soil, all conditions have been dissolved, which arose from the old rural mode of production."[176]

While small peasants' property aids indirectly in the establishment of capitalist agriculture, the development of capitalism threatens its existence by competition. Here are Marx's words on this:

"The free ownership of the self-employing farmer is evidently the most normal form of landed property for small scale production, that is, for a mode of production, in which the possession of land is a prerequisite for the ownership of the product of his own labor by the laborer. . . . The causes which bring about its downfall show its limitations. These causes are: Destruction of rural house industries, which form its normal supplement, as a result of the development of great industries; a gradual deterioration and exhaustion of the soil subjected to this cultivation; usurpation, on the part of the great landlords, of the community lands . . . competition, either of plantation systems or of great agricultural enterprises carried out on a capitalist scale. Improvements of agriculture which . . . bring about a fall in the prices of the products of the soil, and . . . require greater investments and more diversified material conditions of production, also contribute towards this end."[177]

As stated by Marx, the capitalist's "expropriation of the direct producers from the soil" is a "definite form of property in land."[178] By now it should be obvious that there are different forms of property in land. To begin with, there is ownership of land by the feudal landlord who usurps first labor rent, then rent in kind, and money rent from the farmers working on the land. Secondly, there is independent peasants' property without landlordism. And finally, there is ownership by the landlord under capitalism where the capitalist pays money rent to the landlord, with no possession of land by the producers. Marx describes the form of property in land which exists under capitalism as a "separation of private land from capital and labor, or the transformation of all property in land into a form of landed property corresponding to the capitalist mode of production."[179]

In other words, the modern form of ground rent, or differential rent, comes into existence. Without capitalism and its general rate of profit on capital, there could be no theory of differential rent. That is, before there could be a theory of surplus profits from the soil there had to first be a theory of the general rate of profit, and this theory was developed under capitalism.

At this stage in our explanation of ground rent we have arrived at a point where it can be proved once and for all what Marx means by the abolition of private property in land, as he gives an actual example. Our entire purpose in this study of rent has been directed toward proving this particular point, and Marx's quotations are there when the necessary understanding is present to see them. But again we must work up to these quotations gradually, and the explanation must continue.

Now Marx explains that "appropriation of rent is that economic form in which property in land realizes itself." Aside from small peasants' property, ground rent is appropriated from the producers by the landlord. According to Marx, this common element of land ownership, namely, "title to the rent," misleads into overlooking the differences between them. That form of ground rent which exists under capitalism differs from the preceding forms.

"This common element in the various forms of rent . . . that of being the economic realisation of property in land, a legal fiction by grace of which certain individuals have an exclusive right to certain portions of the globe, misleads into overlooking the differences."[180]

By now the idea is beginning to arise that it is "the economic realization of property in land" (ground rent) which is the object of attack, not private ownership of land or the price of land. The difficulty in understanding Marx is that he defines private ownership of land as landlordism because this is the kind of land ownership which exists under capitalism, or in most countries of the world, aside from the colonies. He disregards any deviations, such as the case when the capitalist owns his own land.

It is important to notice Marx's words that when the capitalist owns his own land, this is the "abolition of private property in land." It is important because this is the quotation which proves what Marx means by abolition of private property, as he gives an example of it. Here the abolition of private ownership of land means there is no landlord who appropriates ground rent. This is a statement in direct words that when the landlord and his appropriation of ground rent is gone from economic society, private ownership of land has been eliminated, even though the capitalist is still the legal owner of land.

This means that landlordism is eliminated under the cooperative method just as it is under capitalism when the capitalist owns his own land and buys it as a commodity on the market. In other words, the purchase and sale of land continues untouched by the change.

"If we observe the cases, in which capital may be invested in the land, in a country with capitalist production, *without paying any rent,* we shall find that they imply, all of them, *a practical abolition of private property in land,* even if not a legal abolition, a condition which is found only under very definite circumstances, which are in their very nature accidental."[181]

Marx goes on to explain the favorable results of this lack of payment of ground rent. The price does not have to rise above but only to the price of production of the worst soil before that soil can be cultivated. Also, there is self-management by the owner, which is not the case under landlordism where the landlord is separate from the soil.

"This [abolition of private property in land] may take place when the landlord is himself a capitalist, or the capitalist himself a landlord. In this case he may himself exploit his land, as soon as the market price shall have risen sufficiently to enable him to get the price of production, that is, cost of production plus the average profit, out of what is now land of class A. But why? Because for himself *private property in land is not an obstacle* to the investment of his capital. He can treat his land simply as an element of nature, and can listen wholly to considerations of expediency concerning his capital, to capitalist considerations. Such cases occur in practice, but only as exceptions. Just as the capitalist cultivation of the land presupposes the separation of the active capital from property in land, so it excludes as a rule the self-management of property in land. It is evident, that the opposite is only an exception."[182]

Without going into the question of capital organization, etc., under the cooperative or profit sharing method, some guess can be made here of how conditions will function after the "abolition of private ownership of land" or ground rent by judging how conditions exist under the capitalist form of its abolition. In other words, there is still ownership in the form of the private buying and selling of land by individuals as well as the producers who use the land, but in the case of the cooperative method, management is not identical with private ownership of the profits to the exclusion of the other producers in the enterprise. It can even be imagined that management might exist on and manage the land legally owned by the cooperative enterprise just as they do under capitalism, but aside from salary they would not share in the profits any more than the other workers who give their labor for the enterprise. This is assuming, of course, that the purchase price of the land is gradually returned to the cooperative enterprise out of the profits.

It is difficult to imagine exactly how the cooperative method functions in agriculture. The above idea arises only from picturing what exists under capitalist agriculture, and Marx does say that capitalist agriculture prepares the groundwork for the cooperative method. There is a difficulty involved in describing the cooperative method in agriculture, as agricultural production differs from city industry in that more or less labor-time is required during different seasons of the year. At least the above described change would be one possible means of transforming capitalist agriculture into the cooperative form. The assumption is made in this case that the plantation farmer who hires group labor is also manager of his capitalist enterprise, and he could remain as manager of the cooperative enterprise which assumes its place. A different condition would arise if the manager of a large agricultural enterprise was a hired wage laborer under capitalism. The capitalist in that case would be an unnecessary part of the business. The problem in both cases is for the cooperative producers to buy the land over from the landlord, and the means of production over from the capitalist. Also, as Marx explains, the state and the credit system would aid in the transition.

Marx gives an additional illustration of the abolition of private ownership of land when he describes ownership as it exists in the colonies:

"What makes a colony a colony—we have in mind only true agricultural colonies—is not merely the vast area of fertile lands in a natural state. It is rather the circumstance that these lands are not appropriated, are not brought under private ownership. It is this which makes the enormous difference between the old countries and the colonies, so far as the land is concerned, it is this non-existence, *legal or actual,* of private ownership of land [i.e., the payment of ground rent]. . . . It is quite immaterial here, whether the colonists take possession of the land without further ceremony, or whether they pay to the state a fee for a valid title to the land under the title of a nominal price of land. It is also immaterial, that already settled colonists may be legally the owners of the land. In fact the land ownership is not an obstacle to the investment of capital here, nor to the employment of labor upon land without any capital. The settling of a part of the land by the established colonists does not prevent the newcomers from employing their capital or their labor upon new land."[183]

It should be noticed that Marx writes that in the case of the colonies, there is a different kind of private ownership of land. And then he goes on to say that private title to the land exists, even though the landlord's private ownership of land does not. This would be a direct contradiction in words if it was not understood in the first place what Marx means by private ownership of land. That is to say, ownership of land means title to ownership of the rent, not title to ownership of land. At this point, it should finally be obvious that an abolition of private property in land means an abolition of the landlord as a separate economic class.

In one place, Marx refers to "property in land" as "superfluous even from the point of view of capitalist production."[184] That is, even under capitalism, the producer would prefer to own his own land, as landlordism is a barrier to his self-management of the soil.

"The circumstance that the capitalist tenant might invest his capital at the average profit, if he did not have to pay any rent, is no incentive for the landlord to lend his land to the tenant gratis. . . . To assume that this would be done would be to do away with private property in land [i.e., ownership by the landlord], for its existence is precisely an obstacle to the investment of capital and to the liberal self-expansion of capital through land. This obstacle does not fall by any means before the simple reflection of the tenant that the conditions of the grain price would enable him to get the average profit out of an investment of capital in class A of soil, if he did not have to pay any rent, in other words, if he could proceed as though *private ownership of land did not exist.*"[185]

Again, Marx refers to the non-existence of private ownership of land as the non-payment of ground rent. The number of quotations from *Capital* which define the payment of ground rent to a landlord as private ownership of land are numerous; yet the idea persists that he would destroy the private buying and selling of land—not just ground rent.

The purchase and sale of land is not necessarily connected with landlordism, especially in American surroundings. What exists in the colonies and America is the modern form of land ownership as distinguished from landlordism, or the kind of land ownership that is characteristic of capitalism. But it is only an analysis of the history of ground rent which provides an understanding of its temporary nature. Here are Marx's words on this:

"The fact that, first, rent is limited to the excess above the average profit, and, secondly, that the landlord is depressed by the ruler and manager of the process of production and of the entire social life's process to the position of a mere holder of land for rent, a usurer in land and collector of rent, is a specific historical result of the capitalist mode of production. . . . The fact that private ownership of land assumes forms [i.e., differential rent, etc.] which permit the capitalist mode of production in agriculture, is a product of the specific character of this mode of production. The income of the landlord may be called rent, even under other forms of society. But it differs essentially from the rent as it appears under the capitalist mode of production."[186]

Marx writes more directly of land and landlordism as it exists under capitalism as follows:

". . . land is then naturally the earth monopolized by a certain number of landlords . . . land becomes personified by the landlord . . . land and land monopolized by private owners become identical terms . . . and so does land assume the guise of the source of rent."[187]

We have already seen that Marx's main criticism of landlordism is its tenant form of agriculture. It is "one of the greatest obstacles to a rational development of agriculture, because the capitalistic renter avoids all improvements and expenses, for which he cannot expect any returns during the time of his lease."[188]

That the payment of ground rent is a historical and not a permanent part of society is reflected again in what Marx calls the "trinitarian formula." He writes that labor-power, owners of capital, and landlords form the three great classes under the capitalist mode of production; also, that the mode of distribution of capitalism is reflected in the formula: "Capital—Profit (Profit of Enterprise plus Interest); Land—Ground Rent; Labor—Wages."[189]

Marx then explains that this form of distribution disappears when capitalism is changed into the cooperative method. In other words, ground rent as a part of the trinitarian formula, goes down along with profit on capital and wages of labor.

"Capitalist distribution differs from those forms of distribution which arise from other modes of production, and every mode of distribution disappears with the preculiar mode of production, from which it arose and to which it belongs."[190]

Again, it is the wage system, the general rate of profit on capital, and the payment of ground rent to a landlord which is eliminated with the abolition of capitalism. This is how Marx expresses the idea in still another way:

"The modern changes of the art of production . . . will expropriate in due time the landlord and the cotton lord."[191]

Marx does admit, however, that out of the three—wages, profit and rent—it is "the form of labor as wage labor" which "determines the shape of the entire process and the specific mode of production."[192] But he goes on to say that wages and surplus-value are common to all modes of production. "If we deprive both wages and surplus-value, both necessary and surplus labor, of their specifically capitalist character, then we have not these forms, but merely their foundations, which are common to all social modes of production."[193] Thus, under feudalism, capitalism, and the cooperative method there are wages and surplus-value. But under capitalism, as under feudalism, the producers do not own the surplus-value they produce in addition to their means of subsistence; whereas under the cooperative method they do own both wages and surplus-value.

According to Marx, the fact that the independent farmers' method of production can be brought into line with the forms of revenue which exist under capitalism, that is, with wages, profit and rent, gives the false impression that capitalist conditions are the natural conditions of all modes of production. The passage of time has proved this error in understanding to have had unfortunate results during periods of economic change. For instance, independent farming, which is not capitalism, has been destroyed along with capitalism because of this misunderstanding of economics.

"If an independent laborer—for instance a small farmer, in whose case all three forms of revenue may be used—works for himself and sells his own product, he is, in the first place, considered as his own employer (capitalist), who employs himself as a laborer, and as his own landlord, who employs himself as his own tenant. To himself as a wage worker he pays his wages, to himself as a capitalist he turns over his profit, and to himself as a landlord he pays his rent. . . . Because a form of production not corresponding to the capitalist mode of production may thus be brought in line with its forms of revenue—and to a certain extent not incorrectly—the illusion is strengthened so much the more that the capitalist conditions are the natural conditions of any mode of production."[194]

In concluding this explanation of the historical nature of ground rent, which implies its eventual abolition, it can be understood now

why new theories of ground rent at this stage of development are
unreasonable, because as capitalism goes down, so does its theory
of wages, profit, and rent. As Marx writes, "the analysis of ground
rent from the point of view of modern economics . . . is a theoretical
expression of the capitalist mode of production. . . . Even many of
the more modern writers have not grasped this yet, as is shown by
every renewed attempt to find a 'new' explanation of ground rent.[195]

## Section 5.—The Historical Establishment and Growth of Capital.

It has already been proved that capitalism is not the only method
of value production which grows up in history. There are three
forms of such enterprise. First, there is the form where the independent worker owns his own means of production and value product, or the production of commodities. Second, there is the capitalist
system of industry in which the worker does not own his own means
of production and value product, or production for capital. Marx
refers to the natural transformation of independent workers' enterprise
into the capitalist method as a transition into an opposite form of
property ownership. In the case of independent workers' production the worker owned the product of his labor, while under capitalism he has no part in its ownership.

". . . it is evident that the laws of appropriation or of private
property, laws that are based on the production and circulation of
commodities, become by their own inner and inexorable dialectic
changed into their very opposite. . . . At first the rights of property
seemed to us to be based on a man's own labour. . . . Now, however,
property turns out to be the right, on the part of the capitalist, to
appropriate the unpaid labour of others or its product and to be the
impossibility, on the part of the labourer, of appropriating his own
product. The separation of property from labour has become the
necessary consequence of a law that apparently originated in their
identity."[196]

Just as production owned by the independent worker is changed
into the capitalist form of property ownership, so the capitalist's

ownership of industry is eventually transformed into group workers' property. Cooperative workers' ownership of the means of production and value product, as distinguished from production for capitalist profit, is the final form of value production which grows up in history. The group ownership of co-operative enterprise is the direct opposite of both independent workers' production and the capitalist method as both constitute private ownership by individuals, not the group ownership of associated workers. The cooperative method re-establishes individual ownership of the product by the laborer, but on the basis of cooperation, not isolation. Marx explains it thus:

"The capitalist mode of appropriation, the result of the capitalist mode of production, produces capitalist private property. This is the first negation, of individual private property, as founded on the labour of the proprietor. But capitalist production begets, with the inexorability of a law of Nature, its own negation. It is the negation of negation. This does not re-establish private property for the producer, but gives him individual property based on the acquisitions of the capitalist era; i.e., on cooperation and the possession in common of the land and of the means of production."[197]

We have seen that commodity production is first carried on by private individuals, by the independent laborer who sells his surplus product as a commodity. This petty method of enterprise is eventually transformed into the group commodity production of capitalism. When the owner of the means of production no longer works alongside of his hired laborers because of the increase in size of his business, that is, as soon as he is no longer the mixture of a capitalist and laborer but performs the functions of management alone, his production is capitalistic in form. As capitalist enterprise further enlarges itself, the owner of the means of production hires wage-labor to perform the functions of management, and the capitalist becomes separated from activity in production. Small-scale capitalism is transformed into the large-scale method, which hires many wage-workers. Here is Marx's description of the hierarchy which grows up under large-scale capitalism.

"Just as at first the capitalist is relieved from actual labour so soon as his capital has reached that minimum amount with which capitalist production, as such begins, so now, he hands over the work of direct and constant supervision of the individual workmen, and groups of workmen to a special kind of wage-labourer. An industrial army of workmen, under the command of the capitalist, requires, like a real army, officers (managers), and sergeants (foreman, overlookers), who, while the work is being done, command in the name of the capitalist."[198]

After the social production of capitalism is well established, it gradually destroys by competition practically all independent workers' enterprise. That is to say, it transforms all production into the group system of industry which must form the basis of the cooperative method. Even though the many capitalist enterprises within the various lines of industry gradually become enlarged by the investment of surplus-value in production on a progressive scale, still there is a contradiction which develops as follows: The large-scale capitalist enterprise, because of its more scientific methods of production, is able to sell its commodities at a lower price than either the small scale capitalist or business owned and operated by isolated individuals. Therefore, the larger capital eliminates the smaller one and takes the market lost by it.[199] Here are Marx's words on this:

"This splitting up of the total social capital into many individual capitals or the repulsion of its fractions one from another, is counteracted by their attraction. This last does not mean that simple concentration of the means of production and of the command over labour, which is identical with accumulation. It is concentration of capitals already formed, destruction of their individual independence, expropriation of capitalist by capitalist, transformation of many small into few large capitals. This process differs from the former in this, that it only presupposes a change in the distribution of capital already to hand, and functioning; its field of action is therefore not limited by the absolute growth of social wealth, by the absolute limits of accumulation. Capital grows in one place to a huge mass in a single hand, because it has in another place been lost by many. This is centralisation proper, *as distinct from accumulation and concentration*. The laws of the centralisation of capitals . . . cannot be developed here. A brief hint at a few facts must suffice. The battle of competition is fought by cheapening of commodities. The cheapness of commodities, depends . . . on the productiveness of labour, and this again on the scale of production. Therefore, the larger capitals beat the smaller. It will further be remembered that, with the development of the capitalist mode of production, there is an increase in the minimum amount of individual capital necessary to carry on a business under its normal conditions. The smaller capitals, therefore, crowd into spheres of production which Modern Industry has only sporadically or incompletely got hold of. Here competition rages in direct proportion to the number, and in inverse proportion to the magnitudes, of the antagonistic capitals. It always ends in the ruin of many small capitalists, whose capitals partly pass into the hands of their conquerors, partly vanish." [200]

Ever larger amounts of capital are necessary to carry on a business under normal conditions, and this need for more capital is filled by the capitalist corporation. In some cases, it is the large masses of capital formed by a union of private capitals in stock companies which makes the big capitalist enterprise possible. However, whether large scale enterprise comes to pass by the operation of competition or the mere joining together of separate capitals to form stock companies, the result is the same. There is a centralization of the means of production into large businesses within the various lines of industry. This does not mean that monopolies are established in the different branches of production; it only means that the majority of capitalist enterprises become large scale. Marx explains that the big capitals which form the basis of large-scale industry may be composed of either individual or associated capitals, which shows that when he refers to the centralization of capital he does not mean the centralization of capital into a few productive organizations but a centralization of money capital in the hands of a few individuals:

"[By means of the formation of stock companies] An enormous expansion of the scale of production and enterprises which were impossible for individual capitals.[201] Centralisation supplements the work of accumulation, by enabling the industrial capitalists to expand the scale of their operations. The economic result remains the same, whether this consummation is brought about by accumulation or centralisation, whether centralisation is accomplished by the violent means of annexation, by which some capitals become such overwhelming centers of gravitation for others as to break their individual cohesion and attracting the scattered fragments, or whether the amalgamation of a number of capitals, which already exist or are in process of formation proceeds by the smoother road of forming stock companies. The increased volume of industrial establishments forms everywhere the point of departure for a more comprehensive organisation of the co-operative labor of many, for a wider development of their material powers, that is, for the progressive transformation of isolated processes of production carried on in accustomed ways into socially combined and scientifically managed processes of production.[202] . . . the functions of the industrial capitalists [are transformed] more and more *into a monopoly of great money-capitalists, who may be individuals or associations.*"[203]

Marx mentions that there are decentralizing influences at work which prevent monopoly in the individual spheres, which eliminates the idea that capitalism develops into a monopoly form of commodity production. While there may be a monopoly of money capitalists, the existence of monopoly in all lines of indiustry would mean the collapse of capitalism; that is, because it is a competitive system. Marx would never justify monopoly, as the competitive system continues after capitalism under the cooperative method. Here are his words:

"Generally speaking, the labor of a capitalist stands in an inverse proportion to the size of his capital, that is, to his degree as a capitalist. This divorce of requirements of production here and producers there is inseparable from the nature of capital. It begins with the inauguration of primitive accumulation (Vol. I, chapter XXVI), becomes a permanent process in the accumulation and concentration of capital, and expresses itself finally as a centralisation of already existing capitals in a few hands and a decapitalisation of many (a change in the method of expropriation). This process would soon bring about the *collapse* of capitalist production, if it were not for *counteracting tendencies, which continually have a decentralising effect* by the side of the centripetal ones." [204]

Marx calls the abolition of small money capitalists by larger ones, a change in the method of expropriation. Before it was an expropriation of the individual producer by the capitalist, but now it is an expropriation of smaller capitals by larger ones. In the quotation which follows, Marx compares the abolition of capitalism to the expropriation of independent workers' production by means of capitalist competition:

"The transformation of scattered private property, arising from individual labour, into capitalist private property is, naturally, a process, incomparably more protracted, violent, and difficult, than the transformation of capitalistic private property, already practically resting on socialised [group] production, into socialised [group] property. In the former case we had the expropriation of the mass of the people by a few usurpers; in the latter, we have the expropriation of a few usurpers by the mass of the people." [205]

The material basis of cooperative enterprise, or group production, develops out of the capitalist method, just as capitalism grows up out of the individual form of enterprise which precedes it in history. Cooperative production does not have to establish itself anew, but it is established on the basis of the competitive group enterprises which exist under capitalism. Just as there was a change in the private workers' method of production which preceded the capitalistic system in history, so capitalist enterprise must also undergo a change. Marx describes the historical nature of capitalism in the following words:

". . . every definite historical form [of the labor] process develops more and more its material foundations and social forms. Whenever a certain maturity is reached, one definite social form is discarded and displaced by a higher one. The time for the coming of such a crisis is announced by the depth and breadth of the contradictions and antagonisms, which separate the conditions of distribution, and with them the definite historical form of the corresponding conditions of production, from the productive forces, the productivity, and development of their agencies. A conflict then arises between the material development of production and its social form."[206]

We have just mentioned the centralization of capital as one contradiction which develops under capitalism, and the periodic crisis has been explained as another. There is another contradiction mentioned by Marx which we will only describe briefly. He writes that there is a steady fall in the general rate of profit through a predominance of constant over variable capital. While these various contradictions might be problems under the capitalist method, they are non-existent under cooperative production.

───────

Now that we have seen that capitalism is a historical form of value production which grows up naturally out of independent workers' enterprise, only to be transformed into the cooperative system, let us analyze the question as to whether the cooperative method continues to develop and enlarge production. An answer to this question is found from an analysis of how production is differentiated and developed under the two preceding forms of enterprise. Production is differentiated and enlarged naturally under the private production of commodities as well as under the capitalist method, which is a reflection of the fact that it is a natural power that brings on the establishment of new lines of industry, or an increased division of the labor of society. An increase in the variety of commodities produced does not imply any creative effort on the part of the capitalist in particular, as even the cooperative producers and the isolated producers of commodities develop new types of commodity production. The new enterprises which grow up under capitalism reflect the need for new lines of business; needs which themselves develop as a result of already established enterprises. Just as the capitalist works on the basis of production developed in an earlier period of history, so the cooperative method develops on the basis of enterprises established by the capitalist system in history As new needs and wants for production develop out of the already established ones, production continues to enlarge and differentiate. Here are Marx's words:

"In proportion as machinery, with the aid of a relatively small number of workpeople, increases the mass of raw materials, intermediate products, instruments of labour, etc., the working-up of these raw materials and intermediate products becomes split up into numberless branches; social production increases in diversity. The factory system carries the social division of labor immeasurably further than does manufacture, for it increases the productiveness of the industries it seizes upon, in a far higher degree. . . . Entirely new branches of production, creating new fields of labour, are also formed, *as the direct result either of machinery or of the general industrial changes brought about by it*.[207] A radical change in the mode of production in one sphere of industry involves a similar change in other spheres . . . the revolution in cotton spinning *called forth* the invention of the gin, for separating the seeds from the cotton fiber; it was only by means of this invention, that the production of cotton became possible on the enormous scale at present required. But more especially, the revolution in the modes of production of industry and agriculture *made necessary* a revolution in the general conditions of the social process of production, i.e., in the means of communication and of transport."[208]

In other words, it is the development of production which brings on the establishment of new lines of industry, so that capitalism is only one historical form of the enlargement of production. There is not an end to economic necessity under the cooperative method. New enterprises continue to grow up out of old ones, or entirely new lines of business continue to develop. The difference between capitalism and associated production is that new enterprises grow up in the form of cooperative factories as distinguished from capitalist ones. And as Marx writes, "the credit system is the . . . means for the . . . extension of cooperative factories on a more or less natural scale."[209]

In reference to the change over from the capitalist corporation form of business enterprise into ownership by the individuals at work in production, Marx implies that one of the functions of the newly emancipated workers is the establishment of new business; he implies this when he writes that all essential functions of the capitalist would then be performed by the cooperative producers. That is, whoever establishes a new business which requires production on a group scale would have to establish it on a cooperative basis. He could no longer exploit the workers for his own advancement. Here are Marx's words on this detail of cooperative production:

". . . it is a transition to the conversion of all functions in the process of reproduction, which still remain connected with capitalist private property, into mere functions of the associated producers, into social functions." [210]

Thus Marx writes that all functions connected with capitalist private property are taken over by the associated producers, not the state. It was explained in Section 1 of this chapter how new enterprises will grow up in the already established lines of industry as a result of increases in demand caused by population increase, etc. And it has been assumed that new lines of business will continue to grow up naturally as a result of new wants, etc. But we shall now analyze in more detail the question as to how these new cooperative enterprises will be organized and financed by means of the credit system.

Under the new conditions the workers would own not only that value which reproduces their own value in wages, but also the surplus-value. While under capitalism it is a function of the capitalist to save a portion of the surplus-value for enlargement, this would become a function of the workers under cooperative production. Here are Marx's words on this:

"The notion of 'means of subsistence' would considerably expand . . . on the other hand . . . a part of what is now surplus labor would then count as necessary labor; I mean the labour of forming a fund for reserve and accumulation." [211]

Under its more prosperous conditions, cooperative production would make savings possible for the workers. They—along with capital owners of the preceding method of production—could purchase bonds that would be used in the establishment of new industries. New cooperative enterprises would be established as they are under capitalism, that is, by the savings of the workers, and by credit capital rather than the accumulation of a capitalist. However, there would be a difference in that the supplying of money for production would no longer mean ownership but a definite value to be repaid, the same as credit capital with interest, with group ownership of the means of production and profit by those at work in the enterprise. This is the corporation of the workers as distinguished from the capitalist corporation.

As long as the supplying of money for production determines ownership of the profits, there can be no profit sharing. Contrariwise, take the banking system and bond ownership. This is the credit system, or the supplying of money for production without private ownership of the profits. In the case of bonds, money is borrowed in the form of the issuance of bonds, and it is gradually repaid over a period of time with interest.

It can be proved that Marx refers to bonds as loaned money just as he refers to bank loans as a part of the credit system. This implies the continued use of bonds in the financing of cooperative enterprises. For instance, here is a quotation from Marx mentioned in the section on ground rent where he compares the purchase of land to the purchase of bonds. He writes that bonds are not "productive capital," or capital invested in labor power and means of production for the gain of profit. Here again are those words:

". . . capital invested in the purchase of land . . . is neither first nor running capital, any more than the capital, which some one may invest at the Stock Exchange in the purchase of consols or state bonds, and which represents a personal investment of capital for him, is "invested" in any productive line of industry . . . it . . . constitutes an interest-bearing investment of capital for him."[212]

In a similar way, Marx writes as follows: ". . . it is immaterial for the organization of a new and independent manufacturing business whether another manufacturer of the same line of business invests a portion of his capital in *interest bearing papers*, because he cannot use all of it in his business."[213]

There is thus a difference between the credit system or loaned money and productive capital which is capitalism. In one place Marx gives an actual example of how the issuance of bonds financed production, aside from the capitalist owners of production. The mere fact that he refers to bonds as loans hints at their existence after the abolition of capitalism.

In an American newspaper article entitled, "The Approaching Indian Loan" written in 1858, Marx tells how the East India Company was "prohibited from contracting *interest-bearing debts* without the especial sanction of Parliament." He goes on to say that in times past when the East India Company "set about establishing railways and electric telegraphs in India, it applied for the authorization of Indian *bonds* in the London market, a request which was granted to the amount of 7,000,000 pounds sterling to be issued in *bonds* bearing 4 per cent interest." Later the East India Company applied for another such "*loan* in the amount of eight or ten million pounds sterling."[214]

In the above example of the issuance of bonds by the East India Company, he refers to them in direct words as a loan. According to Marx, such a loan would raise the rate of interest because the demand for money as bonds is the same as the demand for bank loans, that is to say, both are interest bearing debts:

". . . it is true that successive loans by the Indian Company in the London money market would raise the value of money and prevent the . . . further fall in the rate of interest. . . . Any artificial check put upon the downward movement of *the rate of discount* is equivalent to an enhancement in . . . *the terms of credit.*"[215]

The above example of bonds is given only to show that bonds can be considered a part of the credit system just as bank loans are. At least Marx refers to them as loans, not productive capital, and it is Marx that is the object of our understanding. Thus, if bonds were used in times past and present to establish large enterprises such as telegraphs and railways, then they will also be used under the cooperative method. At least there is no objection to their use, considering they are not a part of capitalism but the credit system.

With this taken for granted, the idea of "state aid" as a necessity in the establishment of cooperative production disappears. For instance, there are those who believe that cooperative production must come into existence by state aid, or as proteges of the government.

Marx emphasizes the falsity of such an idea and praises cooperative enterprises as independent creations of the workers. He thus implies indirectly that cooperative production as the creation of the workers is the means for the establishment of new lines of industry. But at the same time he explains that cooperative production should be established on the basis of already established capitalist enterprises, or by what he calls social revolution, not by means of isolated experiments:

"That the workers desire to establish the conditions of co-operative production on a social [i.e., group], and first of all on a national, scale in their own country, only means that they are working to revolutionise the present conditions of production, and *has nothing in common with the foundation of co-operative societies with state aid.* But as far as the present co-operative societies are concerned they are of value only in so far as they are the *independent creations of the workers and not proteges either of the government or of the bourgeoisie.*[216]  [This is] the remedy of the [non-Marxist]. In place of the existing class struggle. . . . Instead of the revolutionary process of transformation of society, the 'socialist organization of the total labour' 'arises' from the 'state aid' that the state gives to the producers' co-operative societies and which the state, not the worker, '*calls into being.*' This is worthy of Lassalle's imagination that one can build a new society by state loans just as well as a new railway [instead of transforming capitalist ownership of industry, which is already established, into workers' ownership]."[217]

When Marx criticizes state created cooperative enterprises in the above words, it should be noted that he opposes cooperative enterprises with state aid, to cooperative production as the independent creations of the workers; that is, it means that enterprise established by the government is not scientifically Marxist. In other words, after there has been a change from capitalism to cooperative production, it is not the state which creates new lines of enterprise; these are the independent creations of associated workers who organize new enterprises on a cooperative basis.

Further, in regard to the cooperative method, Marx praises co-operative enterprises in that the workers are given incentive in production, whereas under capitalism they have no interest because of their separation from ownership:

"It may indeed be said that capital . . . is itself conditioned upon a certain mode of distribution, namely the expropriation of the laborers from the means of production, the concentration of these conditions in the hands of a minority of individuals.[218] ". . . the social nature of labor, the combination of the labor of a certain individual laborer with that of other laborers for a common purpose, stands opposed to that laborer and his comrades as a foreign power, as the property of a stranger which he would not care particularly to save if he were not compelled to economize with it. It is entirely different in the factories *owned by the laborers themselves*, for instance, in Rochdale."[219]

While capitalism is based upon the idea of a lack of bureaucracy, under large-scale industry a minority of capitalist investors, through their ownership of the means of production, live off of the work of the majority of individuals in society. Production is composed of a hierarchy of leadership which represents the interests of the capitalist-class as opposed to the working one. The capitalist's separation from work in enterprise has the same effect as parasitic government bureaucracy since there is a group of stockholders which represent interests separate from those actually at work in production who live as parasites off of business. The following words of Marx describe capitalism as a productive hierarchy, on top of which is an idle group of stockholders:

"Upon the basis of capitalist production, the social character of their production impresses itself upon the mass of the direct producers as a strictly regulating authority and as a social mechanism of the labor process graduated into a complete hierarchy. This authority is vested in its bearer only as a personification of the requirements of labor standing above the laborer.[220] On the basis of capitalist production, a new swindle develops in stock enterprises with the wages of management. It consists in placing above the actual director a board of managers or directors, for whom superintendence and management serve in reality only as a pretext for plundering stockholders and amassing wealth. . . . The proceedings of the court of bankruptcy show, that these wages of superintendence are as a rule inversely proportioned to the actual superintendence performed by these nominal directors."[221]

It should be noticed that Marx refers to the director of production as necessary, but of a board of directors as unnecessary. It is not management which is the object of criticism since management is necessary even under the cooperative method. But management under the corporation form of business enterprise is uncontrolled management.

Ownership of the means of production and profits by a few large-money capitalists is not in harmony with the ideal of freedom of opportunity for all members of society. Because competition has made small scale enterprise impossible, the majority of individuals are compelled to sell themselves as wage laborers for the benefit of a few large capitalists. This majority does not have freedom of enterprise but they labor for the account of stockholders who have no part in production. Ownership of the profits of industry by a minority of society which performs no physical activity in production is not in harmony with the idea that the individual should acquire wealth according to labor performed. With reference to the modern capitalist's method of acquiring wealth, Marx states that he acquires his capital by stock speculation instead of working for it or using direct force to get it as he did at an earlier period in history:

"Gain and loss through fluctuations in the price of these titles of ownership, and their centralisation in the hands of railroad kings, etc., naturally becomes more and more a matter of gambling, which takes the place of labor as the original method of acquiring capital and also assumes the place of direct force."[222]

When ownership of production becomes possible for all members of society, then there is an end to the freedom of some individuals to live off of the labor of others. Under the capitalist corporation, because even the manager of production has no part in ownership of enterprise, all individuals active in business, including the manager, stand in opposition to the owners of the means of production and profit as wage-laborers. Once capitalism has reached this advanced stage it is ready to be changed into the cooperative method. To express this in the words of Marx:

"In the stock companies the function is separated from the ownership of capital, and labor, of course, is entirely separated from the ownership of means of production and of *surplus-labor*. This result of the highest development of capitalist production is a necessary transition to the reconversion of capital into the property of the producers, no longer as the private property of individual producers, but as the *common property of associates,* as *social property outright.* On the other hand it is a transition to the conversion of all functions in the process of reproduction, which still remain connected with capitalist private property, *into mere functions of the associated producers, into social functions.*"[223]

Again Marx refers to cooperative production as a system based on the "common property of associates" not government ownership. He uses the words "social property" in reference to the group carrying on production, without mentioning the word "state."

By now it should be obvious that Marx advocated cooperative production as opposed to government enterprise. That Marx had noble intentions is proved by the fact that he promoted this ideal system and worked for it with his book *Capital,* as against state socialism. Others had advocated cooperative production before; in this he was only one among others. But Marx was different in that he prophesied the abolition of capitalism—he did not just advocate it. Also, he gave a scientific explanation of cooperative production which could dissolve the capitalist system of exploitation; he constantly emphasized that an understanding of economics is necessary in order to transform capitalist production into the cooperative method. Thus, the following words of Marx contain both a prophecy and an explanation of the new system:

". . . as we pre-supposed the limits set by capitalist production, that is to say, pre-supposed the process of social production in a form developed  by purely spontaneous growth, we neglected any more rational combination, directly and systematically practicable with the means of production and the mass of the labour-power at present available.[224] The life-process of society, which is based on the process of material production, does not strip off its mystical veil until it is treated as production by *freely associated men,* and is consciously regulated by them in accordance with a settled plan. This, however, demands for society a certain material groundwork or set of conditions of existence which in their turn are the spontaneous product of a long and painful process of development."[225]

Here Marx refers to regulation of production as conscious regulation by competitive cooperative producers. It is only by means of a voluntary association of competitive producers that production could be regulated without interference by a centralized bureaucracy.

The operation of competition under capitalism that is causing a general establishment of the group method of production, together with centralization of production ownership in the hands of a minority of individuals, will eventually cause the workers to bring about a change in property ownership. The cooperative method of enterprise will then be a present threat to capitalism, a radical economic change. Private ownership of industry will be replaced by group ownership. Our assumption that the abolition of capitalism is something that will inevitably come to pass is in complete accord with the following prophetic words of Marx:

"Both success and failure lead now simultaneously to a centralisation of capital, and thus to an expropriation on the most enormous scale. This expropriation extends here from the *direct producers to the smaller and smallest capitalists themselves.* It is first the point of departure of the capitalist mode of production; its complete accomplishment is the aim of this production. In the last instance it aims at the expropriation of all individuals from the means of production, which cease with the development of social production to be means of private production and products of private production, and which can henceforth be only *means of production in the hands of associated producers, their social property, just as they are social products.*[226] "Centralisation of the means of production and socialisation of labour at last reach a point where they become incompatible with their capitalist integument. This integument is burst asunder. The knell of capitalist private property sounds. The expropriators are expropriated." [227]

### Section 6.—World Imperialism.

Capitalism is a form of production which gives the capitalist of one nation an opportunity to control individuals in others. It must have outlets for its products; therefore, it destroys by competition the production of less developed nations and transforms them into markets for its products. Also, the capitalists establish enterprises in foreign nations, and production thereby assumes an international character. As Marx describes it, there is an "entanglement of all peoples in the net of the world-market, and this the international character of the capitalistic regime." [228]

When one nation is free to control industry and government in other nations, this is contrary to the idea that each nation should be self-governing. Once a large scale enterprise controls the wage-labor of individuals in foreign countries, it is in fact an international despotism.

However, the solution is not as difficult as it would appear. If each branch of a company should be made cooperative, then the large scale enterprise would no longer be an international despotism. It has been mentioned before that the loaning of money to under-developed nations is not capitalism, whereas the investment of capital in labor and means of production is. Once production was co-operative in each individual nation and each nation was independent of foreign rule in government, then there would be no further exploitation of nation by nation. This would be a rejection of empire, and all nations would then be ready to join in peaceful federation.

It is only after capitalism that there can be a federation of nations, since as long as the capitalist method exists, the weaker nation is under the despotic control of the stronger one. However, when capitalist production establishes itself in less developed nations by means of imperialism, it does force the general establishment of modern methods of industry. It performs the service of bringing all nations into civilization and thereby prepares the groundwork for a world federation. The following is Marx and Engels' explanation of how capital accomplishes its historical task of drawing all nations into civilization:

"The need of a constantly expanding market for its products drives the bourgeoisie over the whole surface of the globe. It must elbow-in everywhere, settle everywhere, establish connections everywhere. The bourgeoisie has through its exploitation of the world-market given a cosmopolitan character to production and consumption in every country. . . . In place of the old wants, satisfied by the productions of the country, we find new wants, requiring for their satisfaction the products of distant lands and climes. In place of the old local and national seclusion and self-sufficiency, we have intercourse in every direction, universal interdependence of nations. And as in material, so also in intellectual production. The intellectual creations of individual nations become common property. National one-sidedness and narrow-mindedness become more and more impossible, and from the numerous national and local literatures there arises a world literature."[229]

At this stage of development, the capitalistic regime has brought an interdependence of nations into existence that will make a federation of nations a present possibility. If all nations should eliminate the capitalist class from production and become independent of foreign rule in government, world society would be in preparation for federation and permanent peace. As Marx and Engels prophesy, hostility between nations will cease as soon as capitalism is eliminated:

"In proportion as the exploitation of one individual by another is put an end to, the exploitation of one nation by another will also be put an end to. In proportion as the antagonisms between classes within the nation vanish, the hostility of one nation to another will come to an end."[230]

For Marx, the reign of world peace is conditioned on the abolition of the capitalist system. The question is, is Marx's scientific plan for peace identical with that peace which has been the prophecy of men with vision for centuries? This must be true, because whatever materializes peace is the ideal. If we assume that Marx's scientific plan for peace actually brings peace to pass, then it is that peace which is the will of God, even if the Marxists do refer to peace as the materialization of scientific rather than inspired prophecy. The following is Marx's way of expressing this idea:

"It will be evident that the world has long dreamed of something of which it only has to become conscious in order to possess it in actuality. It will be evident that there is not a big blank between the past and the future, but rather that it is a matter of realizing the thoughts of the past." [231]

# Chapter IV

# NATIONAL SOCIALISM

## Section 1.—A Planned Capitalism.

At this advanced stage in our explanation of associated enterprise it is obvious that the ideas of both state communism and capitalism have been weakened. However, the theory of a planned capitalism still remains as another possible obstacle. There should be no doubt, however, that Marx's theory can destroy even this. As the criticisms develop, so also does his explanation of the new economic system.

It is difficult to understand why there should be an attempt to preserve an economic system which is based on the exploitation of individuals. But for those who have private capital in production the motive is obvious. For them the most overpowering weakness of capitalism is its periodic crisis, even though this is only one weakness among others. They would not think to fear the moral weakness of capitalism, although it is precisely this which inevitably brings on its downfall.

Nevertheless, we shall consider their theory which has developed as a result of the "universal crisis" which occurred in 1929.

### a. *State Control Over Capital Investment and the Banking System*

There is an attempt to control production within the boundaries of the capitalist system under national socialism. The competitive producers in a particular line of production join in association, and the government bureaucracy controls the association. Depending on the plan of the bureaucracy, more or less capital is invested in the various lines of production.

The national socialist believes that it is the over-extension of credit or loans to production which causes crisis, and therefore he arrives at the conclusion that it is state control over the use of borrowed money in production which eliminates crisis. According to Marx, this conclusion is a false one since the cause of crisis is rooted in the accumulation process of capital, not the credit system, which is a servant to the accumulation process and dependent upon it. A control over the credit system cannot eliminate the antagonisms of capitalism:

"The superficiality of Political Economy shows itself in the fact that it looks upon the expansion and contraction of credit, which is a mere symptom of the periodic changes of the industrial cycle, as their cause. As the heavenly bodies, once thrown into a certain definite motion, always repeat this, so it is with social production as soon as it is once thrown into this movement of alternate expansion and contraction. Effects, in their turn, become causes, and the varying accidents of the whole process, which always reproduces its own conditions, take on the form of periodicity."[1]

In Marx's opinion, the bankers interfere in business too much under capitalism, considering they know nothing about production itself. Why then would the state's interference in banking be any improvement over the banker's interference in industry? Here are Marx's words:

"Talk about centralization! The credit system, which has its center in the so-called national banks and the great money lenders and usurers about them, is an enormous centralization and gives to this class of parasites a fabulous power, not only to despoil periodically the industrial capitalists, but also to *interfere into actual production in a most dangerous manner*—and this gang knows nothing about production and has nothing to do with it."[2]

Again here—just as in his explanation of the small farmer—Marx's criticism of the credit system under capitalism does give the wrong impression. Just as peasant agriculture goes by untouched with the abolition of ground rent, so the credit system remains the same after the abolition of private capital. It should be remembered that Marx refers to those who idealize the credit system as "swindlers and prophets."[3]

But when Marx refers to the "expansion and contraction of credit" as a symptom of the periodic crisis, he is referring also to another kind of credit. It is a well known fact that the crisis of 1929 was called a "stock market crash." Therefore, there have been attempts to control stock speculation as well as the banking system.

Marx would call a control over the Stock Exchange an attempt to control "fictitious capital" since the actual capital is already functioning in production. He explains that stocks are mere titles of ownership which assume the form of commodities, and which rise and fall in value according to the high or low profits to be gained from production. Marx describes these securities as follows:

". . . the credit system creates [issues] associated capital [i.e., stocks, and also bonds which are not productive capital]. The papers are considered as titles of ownership, which represent this capital. The stocks of railroads, mines, navigation companies, and the like, represent actual capital, namely the capital invested and used in such ventures. . . . But this capital does not exist twofold, it does not exist as the capital value of titles of ownership on one side and as the actual capital invested, or to be invested . . . on the other. It exists only in this last form, and a share of stock is merely a title of ownership on a certain portion of the surplus-value realized by it. . . . Even when the certificate of indebtedness—the security—does not represent a purely fictitious capital, as it does in the case of state debts, the capital value of such papers is nevertheless wholly illusory."[4]

The following is Marx's explanation of how the market price of a security is determined:

"The independent movement of the value of these titles of ownership, not only of government *bonds*, but also of stocks, adds weight to the illusion that they constitute a real capital by the side of that capital, or that title, upon which they may have a claim. For they become commodities, whose price has its own peculiar movements and is fixed in its own way. Their market value is determined differently from their nominal value, without any change in the value of the actual capital, which expands, of course. On the one hand their market value fluctuates with the amount and security of the yields, on which they have a claim. If the nominal value of a share of stock, that is, the invested sum originally represented by this share, is 100 pounds sterling, and the enterprise pays 10%, instead of 5%, then their market value, other circumstances remaining the same, rises to 200 pounds sterling, so long as the rate of interest is 5%, for when capitalised at 5%, it now represents a fictitious capital of 200 pounds sterling. He who buys it for 200 pounds sterling receives a revenue of 5% on this investment of capital. If the success of the venture is such as to diminish the income from it, the reverse takes place. The market value of these papers is in part fictitious, as it is not determined merely by the actual income, but also by the expected income, which is calculated in advance. But assuming the self expansion of the actual capital to proceed at a constant rate . . . the price of such securities rises and falls inversely as the rate of interest."[5]

It can thus be seen that a control over stock speculation would be of no benefit in abolishing the cause of periodic crisis. Regardless of the rise and fall in the prices of these securities, the real capital in production continues to grow and accumulate in a steady ratio until it reaches its limit in production as a whole, and there is a general economic crisis. However, these stocks and bonds, because their prices are dependent on production itself, do depreciate in value when there is a general overproduction. Marx quotes one credit expert: "When a panic reigns, a business man does not ask himself, how profitably he can invest his bank notes, or whether he will lose 1 or 2% in the sale of his *treasury notes or 3% bonds*. Once . . . he is under the suggestions of fright, he cares nothing about gain or loss; he gets himself into a safe place."[6]

In the case of national socialism it is believed that the government bureaucracy has a more practical ability to control capital investment than those planning production in the enterprise itself because of its knowledge of the activities of production as a whole. Therefore, the bureaucracy interferes with the production of the capitalist producer, and forcibly assumes the role of his representative. The amount of capital used in production is dependent on the decision of the bureaucracy.

An economic system such as capitalism that is based on force in the purchase and sale of wage labor must of necessity imagine such a forced planning of production. Also, regardless of its appearance of reason and order, a planned capitalism is impractical according to Marx's explanation. He explains that production control requires only that (1) capital investment in labor-power and means of production be eliminated, and (2) the cooperative enterprises regulate production by voluntary association. The accumulation of private capital cannot be a cause of crisis once it no longer exists. In the case of associated production, capital is not distributed according to the plan of the bureaucracy; instead, depending on the requirements of the various enterprises which plan production to meet the demand, it is loaned to them. Marx explains that the quantity of the demand for loan capital is dependent upon the prices of the commodities to be purchased with the borrowed money. And these prices, in their turn, are under the control of supply and demand.

"The demand for commodities raises their price, either because it may rise above the average, or because the supply of commodities may fall below the average. If the industrial capitalist or the merchant must now pay 150 pounds sterling for the same mass of commodities for which he used to pay 100 pounds sterling, he would have to borrow 150 pounds sterling whereas he had to borrow but 100 pounds sterling formerly, and if the rate of interest were 5% he would now have to pay 7½ pounds sterling of interest as against 5 pounds sterling of former times. The mass of the interest to be paid by him would rise because he now has to borrow more capital." [7]

This shows directly how the extension of credit is dependent on production itself, not vice versa, the extension of credit a determinant of production. In other words, once production is under control, so is the credit system under control. As Marx explains it, under the associated method it is the demands of society which determine production, not the return on private capital. As more or less commodities are required of the various lines of industry, more or less means of production and labor-power go into them as the quantity of the demand is made known by the purchases of individuals and the cooperative enterprises themselves.

"In the case of socialized production, the money-capital is eliminated. Society [i.e., the demands of society] distributes labor-power and means of production to the different lines of occupation.[8] The barrier of the capitalist mode of production becomes apparent. . . . In the fact that the expansion or contraction of production is determined by the appropriation of unpaid labor and by the proportion of this unpaid labor to materialized labor in general, or . . . is determined by profit and by the proportion of this profit to the employed capital, by a definite rate of profit, instead of being determined by the relations of production to social wants, to the wants of socially developed human beings."[9]

The national socialist identifies the movement of loan capital with that of industrial capital although Marx explains that "loan capital has a different movement than industrial capital."[10] The banking system is only the source of the money necessary for the promotion of the exchange of products among the various groups of production. The following words of Marx show that the volume of products is independent of the money trade, or the banking system:

"So far as money serves as a means of purchase, the volume and number of purchases and sales are quite independent of the money trade. This trade cannot do anything but abbreviate the technical operations that go with buying and selling, and by this means it is enabled to reduce the amount of cash money required to turn the commodities over.[11] The transactions in the market effectuate only the interchange of the individual components of [the] annual product, transfer them from one hand to another, but can neither augment the total annual production, nor alter the nature of the objects produced."[12]

In other words, the amount of money in circulation is dependent on the demands for it in promoting the circulation of commodities. The banking system remains outside of the sphere of production.

". . . the currency of money, generally considered, is but a reflex of the circulation of commodities.[13] Money . . . in its function of means of purchase and of payment . . . does no more than realise the price of the commodity it buys or pays for; and, as hard cash, it is value petrified, never varying.[14] . . . the retardation of the currency . . . reflects the stagnation in the change of form, and therefore, in the social interchange of matter [i.e., the transformation of commodities into money and vice versa]. The circulation itself, of course, gives no clue to the origin of this stagnation. . . . The general public, who, simultaneously, with the retardation of the currency, see money appear and disappear less frequently at the periphery of circulation, naturally attribute this retardation to a quantitative deficiency in the circulating medium."[15]

The national socialist believes that state control over the currency is an aid in the elimination of crisis because be believes the amount of money in circulation is a cause of the rise or fall in the prices of commodities. Marx shows the falsity of such a conclusion by explaining that it is an overproduction of commodities which causes the appearance of an undersupply of money, through a depreciation in the prices of the overproduced commodities. In other words, he shows how the quantity of the currency is dependent upon the prices of commodities.

"Herrenschwand's fanciful notions amount merely to this, that the antagonisms, which has its origin in the nature of commodities, and is reproduced in their circulation, can be removed by increasing the circulating medium. But if, on the one hand, it is a popular delusion to ascribe stagnation in production and circulation to insufficiency of the circulating medium, it by no means follows, on the other hand, that an actual paucity of the medium in consequence, e.g., of *bungling legislative interference with the regulation of currency*, may not give rise to such stagnation." [16]

There is no need for state regulation of the currency since it is regulated naturally by circulation itself. In the quotation which follows Marx explains how the money needed for circulation depends on the total prices of those products which must be transformed into money; that is, he shows how the needed currency is controlled automatically:

"If we . . . consider the sum total of the money current during a given period, we shall find that, given the rapidity of currency of the circulating medium and of the means of payment, it is equal to the sum of the prices to be realized, plus the sum of the payments falling due, minus the payments that balance each other, minus finally the number of circuits in which the same piece of coin serves in turn as means of circulation and payment.[17] The erroneous opinion that it is . . . prices that are determined by the quantity of the circulating medium, and that the latter depends on the quantity of the precious metals in a country; this opinion was based by those who first beheld it, on the absurd hypothesis that commodities are without a price, and money without a value, when they first enter into circulation, and that, once in the circulation, an aliquot part of the medley of commodities is exchanged for an aliquot part of the heap of precious metals.[18] . . . when the industrial cycle is in the phase of crisis, a general fall in the price of commodities is expressed as a rise in the value of money, and, in the phase of prosperity, a general rise in the price of commodities, as a fall in the value of money. The so-called currency school concludes from this that with high prices too little, with low prices too much money is in circulation. Their ignorance and complete misunderstanding of facts are worthily paralleled by the economists, who interpret the . . . phenomena of accumulation by saying there are now too few, now too many wage-labourers." [19]

With the idea taken for granted that the quantity of the currency does not determine the prices of commodities, let us return to the subject of the banking system. The national socialist believes that it is the banking system which advances the capital, or determines the quantity of private capital production. We have seen, however, that it is the demands of production which control the issue of credit. Marx refers to his explanation of the circulation of the total product in Volume II of *Capital* in order to prove that it is an advance of currency not of the capitals which the banking system circulates:

"The difference between the issue of currency and loans of capital is best shown in the real process of reproduction. We have seen, there (Volume II, Part III), in what manner the different component parts of the production are exchanged for one another. For instance, the variable capital [money invested in wages] consists

substantially of the means of subsistence of the laborers, a portion
of their own product. But this is paid over to them piecemeal in
money. The capitalist has to advance this, and it depends very
much on the organization of the *credit system*, whether he can pay
out the new variable capital next week with the old money, which
he paid out last week. The same holds good with regard to the
acts of exchange between the different component parts of the total
social capital, for instance between the articles of consumption and
the means of production of articles of consumption. The money for
their circulation, must, as we have seen, be advanced by one or both
of the exchanging parties. It remains thereupon in the circulation,
but returns after the consummation of the exchange always to him
who actually employed industrial capital. (Volume II, Chapter XX).
Under a developed credit system, when the money is concentrated
in the hands of the banks, it is they, at least nominally, who advance
it. This advance refers only to the money existing in circulation. It
is an advance of currency, not of the capitals, which the credit system circulates." [20]

It is the banking system which supplies the money necessary for
the exchange of products, that is, it does not determine production,
but it is a servant to production. According to the needs of circulation, the reserve fund of the bank is increased or decreased. Again,
Marx writes that "the mass of the loan capital is quite different from
the quantity of the currency":

"By the quantity of the currency we mean . . . the sum of all
bank notes and all hard cash existing and circulating in a country,
including the bullion of precious metals. One portion of this quantity
forms the reserves of the banks, an ever changing magnitude. . . .
The variations of the rate of interest . . . depend upon the supply
of loan capital . . . that is, of the capital loaned in the form of money,
hard cash, and notes." [21]

Marx gives an actual example of what he means when he writes
that "the mass of this loanable capital is different from and independent of the mass of the circulating money." He explains that if
20 pounds sterling were loaned five times a day, then a total money
capital of 100 pounds sterling would be loaned. This is loan capital.

But each of these 20 pounds sterling would serve at least four times as means of purchase and payment, that is, it would be used to purchase commodities, and the seller would use the money again, etc. Looked at from this direction, each of the 20 pounds sterling forms a part of the quantity of the currency.[22]

". . . a low or full circulation means simply a different distribution of the same mass of currency into active circulation and deposits, which serve as an instrument of loans."[23]

Thus, the quantity of the currency is controlled naturally by the needs of circulation, and loans to production are also controlled by productive needs. It has already been explained that "it is . . . credit through which the capital . . . is placed at the disposal of each sphere of production, not in proportion to the capital possessed by the capitalists of this sphere, but *in proportion to its productive needs*—whereas in competition the individual capitals seem to be independent of each other . . . it makes a convenient transition for us from competition between capitals to *capital as credit*."[24]

In other words, the banking system distributes the necessary capital for production without any need of state interference. Marx even hints that since paper securities, or bonds, are a part of the credit system, they are also controlled by productive needs the same as bank loans are. He writes that reserve funds are used temporarily as bank deposits which become bank loans, and they are also used in the purchase of bonds:

"The desire to utilize . . . surplus-value [reserve funds], while accumulating as virtual money capital, for the purpose of deriving profits or revenue from it, finds in the *credit system and paper securities its consummation*."[25]

Because bonds are not productive capital any more than bank loans are, their use in production does not require centralized planning. This idea that there should be state interference in the distribution of capital is another of those false theories which would preserve the capitalist system. As in all other cases, however, Marx's theory is present to disprove any such obstacle to his economic system.

Again, the banking system promotes the distribution of the various commodities, but it does not determine production itself, since "production is determined by demand"[26] As Marx sees it, the banking system is a natural form for the distribution of the total product, but without production as the independent entity it is an empty form:

"The banking system, so far as its formal organisation and centralisation is concerned, is the most artificial and most developed product turned out by the capitalist mode of production. . . . It presents indeed the form of universal bookkeeping and of a distribution of products on a social scale, but only the form."[27]

In other words, the credit or banking system is only an artificial form that is a servant to production, not an organization that can, by means of state interference, abolish the antagonisms of capitalism. Therefore, we know that the plans of national socialism for a control over the credit system are unsound.

It borrows from communism the idea of planning production and yet maintains the capitalist's ownership of production. That is, it destroys the self operation of capitalism as prices are artificially fixed by the state, and the free movement of capital into the various lines of production is retarded. Purchase and sale is still the method of distributing the total product, but free exchange is interfered with by the state. In other words, it is an economic system which maintains the bad points of both state communism and capitalism. It is an economic theory without any scientific basis or reason for existence.

### b. *State Planning in a Reproduction of the Fixed Capital*

Before leaving this criticism of a planned capitalism, there is one more important theory which requires explanation. It involves a theory of Marx's which both the followers of state communism and a planned capitalism have used as proof that he believed in over-all state planning. Its explanation has been deferred until this part of the book because at this point the idea of cooperative production is almost complete. An understanding of cooperative production should be helpful in overcoming any false interpretation of Marx which might arise from his explanation of the "circulation of capital" in volume II. Just as Marx's explanation of differential rent involved detail, so does this theory also. It is important in both cases to realize it is only theory; and theory is not exact in actual practice but only gives a general idea of what occurs in experience. Whether or not it is possible to disprove the theory of over-all planning by the explanation which follows, is open to question. But if it can be done, the followers of state communism as well as those who believe in a planned capitalism should find some benefit from it.

It should be mentioned, to begin with, that in volume II of *Capital* there are some additional reasons given for a control over production by an association of the competitive producers, aside from for the purpose of alleviating the periodic crisis.

For example, Marx discusses the cause of a disturbance in the money and commodity markets as follows: He explains that there are lengthy enterprises undertaken in the construction of "railways, canals, docks, large municipal buildings, iron ships," etc., which require the passage of a long period of time before the commodity is completed, in these cases, a production time of a year or more.* Those who manage and work in these enterprises take commodities out of the circulation in the purchase of raw materials and machinery, etc., in addition to those commodities which comprise means of subsistence. They take these commodities out of the total commodity production for a long period of time without putting any commodity into the circulation, except money. It requires the borrowing of huge sums of money, in the first place, and this causes a disturbance in the money market. In

---

* Further, in regard to this Marx writes: "The working period in certain branches of production may be shortened by the mere extension of cooperation. The completion of a railroad is hastened by the employment of huge armies of laborers and the carrying on of the work in many places at once. The time of turn-over is in that case hastened by an increase of the advanced capital." *Capital*, vol. II, p. 268.

the second place, because large quantities of commodities are taken out of the market without any commodities being supplied to it, the "demand of cash payers for products increases without supplying any elements for purchase. Hence a rise in prices, of means of production and of subsistence . . . in those lines of business in which production may be rapidly increased, such as manufacture proper, mining, etc., the rise in prices causes a sudden expansion, which is soon followed by a collapse."[28]

In the above criticism of lengthy enterprises, Marx does not refer to that building which is necessary as means of production of a commodity, but the large scale construction of use values which require "a year or more" for completion. He goes on to advise some limitation in the simultaneous construction of too many of these lengthy productions which take commodities out of the circulation without supplying any commodity to it. This implies he wanted to avoid disturbances in the money and commodity markets; he did not advocate an abolition of the credit or money system. He writes that this situation of some commodities requiring long periods of production exists under both capitalist and cooperative production, but in the case of cooperative production he advises one possible means of avoiding such disturbances in the market.[29]

It should be remembered that those commodities which require a year or more for completion form a small part of the total production. In fact, this only involves the construction industry, or particular branches of it. Therefore, assuming there was a voluntary association of those enterprises engaged in large-scale construction, they could deliberately limit the simultaneous construction of too many of those lengthy enterprises which require a year or more for completion.

It should be noted that in the case of the large-scale construction imagined here, there is no problem of an oversupply in their commodities since demand precedes the supply, or production is for order. Therefore, aside from this particular problem mentioned in connection with lengthy enterprises, if demand precedes the supply, or production is for order in a particular line of business, there would seem to be no need for association in that line. In other words, the important thing is that all enterprises be made cooperative (profit-sharing). There is no need for asssociation unless a reason for planning exists. However, since the majority of production under both the capitalist and cooperative method is for an unknown market where the "supply forces the demand," those types of enterprise where demand precedes the supply are deviations from the general rule. In the majority of cases, associated planning is necessary.

---

With this portion of Marx's theory thus under control, we shall go on to a still more detailed explanation found in volume II. This, also, would seem to imply a different kind of control over production by the associated producers, but in practice it only requires an understanding of conditions which already exist under capitalism.

During the course of Marx's explanation of the circulation of the total product under capitalism, he encounters a problem in the explanation of theory. The result of this has been that his followers have interpreted it as a cause for crisis in production and an end to all commodity enterprise. However, in this case as in others, it is possible to find a solution to the problem. Only the essentials of Marx's theory will be given here, or enough of it to overcome the difficulty.

Marx begins by explaining that the total product produced by society each year is divided into two great sections, namely, those that comprise (1) means of production and (2) means of consumption. The means of production are composed of commodities having a form in which they pass into productive consumption such as "buildings, machinery, tanks, raw and auxiliary materials," etc. The means of consumption are composed of commodities which are used for the individual consumption of the capitalist and working class.

He goes on to explain that the capital in each of these two departments is divided into two parts, namely, into variable and constant capital. The variable capital is composed of the sum of the wages paid out to the workers in the given department, and the constant capital is equal to the total value of all the means of production used in that department. As in our previous explanation of commodity value, the total value of the product in each department is equal to the value of the means of production consumed and transferred to the product, plus the new value added in the form of wages and surplus-value. As Marx explains it, the value of the annual product of each department may be expressed in the formula: "c plus v plus s." [30]

Marx bases his analysis of simple reproduction on the diagram which follows, in which c stands for constant capital, v for variable capital, and s for surplus-value, with the rate of surplus-value between v and s assumed to be 100%.

"I. *Production of means of Production*
Capital..............................................................4000c + 1000v = 5000.
Product in Commodities......4000c + 1000v + 1000s = 6000.
These exist in the form of means of production.

II. *Production of Means of Consumption.*
Capital..............................................................2000c + 500v = 2500.
Product in Commodities........2000c + 500v + 500s = 3000.
These exist in articles of consumption.

Recapitulation: *Total annual product in commodities*:

I. 4000c + 1000v + 1000s = 6000 means of production.

II. 2000c + 500v + 500s = 3000 articles of consumption." [31]

After giving this diagram, Marx then examines the transactions which dispose of this total annual product in commodities. To begin with, the wages of the workers in department II represented by 500v and the surplus-value of the capitalists represented by 500s are to be spent for articles of consumption, and these are produced by capitalists within this same department. Once the capitalists and workers of department II purchase their means of subsistence, 500v and 500s in money are returned to the producers of means of subsistence, and a quantity of articles of consumption to the amount of 1,000 (500v + 500s) disappear as a part of the total product of department II.

In the same way, 1000v and 1000s of department I must also be used to purchase means of consumption. They are exchanged for the 2000c of department II in the following way. The workers and capitalists of department I (1000v + 1000s) purchase 2000 in commodity value from the producers of means of subsistence, represented in the diagram by 2000c of department II, thus disposing of the total product of department II. Department II uses the money so received from the capitalists and laborers of department I to purchase its necessary means of production to the amount of 2000c represented in department I by 1000v + 1000s. The commodity value represented by 1000v and 1000s of I thus disappears from the total product of I, along with the 2000c of department II.

At this point there remains only the 4000c of department I to be disposed of, and this is accomplished in the following way: These commodities are in the form of means of production which can be disposed of only in department I, as 4000 is the value in new means of production which is required of this department. "They serve for the reproduction of its consumed constant capital and are disposed of by the mutual exchange between the individual capitalists of I."[32] The capitalists purchase 4000 in means of production of department I, even though they are a part of this department.

In reference to this exchange of the total product, Marx implies in the words to follow that production will be distributed just as naturally under cooperative production as it is under capitalism; he also implies that money is a necessity in this circulation:

"If production were socialized, instead of capitalistic, it is evident that these products of department I would just as regularly be redistributed as means of production to the various lines of production of this department, for purposes of reproduction, one portion remaining directly in that sphere of production which created it, another passing over to other lines of production of the same department, thereby entertaining a constant mutual exchange between the various lines of production of this department.[33] The transactions disposing of the annual product in com-

modities can no more be dissolved into a mere direct exchange
of its individual elements than the simple circulation of commodities can be regarded as identical with the simple exchange of
commodities. Money plays a specific role in this circulation." [34]

As Marx explains that the banking system is the nominal source
of the money necessary for the total circulation under capitalism,
and as the banking or credit system is maintained under the cooperative method, there is still a natural interchange of products
among the various branches of production under the cooperative
method. In the following quotation, Marx describes how the
banking system nominally advances the money for circulation
under capitalism. It would be the same under cooperative production except that the productive capitalist would no longer exist:

". . . if a money capitalist [banker] stands behind the producer
of commodities and advances to the industrial capitalist money-
capital *(using this term in its strictest meaning, that is to say, capital-
value in the form of money)*, the final point of reflux for this money
is the pocket of this money-capitalist. In this way the mass of the
circulating money belongs to that department of money-capital
which is concentrated and organized in the form of banks, etc.,
although the money circulates more or less through all hands." [35]

In the case of cooperative production there is a circulation of the
total product by means of money, but money capital as it exists under
capitalism would no longer exist. Money capital means the investment
of money in variable and constant capital for the gain of profit, and
this involves certain complications which do not exist under the cooperative method. As Marx expresses it, "capitalist production implies the
role which money is playing not only as a medium of circulation, but
also as money capital, and creates conditions peculiar for the normal
transaction of exchange under this mode of production. . . . These
conditions become so many causes of abnormal movements. . . . The
continual offer of labor-power on the part of the working class of
I, the reconversion of a portion of the commodity-capital of I into the
money-form of variable capital, the renewal of a portion of the commodity-capital of II by natural elements of the constant capital of
IIc—all these are necessary premises dovetailing into one another,

but they are promoted by a very complicated process including *three processes of circulation* which occur independently of one another, but intermingle. The complicatedness of this process presents so many opportunities for abnormal deviations."[36]

The abnormal deviations mentioned above do not require any further explanation, as they are minor deviations which do not involve any major economic crisis. At least Marx does not imply any major economic crisis in his explanation of this. It is enough to say that with an end to the investment of money in labor-power on the part of the capitalist, the circulation of the total product is rendered less complicated. Instead of the three processes of circulation mentioned above, there will be only two, as labor-power will no longer form a commodity purchase. The new value produced $(v + s)$ will exist completely in the form of wages of labor, with the money form of all this value owned by the workers themselves; that is, aside from that part of the surplus-value which is saved for an enlargement of production, and assuming that all credit or bank loans have been disposed of.

Marx gives a different diagram for production organized on the basis of accumulation, where the capitalist does not consume his complete surplus-value but uses some of it for an enlargement of production. Since he encounters no difficulty in this explanation any more than under his explanation of simple reproduction as explained above, there is no reason to repeat it here. The details of it require an involved explanation, and these can be found from a study of volume II. However, Marx does encounter one difficulty in his further explanation of simple reproduction; it is this difficulty which is the real source of the idea that Marx believed in over-all centralized planning, when this was not his intention. The difficulty arises in connection with his explanation of the reproduction of fixed capital by department I for II. Because of the unusual importance given to this part of Marx's theory by modern economists, we shall go into a brief explanation of it. It is only a question of theory with Marx, but with other economists it has become an obstacle to reasonable economic change.

Marx begins this part of his theory by writing that "a great difficulty in the analysis of the transactions in annual reproduction" has to do with the reproduction of the fixed capital.[37] He then repeats his original diagram for simple reproduction as follows:

(*Capital*, II, p. 522)

I. 4000c + 1000v + 1000s +        [means of production]
II. 2000c + 500v + 500s = 9000.    [means of consumption]

[6000c]

Now the total value of the constant capital used in the two departments is 6000c. One portion of the value of this constant capital, namely that portion of it which is composed of means of production, has its value transferred to the product gradually; that is, that part of its value which is lost by depreciation is transferred to the value of the new product, while the instruments of production, etc., continue to serve in the productive process.

Since the above diagram is based on the total annual product in commodities, if an element of fixed capital lasts a year or less, then it is reproduced out of the total annual production the same as other elements of constant capital such as raw materials, etc., and requires no additional explanation.[38]

But some fixed capital in the form of machinery, buildings, etc., is not worn out during the course of one year. For example, a $10,000 machine might last for 10 years, which would mean that a $1,000 value in wear and tear would be transferred yearly to the annual product in commodities. "But the money received through the sale of commodities so far as it represents the value of the wear and tear of fixed capital [i.e., $1,000 yearly], is not reconverted into that component part of productive capital whose loss in value it makes good. It settles down beside the productive capital and retains the form of money. This precipitation of money is repeated until the period of reproduction . . . has elapsed. . . . As soon as the fixed element, such as buildings, machinery, etc., has been worn out and can no longer serve in the process of production, its value exists fully in money. . . . This money then serves to replace the fixed capital."[39]

Marx then gives the following diagram to further his explanation:

I.   $4000c + \underline{1000v + 1000s}$                    (II, p. 526, Ibid.)
II.   .............................2000c        $+ 500v + 500s$

We have already seen in the previous explanation how 2000c of II was exchanged for $1000v + 1000s$ of I. But this exchange was conditioned on the assumption that "the entire 2000 IIc are reconverted from their natural form into that of the elements of the constant capital of II, produced by I."[40] A part of the commodity value of 2000c in II is made up of depreciation from fixed capital (in addition to the reappearance of the value of raw materials, etc.,) used in production. Upon the sale of a 2000 value in commodities by department II, this value in depreciation is returned (along with the value of the consumed raw materials, etc.) to the capitalist, and it is held in the form of money. On the other hand, every year some fixed capital in department II does require reproduction as it has become worn out, and the necessary money has been accumulated in the form of a hoard.[41]

Aside from further details, Marx then gives another diagram, with w representing the value in wear and tear of fixed capital.

I.   1000v plus 1000s
II.      1800c          plus 200w            (II, p. 530, Ibid.)

The exchange of the product then proceeds in the following way. The laborers of I (1000v) buy means of consumption to the amount of 1000c from department II. Department II buys with the money received, means of production from I to the amount of 1000v. Thus 1000v of I and 1000c of II have been disposed of. Department II then advances 400 in money to purchase additional means of production from I which disposes of 400s in I, and Is uses this same 400 to purchase means of consumption to the amount of 400c from II. Dept. I then advances 400 in money to purchase 400c in means of consumption from II, and II returns the money to I by purchasing 400s in means of production. 1000v and 800s of I have thus disappeared from the diagram and 1800c of II.

There seems to be a problem arising here as there still remains 200s in means of production of department I, and on the side of II there remains 200c (w) in articles of consumption.

Department I buys with 200 in money the articles of consumption represented by 200w in II. But II holds this 200 money value in the form of a hoard as it represents the wear and tear on its fixed capital. In other words, the 200s of I, that was passed on to IIc (w) in the form of money is not returned to it, because IIc (w) does not use it to purchase 200s in means of production from I. It would seem there was an overproduction of 200s in means of production of I, as II does not purchase it.[42]

But Marx does find one possible way of explaining how this 200s in means of production is disposed of. He assumes that two sections of capitalists exist simultaneously in department II. One portion of them are accumulating money in the form of a hoard for a future purchase of machinery, etc., while the others have accumulated the necessary money as a result of the wearing out of their old fixed capital and are ready to purchase new. In the following diagram, (1) represents those capitalists who have the money to purchase new instruments of production, and (2) those that accumulate for future purchase.[43]

I. 200s in commodities

II. (1) 200c in money plus (2) 200c in commodities

Under these conditions, section 1 of the capitalists of II, represented in the diagram by (1) 200c in money, buys 200s in commodities of department I. I buys with this money 200c in commodities of II, represented in the diagram by (2) 200c, which monetizes the value of the depreciated fixed capital for those capitalists of II who accumulate the money as a hoard. This same process continues every year until section 2 of the capitalists of II recover the complete value of their depreciated capital and purchase new machinery, etc.[44]

With the above explanation, the entire production has now been disposed of. But according to Marx, this ideal is accomplished only under the assumption that "this fixed element of constant capital II, which must annually be reconverted into money to the full extent of its value and, therefore, entirely reproduced in its natural form (section 1), should be equal to the annual depreciation of the other fixed element of constant capital II [i.e., section 2], which continues its function in its old natural form and whose depreciation, represented by the value transferred by it to the commodities produced by it, is first accumulated in money."[45]

Marx goes on to explain that such a balance of value is conditioned on "a law of reproduction on the same scale." By this he means that the "proportional division of labor in department I which puts out means of production" remains constantly the same to the extent that it produces a given quantity of fixed capital (in the form of machinery, etc.) and another given quantity of circulating capital (raw materials, etc.) which replaces the constant capital of department II.[46]

Marx then analyzes what the results might be if the remaining amount of IIc (1) in money ready to purchase new fixed capital is not equal to the remainder of IIc (2) in commodities of department II which represents the value of the annual depreciation of machinery. He writes that section 1 might be either larger or smaller than section 2, and he proceeds to analyze each case separately as follows:

## "FIRST CASE"

I. 200s   [in commodities]                    (II, p. 541, Ibid.)
II. (1) 220c in money plus (2) 200c in commodities

Under these conditions IIc (1) purchases 200 in fixed capital from 200s in I, and I buys with this same money 200c (2), or those commodities in II which return the depreciated element of fixed capital. But a problem arises in that 20c (1) in money of II remains which cannot purchase new means of production from I, as 200s has already been disposed of. In this case there is a shortage of means of production, and a money surplus of 20c in section 1, II.

## "SECOND CASE"

I. 200s in commodities
II. (1) 180c in money plus (2) 200c in commodities. (II, p. 542, Ibid.)

Section 1 of department II buys 180 in fixed capital from department I, or 180s. I buys with this money 180c in commodities from section 2 of II. In this case there is 20s of I left unsaleable and 20c in commodities of II (2) left over. There is also a deficit of 20s in money in department I, and a deficit of 20c in money in section 2 of II, as a result of the unsaleable commodities, or a total value of 40.[47]

But again Marx comes up with a possible solution to the problem. He suggests that if IIc (1) is greater than IIc (2), where the result is a shortage in means of production, then "the importation of foreign commodities is required for the employment of the money-surplus in [IIc (1)]. If IIc (1) is smaller than IIc (2), then an exportation of commodities (articles of consumption) is required for the realization of the value of the depreciation of IIc [2] in means of production. In either case, foreign trade is necessary."[48]

The fact that Marx brings the question of world trade into his argument implies, to begin with, that he did not advocate the state planning of production which some economists have imagined from studying this part of his writings. He is not describing the cause of a general crisis in production, but only a problem in theory which implies minor disturbances. We have already seen in the chapter on capitalism that it is the process of capital accumulation meeting its limits which is the cause of the periodic economic crisis. Marx's explanation of the "reproduction of fixed capital" is another of his explanations for minor disturbances in the market. And he does come up with a solution to the problem, which does require understanding but not any government interference.

However, before presenting Marx's solution to the problem, a further understanding of the problem itself is necessary. For example, Marx proceeds with his argument as follows: He writes that "if a larger portion of the fixed element of IIc expires this year than last and must be reproduced in its natural form . . . then that portion of the fixed capital which is as yet only declining and must be temporarily accumulated in money until its term of expiration arrives, must decline in the same proportion, since we have assumed that the sum of the fixed capital serving in II (also the sum of its values) remains unchanged."[49]

Marx then describes the following consequences. He writes that if a greater portion of the commodity capital of I consists of elements of the fixed capital of IIc, then a smaller part of I consists of circulating elements (raw materials, etc.) for IIc, since the total product produced by I for II remains unchanged. "If one of these portions increases, then the other decreases and vice versa." But then the total production of II is assumed to remain unchanged, and "how is this possible if the production of its raw materials, half-wrought products, and auxiliary materials (the circulating elements of the constant capital of II) decreases? On the other hand, a larger portion of fixed capital of IIc in its money form is paid out to department I to purchase new means of production in the form of fixed capital. This money, however, does not return completely to department II, as there are fewer commodities which represent the value which replaces the depreciation on fixed capital and which is to be held in money. "More money would have flown from II into I for onesided purchases, and there would be fewer commodities of II which would stand only in the relation of a [seller] toward I. Under these circumstances a great portion of Is . . . would not be convertible into commodities of II, but would be held in the form of money."[50]

In this case there is a shortage of means of consumption, and according to Marx, it implies "a crisis in production." He writes that unless there is a "constant proportion between expiring (and about to be renewed) fixed capital and still continuing (merely transferring the value of its depreciation to its product) fixed capital is assumed," a problem arises. In order for department II to continue production on the same scale, if it purchases more fixed capital one year than another from department I, I would also have to maintain its same production of circulating elements of capital for II, not decrease it because of the increase in production of fixed capital for this department. "The aggregate production of I would have to increase, or, there would be a deficit in the reproduction, even aside from money matters."[51]

Marx then imagines the opposite situation in which the amount of fixed capital in department II to be purchased in its new form should decrease and the value of fixed capital in II which is to be accumulated in money increases in proportion. In this case, the quantity of the circulating elements of the constant capital of II, reproduced by I would remain the same "while that of the fixed elements about to be reproduced would have decreased." There would then be either a decrease in the total production of I, or a surplus which could not be converted into money because department II did not purchase it.

Marx writes that in the first example where there is a shortage of means of consumption, the same labor might supply a greater product with an increase in productivity and make up for the deficit in production, "but there would be a depreciation [in the value] of the product of I." In the second example where I would have to decrease its production or produce a surplus, this would also cause complications which would imply market disturbances.[52]

But again Marx brings in the question of world trade, which is at least a theoretical answer to the problem. "Foreign trade could relieve the pressure in either case. In the first case it would convert products of I held in the form of money into articles of consumption, in the second case it would dispose of the surplus of commodities [in I]." [53] However, in the final analysis, Marx does not depend on world trade to solve this theoretical problem as it only enlarges the difficulty. But he proposes another solution which appears equally as reasonable. He describes how the situation should exist under cooperative production as follows:

He assumes to begin with that "the magnitude of the expiring portion of fixed capital, which must be reproduced in its natural form every year (which served in our illustration for the production of articles of consumption) varies in successive years. It is very large in a certain year . . . then it is so much smaller in the next year." [54] This circumstance exists under both capitalist and cooperative production. But then Marx imagines conditions under the cooperative method as follows: "The quantity of raw materials, half wrought articles and auxiliary materials required for the annual production of the articles of consumption . . . does not decrease in consequence. Hence the aggregate production of means of production [fixed plus circulating capital] would have to increase in the one case and decrease in the other."[55]

But how would it be known beforehand whether the fixed capital will depreciate more, or less rapidly in different years? The solution Marx proposes is that there be a "continuous relative overproduction" of means of production,[56] so that if more fixed capital is required one year than another, then the necessary supply will be present. Likewise, in the case of commodities which represent circulating capital such as raw materials, etc, there would be a relative overproduction in these spheres, so that even though the production of fixed capital might be more one year than another, there would still be a sufficient supply of circulating capital produced by I for II, and the total production of II would not have to decrease as a consequence. Thus Marx writes, "There must be on the one hand a certain quantity of fixed capital in excess of that which is immediately required; on the other hand, there must be above all a supply of raw materials, etc., in excess of the actual requirements of annual production (this applies particularly to [raw materials, etc., needed in the production of] articles of consumption)."[57]

The false impression might arise here that if there should be a continuous relative overproduction of means of production, including both commodities which compose fixed and circulating capital, under cooperative production, the result would be a fall in prices and crisis. But this is not the case if it is a conscious formation of a supply, that is, if it is assumed that the producers in the individual lines of production of "means of production" consciously regulate their output in that line. For example, the producers of a particular kind of machinery might deliberately produce a quantity of their product that is slightly in excess of what they anticipate will be required of the market. It is not that these commodities will not be sold in the end. It is only that they exist over a longer period of time in the market than the others, before they are sold and replaced by new commodities.

Marx explains that where a longer period of time is required to transform a commodity into money, a reserve fund is needed to maintain the same scale of production, or credit capital might be used until the necessary money is returned. "Generally speaking, reserve capital in the form of money is always necessary in order to be able to work without interruption, regardless of the rapid or slow reflux of the . . . capital value in money."[58]

Marx writes that it is only under associated production where there is a conscious regulation of the total product produced in each sphere that there can be such a relative overproduction of commodities; under capitalism "it is an element of anarchy."[59] But he does describe a similar situation which exists under capitalism. For example, he differentiates between an intentional and unintentional formation of a supply. An unintentional formation of a supply implies an overproduction of commodities and a fall in prices. But an intentional formation of a supply on the market does not involve any overproduction which would cause a fall in prices. Thus, even under capitalism the total product is not purchased immediately; a supply must exist at least in the hands of the retail merchants, and it is gradually absorbed. Marx describes an intentional formation of a supply as follows:

"The seller seeks to get rid of his commodity as much as ever. He always offers his product as a commodity. . . . The commodity-supply must have a certain size, in order to satisfy the demand during a given period. The continual extension of the circle of buyers is one of the factors in the calculation. For instance, in order to last to a certain day, a part of the commodities on the market must retain the form of commodities while the remainder continue to flow and are converted into money. The part which is delayed while the rest keep moving decreases continually, to the extent that the size of the entire supply decreases until it is all sold. The delay of the commodities is thus calculated on as a necessary requirement of their sale. *The size of the supply must be larger than the average sale or the average extent of the demand.* At the same time the supply must be *continually renewed,* because it is *continuously dissolved.* . . . The expenses of the formation of a supply fall either on the shoulders of the producers or on those of a series of merchants from A to Z."[60]

It should be noticed in the above quotation that the voluntary formation of a supply which Marx describes as existing under capitalism are the very conditions he advocates under cooperative production, that is, that *"there must be . . . a certain quantity of fixed capital in excess of that which is immediately required,"* etc.

In other words, there is no real problem here. We have already seen in the chapter on Capitalism (Section 1, Competition) how a relative overproduction can and does exist under capitalism without a fall in prices and crisis; that is, assuming it is a deliberate formation of a supply in anticipation of future demand. Here again is that quotation:

"That *relative overproduction,* which is itself identical with accumulation takes place even with *average prices,* whose stand has neither a paralyzing nor an exceptionally stimulating effect upon production. This takes place in agriculture as well as in all other capitalistically managed lines of production. Under *different modes of production,* this *relative overproduction* is effected directly by the increase of population, and in colonies by continual immigration. The demand increases constantly, and in anticipation of this new capital is continually invested in new land. . . . It is the formation of new capitals which in itself brings this about."[61]

The possibility of a deliberate relative overproduction of constant capital under cooperative production (in anticipation of future demand) poses no threat to the market system since it already exists under deliberate circumstances in the case of capitalism, without any unfavorable effect on the price system. Economists have thus overemphasized the importance of Marx's explanation of "the reproduction of the fixed capital" and its threat to reasonable economic change.

In reference to his explanation, Marx has only to say that "this illustration of fixed capital, on the basis of an unchanged scale of production, is convincing."[62] It was in fact too convincing for the best of economists, even to the extent of their accepting the idea of over-all centralized planning as a result of it. By now it should be obvious that Marx did not advocate government planning because of this problem in detail connected with his explanation of the circulation of the total product in volume II of *Capital.*

———

The following words of Marx summarize the essentials of his theory from volume II which we have now discussed, namely, (1) the necessity of money in the circulation of the total product of society, (2) the problem of commodities with long working periods, and (3) the reproduction of the fixed capital:

"The natural flux and reflux of money by the exchange of the annual products on the basis of capitalist production; the advances of fixed capital in one bulk to the full value and the gradual and prolonged recovery of this outlay from the circulation in the course of successive years . . . the different length of time in which money is advanced according to the duration of the periods of reproduction of commodities . . . the differences in the magnitude and period of the reflux according to the relative size or condition of the productive supplies in the various lines of business and in the individual businesses of the same line . . . all this taking place during the year of reproduction, it was necessary that all these different facts should be noted and brought home by experience in order to give rise to a systemization of the mechanical aids of the credit-system, and to an actual discovery of whatever capital was available for lending."[63]

It is as if Marx was saying in confident prophecy that both problems discussed in this section—first, the reproduction of the fixed capital and the formation of a market supply which it requires, and second, the problem of commodities with long working periods —will find a solution in the end with the growth in an understanding and use of the credit system. It is their misunderstanding of the credit and money system which caused modern economists to misinterpret what Marx meant by "planning." The followers of both state communism and a planned capitalism have become unnecessarily concerned over these problems in theory found in volume II.

———

It would seem that we have deviated some from our discussion of a planned capitalism under national socialism; however, it is only

Marx's theory as explained above which is powerful enough to disprove the idea of over-all centralized planning, which even theorists of capitalism have accepted as reasonable.

## Section 2.—Private Ownership of Profit.

The property relations of national socialism are the same as those of capitalism. The private capital investor owns the means of production and profit of enterprise, with the working-class having no part in the ownership of industry. There is evidently a fear of giving up the capitalist as the owner of production, as if his existence was an eternal law of nature. The capitalist is admired, and even the working class may find satisfaction in idealizing the capitalist class as men of enterprise, etc.

It would be incomplete not to admit that such men with "a touch of enterprise" do perform a service, but as conditions exist under capitalism, they are free to exploit the labor of other less aggressive individuals. They could just as well be managers under the cooperative method without this freedom to use others for their own benefit. This is not to say there need be any animosity toward the capitalist since capitalism is a system of spontaneous growth, or the individual capitalist did not plan its organization. Nevertheless, when some individuals are free to rob others of their freedom and individuality, as is the case under capitalism, this is obviously a temporary situation, and it would be wise that the capitalist submit to the cooperative method once and for all. The majority of society cannot remain ignorant of their right to freedom, indefinitely. The system of feudal nobility went down and so must the capitalist type of despotism.

The national socialist, however, misses the entire point of freedom. He would maintain the capitalist as ruler at all costs, and the workers are of secondary importance. His first goal is to eliminate crisis in production and extremes of poverty. In some cases there is even a reduction of the dividends on investment to the general rate of interest, and any profit gained from production over the general rate of interest becomes the property of the government bureaucracy.

What the national socialist accomplishes by the transformation of all capital into interest-bearing capital is not the elimination of exploitation but the abolition of the aims of capitalism itself, that is, profit on capital investment. It is changes in the rate of profit on capital investment which determines production under capitalism. Therefore, if profit should be reduced to the general rate of interest, a rate which is determined differently than the general rate of profit, capitalist production would come to a practical standstill. Just as Marx writes, interest-bearing capital is entirely different from profit on capital investment:

"The general rate of profit is . . . determined, 1) by the surplus-value produced by the capital; 2) by the proportion of this surplus value to the value of the total capital; and, 3) by competition, but only to the extent that this is a movement, by which capitals invested in particular spheres seek to draw equal dividends out of this surplus-value in proportion to their relative magnitudes. The general rate of profit, then, derives its determination actually from causes, which are quite different and far more profound than those of the market rate of interest, which is directly and immediately determined by the proportion between supply and demand."[64]

The payment of interest also comes from a part of the product produced by the working-class, that is, interest is also surplus-value taken without an equivalent paid to the worker who produced it by the owner of the means of production. It is still capitalist production and private property as long as private money-capital gives owner-ship of the means of production and any part of the surplus-value produced by the workers. It has already been explained that in the case of bond ownership and bank loans there is interest paid on loans, but once they are repaid, there is no more interest due. How-ever, in the case of national socialism interest is paid indefinitely to the owners of the means of production; there is thus a continuation of capitalist exploitation. As Marx expresses it, just because the total profit is divided into interest and profit of enterprise, this does not abolish the fact that both parts are surplus-value taken from the worker by the owner of the means of production.

"The antagonistic form of the two parts, into which profit, or surplus-value is divided, leads him [the capitalist] to forget, that both parts are surplus-value, and that this division does not alter the nature, origin, and living conditions of surplus-value." [65]

Under associated production both the private appropriation of interest from production and the private ownership of the profit of enterprise by the owner of the means of production is eliminated. When the banking system loans money out to production that is deposited by the various enterprises as reserve funds and by all members of society as savings, this does away with the "private character" of capital, as the banking system which loans the money is not the private owner of the capital, and neither are those that use it in production its private owners. Here is another quotation from Marx on the banking system which further clarifies this point:

"[The] social character of capital is promoted and fully realised by the complete development of the *credit and banking system*. On the other hand this goes still farther. It places at the disposal of the industrial and commercial capitalists all the available, or even potential, capital of society, so far as it has not been actively invested, so that neither the lender nor the user of such capital are its real owners or producers. *This does away with the private character of capital and implies in itself, to that extent, the abolition of capital.*" [66]

The national socialist, however, does not accept the fact that the private capital investor is rendered superfluous by the development of the credit system. If he could have given up his idealization of the capitalist investor, he might have imagined a continuation of bond ownership and the banking system as a means to finance that business which is required of society.

### Section 3.—Despotism in Government.

As mentioned before, the follower of national socialism believes that the capitalistic method is the only possible form of business organization, that is, the labor-capital relations of capitalism are considered permanent. Marx would call the national socialist an ideologist of capitalism:

"The practical agents of capitalistic production and their . . . ideologists are as unable to think of the means of production as separate from the antagonistic social mask they wear to-day, as a slave-owner to think of the worker himself as distinct from his character as a slave."[67]

The national socialist does not recognize the presence of two separate classes in production. The capitalist is thought of as a worker laboring side by side with the hired workers, even though as the owner of the means of production he stands in direct opposition to his wage-laborers. Here is Marx's explanation of how the capitalist justifies his own economic existence and how false reasoning leads him to forget that his function as a capitalist consists in exploiting labor-power under the most economical conditions:

"In distinction from interest, his profit of enterprise appears to him [the capitalist] as independent of the ownership of capital, it seems to be the result of his function as a non-proprietor—a laborer. Under these circumstances his brain necessarily conceives the idea, that his profit of enterprise, far from being in opposition to wage-labor and representing only the unpaid labor of others, is rather itself wages of labor, wages of superintendence of labor. . . . The fact that his function as a capitalist consists in creating surplus-value, which is unpaid labor, and to create it under the most economical conditions, is entirely forgotten over the contrast, that the interest falls to the share of the capitalist, even if he does not perform any capitalist function and is merely the owner of capital; and that, on the other hand, the profit of enterprise falls to the share of the investing capitalist, even if he is not the owner of the capital, which he employs."[68]

Even though members of the working-class are hired by the capitalist-class and lose their independence as individuals because of it, the national socialist still believes that freedom exists under capitalism. Capitalism is considered a contract between equals regardless of its purchase and sale of wage-labor. They would turn an antagonistic method of production into a false association. Here is what Marx writes in reference to this:

"All well-developed forms of capitalist production being forms of co-operation, nothing is . . . easier than to make abstraction from their antagonistic character and to transform them by a word into some form of free association."[69]

There cannot be brotherhood between an independent individual and one that is not independent. As long as the capitalist class is free to hire wage-labor, complete freedom of the individual is impossible. According to Marx, class rule is not a law of nature, but it appears natural because of "education, tradition, habit":

"The advance of capitalist production develops a working-class, which by education, tradition, habit, looks upon the conditions of that mode of production as self-evident laws of nature. The organization of the capitalist process of production, once fully developed, breaks down all resistance."[70]

Just as the customs of capitalist production replaced the customs of feudalism, so the free association of cooperative production will eventually become an accustomed method of enterprise. It will differ from all preceding methods of production because it brings an abolition of classes and class antagonisms.

National socialism seeks to reconcile irreconcilables, that is, it seeks to reconcile the opposing classes of capital and labor. For Marx, there cannot be a union of these opposing classes because the economic interests of capital are in direct opposition to those of wage-labor. While the aim of capital is higher profits, the aim of the laborer is higher wages, and in the conflict of interests either one or the other must lose as the other gains.

"The share of capital, profit, rises in the same proportion in which the share of labor, wages, sinks; and inversely. The rise in profit is exactly measured by the fall in wages and the fall in profit by the rise in wages."[71]

Under national socialism the capitalist-class continues as a superior class entering into relations with the working-class, a class it looks down upon and treats as an inferior class because of its freedom to purchase it. The class antagonism continues because of the old labor-capital organization of industry, and the government bureaucracy settles differences which arise between the two classes.

If production should be made associated, the working-class would not be an inferior class but a group of free and independent individuals who share in ownership of the profits of enterprise, and meet each other as equals, if not in physical characteristics, at least before the law. The difference in individual ability would be accounted for by the same wage scale as under capitalism, and the ideal of freedom and equality for all would be materialized in an equality of profit ownership.

In the case of national socialism and similar theories, the antagonism and inequality of capitalistic ownership of the profit is idealized, even though the separation of the capitalist from production under the corporation renders him superfluous as a mere source of money-capital and an exploiter of the labor of others. Marx does not idealize the private money capitalist as does the national socialist; in fact, he writes that the capitalist lives off of or exploits the work of his wage-laborers just as the slave owner exploited his slaves:

". . . capital (the capitalist is merely capital personified and functions in the process of production as the agent of capital), in the social process of production corresponding to it, pumps a certain quantity of surplus labor out of the direct producer, or laborer. It extorts this surplus without returning an equivalent. This surplus labor always remains forced labor in essence, no matter how much it may seem to be the result of free contract. This surplus labor is represented by a surplus-value, and this surplus-value is materialized in a surplus product. It must always remain surplus labor in the sense that it is labor performed above the normal requirements of the producer. In the capitalist system as well as in the slave system, etc., it merely assumes an antagonistic form and is supplemented by the complete idleness of a portion of society."[72]

Under national socialism the group active in production do not own their own means of production and profit of enterprise; instead, large numbers of individuals are submissive before the capitalist owners of industry who are their rulers. The national socialist idealizes leadership in production as opposed to those working in production. In referring to leadership under capitalism, Marx states that the capitalist rules production, not because he is a leader of industry, but because he is the owner of production or a capitalist.

". . . when considering the capitalist mode of production, he [the political economist] treats the work of control made necessary by the co-operative character of the labor process as identical with the different work of control, necessitated by the capitalist character of that process and the antagonism of interests between capitalist and laborer. It is not because he is a leader of industry that a man is a capitalist; on the contrary, he is a leader of industry because he is a capitalist."[73]

The national socialist's belief in minority rule in the productive organization includes a belief in government tyranny. Government under national socialism is grounded upon the idea of the rule of the superior over the inferior. Only superior individuals are considered worthy of governing, and because representative government includes control by inferior individuals, the dictatorship of superior human beings in national government is said to be better than the majority rule of democratic government. First, the capitalist rules the workers in production, that is, the workers in the capitalist enterprise are required to be submissive to the will of the capitalist, and there is no self-government of the producers. Second, the government bureaucracy rules the actions of the capitalist. And last of all, the dictator rules the entire nation.

This is the idea of capitalistic class rule carried to its ultimate conclusion. It is almost unbelievable that such a theory could have come into existence at this advanced stage in history, but it did. Such a theory manifests the complete confusion of those who realize the contradictions of capitalism, and yet have a fear of something new. Still, there is an instinctive fear of representative government in this theory which was well grounded. The republican method, as it exists in the United States and Switzerland, for example, represents the first beginnings of freedom and its existence implies the destruction of anything unlike itself, even if it involves an unfree organization within the productive process.

## Section 4.—Peasant Agriculture.

There is no alteration in land ownership under national socialism;

the private landlord continues to collect ground rent. It should be mentioned, however, that the followers of national socialism had no idea as to what Marx meant by the abolition of private property in land. If they had known what Marx meant, their fear of Marxism might have been lessened. But the fact remains they did not understand Marx's intentions, and it is interesting to see what ideas they considered as superior to cooperative production.

To begin with, the theory of land ownership is idealized under national socialism. The landlord's ownership of land is considered one and the same as the small farmers' type of land ownership. While Marx has words of criticism for both private farming and the private landlord, it is only landlordism which goes down with the "abolition of private property" in land. In Marx's opinion, the landlord is even more superfluous as a part of production than is the capitalist since he does not even perform the function of exploiting labor-power but is completely idle:

"The capitalist performs at least an active function himself in the development of surplus-value and surplus-products. But the land owner has but to capture his growing share in the surplus-product and the surplus-value created without his assistance."[74]

The national socialist not only justifies the landlord's existence; he also rejects the idea of any establishment of the cooperative method in agriculture. By his rejection of the cooperative method in agriculture, he also rejects the specialized and scientific agriculture that is developed under capitalism in the form of plantations and large scale agriculture, where even management is a hired worker. This is already agriculture on a cooperative basis, even though the ownership is not yet cooperative or profit sharing. Here are Marx's words on this:

"The rationalisation of agriculture on the one hand and thus rendering it capable of operation on a social scale, and the reduction ad absurdum of private property in land on the other hand [i.e., small peasants property], these are the great merits of the capitalist mode of production."[75]

Those who believe in national socialism would prefer to hold on to customary methods of production instead of going forward in history. In the place of specialized and scientific agriculture they would perpetuate a state of society in which the independent farmer produces a variety of agricultural products, a part of which is produced for sale, while the other portion is produced for his individual consumption. Because the freedom and independence of the small farmer is idealized, his existence is made general; that is, even though the establishment of large scale agriculture under capitalism implies a change in these enterprises the same as in city industry as a result of competition. We have already seen in the chapter on ground rent that peasant agriculture is not capitalism and therefore could not be changed into cooperative production. In other words, it goes by untouched with an abolition of capitalism. Here are Marx's words on this:

"We Communists have been reproached with the desire to abolish the right of personally acquiring property as the fruit of man's own labor. . . . Hard-won, self-acquired, self-earned property! Do you mean the property of the petty artisan and of the small peasant, a form of property that preceded the bourgeois form? There is no need for us to abolish that; the development of industry has to a great extent already destroyed it, and is still destroying it daily."[76]

It has already been proved in the chapter on ground rent that small peasants' property is neither capitalism nor private ownership of land as personified by the landlord. As it is the "cotton lord and the landlord" which go down with an abolition of capitalism, the small farmer continues his production. This does not mean that he is made free from the competition of large scale agriculture, however. The following is Marx's explanation of how large scale scientific methods are established in agriculture:

"In the sphere of agriculture, modern industry has a more revolutionary effect than elsewhere, for this reason, that it annihilates the peasant, that bulwark of the old society, and replaces him by the wage labourer. Thus the desire for social changes, and the class antagonisms are brought to the same level in the country as in the towns. The irrational old-fashioned methods of agriculture are replaced by scientific ones.[77] . . . that kind of agriculture on a large scale, which corresponds to the epoch of manufacture . . . is distinguished from peasant agriculture, mainly by the number of labourers simultaneously employed, and by the mass of the means of production concentrated for their use."[78]

It should be noticed that Marx answers the question here as to where peasant agriculture ends and capitalism begins. Capitalism begins under large scale agriculture where a group of laborers are simultaneously employed. This idea is important, as it is only capitalist agriculture which is transformed into the cooperative method.

Under national socialism the state is given the responsibility of ordering the many producers what and how much to produce, or they allow the farmers to go their own way in production and the state pays the farmer the difference between the normal price of the product and its depreciated market price. The existence of the independent farmer is thereby perpetuated artificially, while under normal conditions he would be forced to give up his unstable economic existence and submit to the competition of large scale capitalist farming. In either case, the state bureaucracy is steadily increased and not decreased as it is under cooperative production. The independent  farmer loses his freedom because of government control over his actions.

Marx does not advocate any control over the small farmer's production. In fact, he does not even recognize its existence in connection with a control over the productive forces, as its individual contribution to the total product is small. Marx acknowledges that "the capitalist mode of production" is not "as uniformily developed in agriculture as in manufacture,"[79] but this does not prevent him from advocating cooperative enterprise wherever the capitalist method in agriculture does exist. It has already been explained that the small farmers' type of agriculture existed even in ancient times, and it will probably continue to exist for a long time into the future. But wherever the wage system of capitalism exists, the cooperative method follows after. The development of the wage system in both manufacture and agriculture implies the cooperative method in both spheres. Here are Marx's words on this:

"Capitalist production completely tears asunder the old bond of union which held together agriculture and manufacture in their infancy. But at the same time it creates the material conditions for a higher synthesis in the future; viz., the union of agriculture and industry *on the basis of the more perfected forms* they have acquired during their temporary separation." [80]

The national socialist's main criticism of communism is its abolition of independent farming, even though Marx writes in direct words that this is not his intention. He would establish cooperative agriculture only where group agriculture has already been established under capitalism, not by means of an expropriation of the small farmer. In addition, associated enterprise does not artificially perpetuate the small farmers' method of production but allows it to disappear naturally of itself.

When associated production brings large scale enterprise in agriculture under control by a voluntary association of the competitive producers in the individual lines, it accomplishes something which national socialism does not, that is, stability of prices in the field of agriculture. Also, under national socialism, farming production is separated from city industry, and half of society, that is to say the farmers, labor under difficult conditions. But if it is assumed that the capitalist method does function in agriculture along with city industry, the possibility of crisis as a result of capitalist agriculture does exist. That is, the two great branches of production intermingle, and with farming industry weakened by overproduction and crisis, city industry must become affected by it. Because the raw materials produced in agriculture pass over into city industry as means of industrial production, any revolution in the price of raw materials affects the prices of the products of city industry. The general issues are described by Marx as follows:

". . . a rise in the prices of raw material can curtail or clog the entire process of reproduction, since the price realised by the sale of the commodities may not suffice to reproduce all the elements of these commodities.[81] Violent fluctuations of price thereby cause interruptions, great collisions, or even catastrophes in the process of reproduction. It is especially the products of agriculture, raw materials taken from organic nature, which are subject to such fluctuations of value in consequence of changing yields, etc. . . . The same quantity of labor may, in consequence of uncontrollable natural conditions, the favor or disfavor of seasons, etc., be incorporated in very different quantities of use-values, and a definite quantity of these use-values may have very different prices." [82]

In the case of cooperative enterprise when both farming and city industry are brought under control by a voluntary association of the competitive producers, the demand for both agricultural and industrial products is assured and steady. Marx is of the opinion that a steady demand will bring on an improvement in agricultural production. He also mentions the fact that agriculture needs the control of associated producers *under a competitive system.* It should also be noticed he mentions the self-employing small farmer as having a regulating effect on production:

"An actual improvement of raw materials in such a way that not only their quantity, but also their quality would come up to expectations, for instance supplying cotton of American quality from Indian fields, would necessitate a long continued, progressively growing, and steady European demand (quite aside from the economic conditions under which the Indian producer labors in his country). As it is, the sphere of production of raw materials is extended only convulsively, being now suddenly enlarged, and then violently contracted. All this, and the spirit of capitalist production in general, may be very well studied in the cotton crisis of 1861-65, which was further aggravated by the fact that raw materials were at times entirely missing which are one of the principal factors of reproduction. . . . The moral of this story, which may also be deduced from other observations in agriculture, is that the capitalist system works against a rational agriculture, or that a rational agriculture is irreconcilable with the capitalist system, although technical improvements in agriculture are promoted by capitalism. But under this system, agriculture *needs either the hands of the self-employing small farmer, or the control of associated producers.*" [83]

This is the only quotation given by Marx where he directly advocates the control of associated producers under a competitive system. If this is what the control of associated producers means under capitalism, then it means the same thing under cooperative production. That is to say, it does not imply monopoly under cooperative production any more than it does under capitalism. The implication is that when production is under the control of associated producers the sale of products would no longer be accidental or occasional, and prices would be maintained stable. Here is Marx's further explanation of this:

"In order that the prices at which commodities are exchanged with one another may correspond approximately to their values. . . . The exchange of the various commodities must no longer be accidental or occasional.[84] It is one of the great outcomes of the capitalist mode of production, that it transforms agriculture from a merely empirical and mechanically perpetuated process of the least developed part of society into a consciously scientific application of agronomics.[85] But the dependence of the cultivation of particular products of the soil upon the fluctuations of market prices, and the continual changes of this cultivation with these fluctuations of prices, the whole spirit of capitalist production, which is directed toward the immediate gain of money, contradicts agriculture, which has to minister to the entire range of permanent necessities of life required by a network of human generations."[86]

Associated production accomplishes what capitalism and national socialism do not, that is, stability of prices and a planning of production in agriculture as well as in city industry. Only a voluntary association of the competitive producers in the individual lines of production could control the productive forces in agriculture without excessive government bureaucracy. According to Marx, there are occasional associations of producers to regulate production in agriculture, even under capitalism, but these are only temporary. He mentions that they soon return to the price system alone as a means to regulate the supply. The following words of Marx prove there can be a regulation of the supply without an abolition of the price system, or a system of competitive producers. He gives an actual example of this voluntary planning and emphasizes the planning as more important than what the everyday prices happen to be:

"During the period in which raw materials are high, the industrial capitalists get together in *associations for the purpose of regu-*

*lating production*. So they did, for instance, after the rise of cotton prices in 1848, in Manchester, and a similar move was made in the production of flax in Ireland. But as soon as the immediate impulse has worn off, and the principle of competition reigns once more supreme, according to which one must 'buy in the cheapest market' (instead of stimulating production in the most favored countries, as those associations attempt to do, without regard to the monetary prices at which those countries may just happen to supply their product), the regulation of the supply is left once more to 'prices.' All thought of a common, far-reaching, circumspect control of the production of raw materials gives way once more to the belief that demand and supply will mutually regulate one another. And it must be admitted that such a control is on the whole irreconcilable with the laws of capitalist production, and remains forever a platonic desire, or is limited to exceptional co-operation in times of great stress and helplessness." [87]

Thus, it is Marx's idea that there should be a "common, far reaching, circumspect control over the production of raw materials" just as such control occasionally exists under capitalism through an association of capitalists.

But to return to the question of peasant agriculture, that method of farming which is idealized by national socialism, it is a form of agriculture which is not ready to assume equality with city industry, and it must therefore remain outside of the discussion of scientific production methods.

### Section 5.—A Forceful Establishment.

The national socialist idealizes force as a method of attaining goals. He organizes mob violence and stirs up hatred for individuals. Like state communism, national socialism is established by means of a physical overthrow of the government in power, not by voting strength.

The legal method of establishment is always to be preferred over the forceful elimination of the group in power because it is a more democratic method. However, those nations which have not yet established the republican form of government cannot establish economic change peacefully. The forceful overthrow of the group in power in such nations would seem inevitable.

Again, the forceful method of change should not be advocated; that is, regardless of the fact that Marx emphasizes that any economic change when it does occur, has to be accomplished during a certain period of time in history. According to Marx's prophecy, when the time is ripe, capitalism will be changed into the cooperative method by the conscious action of society, and there need be no doubt as to the truth of his prophecy.

But prophecy alone is not enough here. It is obvious that an enthusiasm for reform has to be present just as it had to be present at the time of the abolition of slavery in America. It is impossible that cooperative production would involve any civil war such as was necessary to abolish slavery since slavery was a more obvious evil. Still, the same enthusiasm for change would have to be present for an abolition of capitalism. It is a simple process to transform an enterprise which is already established on a group scale into a cooperative or profit sharing one, but nevertheless it does involve something new and therefore requires pursuasion.

It is at least to be hoped that the threat of a world war or other types of martyrdom will not be the means to arouse the necessary enthusiasm. However, the sublime goal of world peace which it involves makes it of more importance than other types of reform, and it cannot be known for sure what unusual means might be necessary to accomplish it. The mere fact that Marx was generally misinterpreted in the first place is unusual.

But aside from humane incentives, it is the economic theory of Marx which is the real power behind the change. The national socialists realized this, and hence their attempt to stir up hatred for the communists in particular. Such methods in the final analysis are unsuccessful as the attacks are on personalities not ideas. Even though Russian communism is not the ideal form of socialism, it does represent an attempt to materialize the theories of Karl Marx. And because these theories have as their goal freedom, not bondage, the national socialist is powerless to destroy them. The Russian form of communism can only be dissolved by a higher form of socialism, not by the capitalist system. The theory of national socialism has the capitalist system as its basis, and because the system of capitalism is based on an unfree idea, it is a temporary one. Because its basis is temporary, so also is national socialism temporary. The Marxist, however, has as his antagonist the unfree idea of capitalism, and therefore he could eventually be the victor over both systems. Without an attack on personalities but only on an unfree idea, that idea can be overthrown. As soon as the idea of capitalism is replaced by a higher idea of freedom, the capitalist class would soon be separated from production.

In other words, it is first a question of allowing Marx's theory to assume leadership in the field of economics. And there is no doubt that the world will know when capitalism, as a theory, has lost its power. Just as Marx writes, "Communism . . . is the riddle of history solved and knows itself as this solution."[88]

The above reasoning is in harmony with Marx's idea that the criticism of evils outside of us transforms what would otherwise be a physical battle into a battle of ideas, or struggles of thought:

"Absolute criticism has at least learned from Hegel's Phenomenology the art of transforming real, objective chains existing outside me into merely ideal, merely subjective chains existing in me and hence the art of transforming all external, sensuous struggles into mere struggles of thought."[89]

The peaceful theorist who does no physical harm to the capitalists or state communists has a greater power to withstand their rule than those who resort to the use of force. Karl Marx, for example, spent his entire lifetime writing *Capital*. It is theory which poses a threat to unfree systems, not the existence of individuals. The words of economic theory that point the way are a power which cannot be destroyed.

In one place, Marx describes the theoretical explication of communist ideas as a danger because of the moral power which accompanies them. For example, it is obvious that morality is on the side of the workers as opposed to the capitalist class, and the conscience of man eventually forces the destruction of inequalities:

"We are firmly convinced that it is not the practical effort but rather the theoretical explication of communistic ideas which is the real danger. Dangerous practical attempts, even those on a large scale can be answered with cannon, but ideas won by our intelligence, embodied in our outlook, and forged in our conscience are chains from which we cannot tear ourselves away without breaking our hearts; they are demons we can overcome only by submitting to them."[90]

While a scholar in pursuit of truth can bring on an economic change by the mere use of words, it is doubtful that the opposing classes would submit to expropriation without using some force. The interference in private money matters, which would be necessary, could be sufficient to stir the meanest and most malignant passions in the capitalist class. Marx mentions the danger which accompanies any criticism of existing property relations:

"In the domain of Political Economy, free scientific inquiry meets not merely the same enemies as in all other domains. The peculiar nature of the material it deals with, summons as foes into the field of battle the most violent, mean and malignant passions of the human breast, the Furies of private interest. The English Established Church, e.g., will more readily pardon an attack on 38 of its 39 articles than on 1/39 of its income. Now-a-days atheism is *culpa levis,* as compared with criticism of existing property relations."[91]

However, regardless of the "Furies of private interest," if the intellectual rule of the capitalist class is destroyed, this class would be helpless to prevent its own demise. An enthusiasm for economic change would come into existence, and the capitalist system would be eliminated. As for the individuals that give the theory, as in the case of Karl Marx, his work was done once the ideas were written and published. What followed was (and is) in the impersonal hands of history.

According to Engels, Marx admitted the possibility of a peaceful and legal revolution but doubted that the capitalist class would submit without a "pro-slavery rebellion."

". . . we can almost calculate the moment when the unemployed, losing patience, will take their own fate into their own hands. Surely, at such a moment, the voice ought to be heard of a man [Karl Marx] whose whole theory is the result of a life-long study of the economic history and condition of England, and whom that study led to the conclusion that, at least in Europe, England is the only country where the inevitable social revolution might be effected entirely by peaceful and legal means. He certainly never forgot to add that he hardly expected the English ruling classes to submit, without a 'pro-slavery rebellion,' to this peaceful and legal revolution."[92]

We see, then, that a peaceful and legal revolution is not an impossibility, that is, in such nations as England and America where the republican form of government is well established, but the resistance of the capitalist class might cause some conflict between classes.

### Section 6.—World Rule by Superior Nations.

Under national socialism the superior nations rule the world by empire and world dictatorship. The backward and small nations are exploited and controlled by the stronger ones, and nations with similar interests join into alliances against other nations. The national socialist worships war as a means of attaining national goals and believes conflict between nations is a permanent part of world society.

War between nations is not destined to exist in all periods of history. But as long as capitalism remains and strong nations are free to exploit the weaker ones, war is inevitable. If capitalism was destroyed and the large and small nations were joined in federation, world harmony would be established. Permanent warfare between nations would be cast down and replaced by permanent peace.

# NOTES
## and
# BIBLIOGRAPHY

# NOTES

CHAPTER I—

1. Marx, *Capital*, vol. III, pp. 314-380.
2. Ibid., vol. II, p. 149.
3. Marx, *The Civil War in France*, p. 77.
4. Marx, *Capital*, vol. III, pp. 986-987.
5. *Communist Manifesto*, p. 46.
6. Marx, *Capital*, vol. I, pp. 580-581.
7. Ibid., vol. III, p. 438.
8. Ibid., pp. 519-520.
9. Ibid., p. 412.
10. Ibid., p. 416.
11. Ibid., p. 473.
12. Ibid., p. 551.
13. Ibid., pp. 711-712.
14. Ibid., p. 430.
15. Ibid., p. 429.
16. Ibid., p. 100.
17. Ibid., p. 987.
18. Ibid., vol. I, pp. 533-534.
19. Ibid., vol. III, p. 992.
20. Ibid., vol. I, p. 698.
21. Ibid. vol. III, pp. 302-303.
22. Ibid., vol. I, p. 581.
23. Ibid., vol. III, p. 919.
24. Ibid., vol. I, p. 363.
25. Ibid., vol. III, p. 456.
26. Ibid., p. 450.
27. Marx, *The Civil War in France*, p. 76.
28. Ibid., p. 76.
29. Marx, *Critique of the Gotha Programme*, pp. 18-19.
30. Marx, *Capital*, vol. III, pp. 724-725.
31. Ibid., p. 966.
32. Ibid., p. 106.
33. Ibid., vol. I, pp. 823-824.
34. Ibid., vol. III, p. 713.

CHAPTER II—

1. Marx, *Capital*, vol. I, p. 785.
2. Marx, *Theories of Surplus Value*, pp. 386-387.
3. Marx, Capital, vol. I, pp. 169-170.
4. Ibid., vol. II, pp. 38-39.
5. Engels, *Socialism: Utopian and Scientific*, pp. 83-85.
6. Marx, *Capital*, vol. II, p. 552.
7. Ibid., p. 412.
8. Ibid., p. 525.
9. Ibid., vol. III, pp. 954-955.
10. Ibid., pp. 744-745.
11. Ibid., vol. I, p. 106.
12. Marx, *Critique of the Gotha Programme*, pp. 8-9.
13. Engels, *Socialism: Utopian and Scientific*, pp. 71-72.
14. Ibid., pp. 86-87.
15. Marx, *Value, Price and Profit*, pp. 169-170.
16. Marx, *Critique of the Gotha Programme*, p. 18.
17. *Communist Manifesto*, p. 20.
18. Engels, *Socialism: Utopian and Scientific*, pp. 76-77.
19. Marx, *Capital*, vol. I, p. 14.
20. Ibid., p. 624.
21. Marx, *Critique of the Gotha Programme*, p. 16.
22. *Communist Manifesto*, pp. 42-43.
23. Marx, *Critique of the Gotha Programme*, p. 13.
24. *Communist Manifesto*, p. 50.
25. Ibid., p. 50.
26. Marx, *The Civil War in France*, pp. 76-77.

CHAPTER III—
1. Marx, *Capital,* vol. III, p. 993, footnote.
2. Ibid., p. 1004.
3. Ibid., p. 992.
4. Ibid., pp. 1007-1008.
5. Ibid., p. 1026.
6. Ibid., p. 964.
7. Ibid., p. 56.
8. Ibid., p. 431.
9. Ibid., pp. 1007-1008.
10. Ibid., vol. I, p. 589.
11. Ibid., vol. III, p. 221.
12. Ibid., vol. I, p. 45.
13. Ibid., p. 220.
14. Ibid., p. 634.
15. Ibid., p. 217.
16. Ibid., vol. III, pp. 213-214.
17. Ibid., p. 228.
18. Ibid., p. 673.
19. Ibid., p. 227.
20. Ibid., pp. 214-215.
21. Ibid., pp. 219-221.
22. Ibid., pp. 745-746.
23. Ibid., pp. 750-751.
24. Ibid., p. 50.
25. Ibid., p. 218.
26. Ibid., p. 223.
27. Ibid., p. 226.
28. Ibid., vol. I, pp. 347-350.
29. Ibid., vol. III, p. 208.
30. Ibid., pp. 306-307.
31. Ibid., vol. I, pp. 482-483.
32. Ibid., vol. III, p. 209.
33. Ibid., pp. 228-229.
34. Ibid., pp. 223-224.
35. Ibid., pp. 226-227.
36. Ibid., pp. 209-210.
37. Marx, *The Poverty of Philosophy,* pp. 58-59.
38. Marx, *Capital,* vol. II, p. 86.
39. *Marx-Engels Correspondence,* Letter 109, Marx to Kugelman, pp. 246-247.
40. Marx, *Capital,* vol. III, pp. 786-787.
41. Ibid., p. 1002.
42. Ibid., p. 219.
43. Ibid., p. 649.
44. Ibid., pp. 312-313.
45. Ibid., p. 294.
46. Ibid., vol. II, pp. 574-575.
47. Marx, *Theories of Surplus Value,* p. 356.
48. Marx, *Capital,* vol. III, p. 300.
49. Ibid., vol. I, p. 26.
50. Ibid., vol. III, p. 214.
51. Ibid., pp. 566-567.
52. Ibid., p. 297.
53. Ibid., vol. II, pp. 475-476.
54. Ibid., vol. III, pp. 297-298.
55. Ibid., pp. 298-299.
56. Ibid., vol. I, p. 695.
57. Ibid., vol. III, p. 575.
58. Ibid., p. 607.
59. Ibid., vol. II, p. 163.
60. Ibid., vol. III, pp. 595-596.
61. Ibid., vol. II, p. 120.
62. Ibid., vol. III, p. 293.
63. Ibid., p. 221.
64. Ibid., pp. 301-303.
65. Ibid., pp. 516-517.
66. Ibid., p. 456.
67. Ibid., p. 455.
68. Ibid., p. 449.
69. Ibid., p. 455.
70. Ibid., p. 516.
71. Ibid., p. 519.
72. *Marx-Engels Correspondence,* letter 108, Marx to Engels, p. 243.
73. Marx, *Capital,* vol. III, p. 521.
74. Ibid., pp. 456-457.
75. Marx, *Civil War in France,* pp. 79-80.
76. Marx, *Capital,* vol. III, p. 310.
77. Ibid., p. 522.
78. Marx, *Theories of Surplus Value,* p. 254.
79. Marx, *Capital,* vol. I, pp. 632-633.
80. Ibid., pp. 676-677.
81. Ibid., p. 698.
82. Ibid., p. 702.

83. Ibid., p. 363.
84. Ibid., pp. 534-535.
85. Ibid., pp. 680-681.
86. Ibid., vol. III, p. 909.
87. Ibid., p. 1029.
88. Ibid., pp. 45-49.
89. Ibid., p. 55.
90. Ibid., pp. 61-62.
91. Ibid., p. 172.
92. Ibid., pp. 176-177.
93. Ibid., p. 230.
94. Ibid., p. 244.
95. Ibid., p. 204.
96. Ibid., p. 182.
97. Ibid., pp. 183-184.
98. Ibid., p. 185.
99. Ibid., p. 190.
100. Ibid., pp. 187-188.
101. Ibid., p. 188.
102. *Marx-Engels Correspondence,* letter 108, Marx to Engels, p. 243.
103. Ibid., p. 131.
104. Marx, *Capital,* vol. III, p. 985.
105. Ibid., pp. 897-898.
106. Ibid., p. 761.
107. Ibid., p. 762.
108. Ibid., p. 760.
109. Ibid., p. 754.
110. Ibid., p. 759.
111. Ibid., pp. 724-725.
112. Ibid., pp. 773-774.
113. Ibid., pp. 901-902.
114. Ibid., p. 770.
115. Ibid., pp. 884-885.
116. Ibid., p. 765.
117. Ibid., p. 879.
118. Ibid., p. 870.
119. Ibid., p. 792-793.
120. Ibid., p. 792.
121. Ibid., p. 803.
122. Ibid., pp. 851-852.
123. Ibid., pp. 808-809.
124. Ibid., p. 855.
125. Ibid., p. 809.
126. Ibid., p. 904.
127. Ibid., p. 773.
128. Ibid., pp. 879-880.
129. Ibid., p. 880.
130. Ibid., p. 882.
131. Ibid., p. 882.
132. Ibid., p. 888.
133. Ibid., p. 885.
134. Ibid., p. 886.
135. Ibid., p. 887.
136. Ibid., pp. 892-893.
137. Ibid., pp. 896-897.
138. Ibid., pp. 934-936.
139. Ibid., p. 783.
140. Ibid., p. 902.
141. Ibid., p. 742.
142. Ibid., p. 939.
143. Ibid., p. 759.
144. Ibid., p. 759.
145. Ibid., p. 725.
146. Ibid., pp. 899-900.
147. Ibid., p. 888.
148. Ibid., pp. 1015-1016.
149. Marx, *The American Journalism of Marx and Engels,* pp. 230-232.
150. Marx, *Capital,* vol. III, pp. 762-763.
151. Ibid., p. 762.
152. Ibid., pp. 726-727.
153. Ibid., p. 907.
154. Marx, *The American Journalism of Marx and Engels,* pp. 95-96.
155. Marx, *Capital,* vol. III, pp. 943-944.
156. Ibid., pp. 935-936.
157. Ibid., p. 936.
158. Ibid., pp. 942-943.
159. Ibid., p. 782.
160. Ibid., pp. 939-940.
161. Ibid., p. 939.
162. Ibid., pp. 941-942.
163. Ibid., pp. 900-901.
164. Ibid., pp. 944-945.
165. Ibid., pp. 912-913.
166. Ibid., pp. 919-920.
167. Ibid., p. 923.
168. Ibid., p. 922.
169. Ibid., p. 923.

170. Ibid., pp. 933-934.
171. Ibid., p. 921.
172. Ibid., pp. 925-927.
173. Ibid., p. 937.
174. Ibid., p. 928.
175. Ibid., p. 790.
176. Ibid., p. 929.
177. Ibid., pp. 937-938.
178. Ibid., p. 1024.
179. Ibid., p. 1031.
180. Ibid., p. 743.
181. Ibid., p. 871.
182. Ibid., pp. 871-872.
183. Ibid., pp. 877-878.
184. Ibid., pp. 729-730.
185. Ibid., pp. 870-871.
186. Ibid., p. 1029.
187. Ibid., p. 960.
188. Ibid., p. 727.
189. Ibid., p. 947.
190. Ibid., p. 1030.
191. Marx, The American Journalism of Marx and Engels, p. 79.
192. Marx, Capital, vol. III, p. 1028.
193. Ibid., p. 1022.
194. Ibid., pp. 1020-1021.
195. Ibid., p. 908.
196. Ibid., vol I, pp. 639-640.
197. Ibid., p. 837.
198. Ibid., p. 364.
199. Ibid., p. 836.
200. Ibid., pp. 686-687.
201. Ibid., vol. III, p. 516.
202. Ibid., vol. I, p. 688.
203. Ibid., vol. II, p. 122.
204. Ibid., vol. III, p. 289.
205. Ibid., vol. I, p. 837.
206. Ibid., vol. III, p. 1030.
207. Ibid., vol. I, pp. 486-487.
208. Ibid., pp. 418-419.
209. Ibid., vol. III, p. 521.
210. Ibid., p. 517.
211. Ibid., vol. I, p. 581.
212. Ibid., vol. III, p. 939.
213. Ibid., pp. 873-874.

214. Marx, The American Journalism of Marx and Engels, pp. 170-172.
215. Ibid., p. 174.
216. Marx, Critique of the Gotha Programme, p. 17.
217. Ibid., p. 16.
218. Marx, Capital, vol. III, p. 1024.
219. Ibid., p. 102.
220. Ibid., p. 1027.
221. Ibid., pp. 458-459.
222. Ibid., p. 561.
223. Ibid., p. 517.
224. Ibid., vol. I, p. 668.
225. Ibid., p. 92.
226. Ibid., vol. III, p. 520.
227. Ibid., vol. I, p. 837.
228. Ibid., p. 836.
229. Communist Manifesto, pp. 34-35.
230. Ibid., pp. 50-51.
231. Marx, Writings of the young Marx on Philosophy and Society, p. 214.

CHAPTER IV—
1. Marx, Capital, vol. I, p. 695.
2. Ibid., vol. III, p. 641.
3. Ibid., p. 522.
4. Ibid., p. 549.
5. Ibid., p. 549-550.
6. Ibid., p. 488.
7. Ibid., pp. 603-604.
8. Ibid., vol. II, p. 412.
9. Ibid., vol. III, p. 303.
10. Ibid., p. 688.
11. Ibid., p. 379.
12. Ibid, vol. I, p. 635.
13. Ibid., p. 136.
14. Ibid., p. 185.
15. Ibid., p. 136.
16. Ibid., p. 137, footnote.
17. Ibid., p. 156.
18. Ibid., p. 139.
19. Ibid., pp. 679-680.
20. Ibid., vol. III, pp. 623-624.
21. Ibid., pp. 586-587.

22. Ibid., p. 587.
23. Ibid., p. 622.
24. Marx, *Theories of Surplus Value*, p. 254.
25. Marx, *Capital*, vol. II, p. 582.
26. Ibid., p. 543.
27. Marx, *Capital*, vol. III, p. 712.
28. Ibid., vol. II, pp. 361-363, p. 556.
29. Ibid., p. 412.
30. Ibid., pp. 457-458.
31. Ibid., p. 459.
32. Ibid., pp. 459-460.
33. Ibid., p. 493.
34. Ibid., p. 525.
35. Ibid., p. 478.
36. Ibid., pp. 578-579.
37. Ibid., p. 522.
38. Ibid., p. 522.
39. Ibid., p. 524.
40. Ibid., pp. 526-527.
41. Ibid., p. 527.
42. Ibid., pp. 530-531.
43. Ibid., pp. 534-535.
44. Ibid., pp. 540-541.
45. Ibid., p. 541.
46. Ibid., p. 541.
47. Ibid., pp. 541-542.
48. Ibid., p. 543.
49. Ibid., pp. 543-544.
50. Ibid., p. 544.
51. Ibid., p. 545.
52. Ibid., p. 545.
53. Ibid., p. 546.
54. Ibid., p. 546.
55. Ibid., p. 546.
56. Ibid., p. 546.
57. Ibid., p. 546.
58. Ibid., p. 518.
59. Ibid., p. 546.
60. Ibid., pp. 166-167.
61. Ibid., vol. III, pp. 786-787.
62. Ibid., vol. II, p. 546.
63. Ibid., p. 559.
64. Ibid., vol. III, p. 431.
65. Ibid., p. 447.
66. Ibid., pp. 712-713.
67. Ibid., vol. I, p. 667.
68. Ibid., vol. III, pp. 446-447.
69. Ibid., vol. I, pp. 584-585 footnote.
70. Ibid., p. 809.
71. Marx, *Wage Labor and Capital*, p. 101.
72. Marx, *Capital*, vol. III, p. 953.
73. Ibid., vol. I, pp. 364-365.
74. Ibid., vol. III, p. 748.
75. Ibid., p. 724.
76. *Communist Manifesto*, p. 45.
77. Marx, *Capital*, vol. 1, p. 554.
78. Ibid., p. 368.
79. Ibid., vol. III, p. 792.
80. Ibid., vol. I, p. 554.
81. Ibid., vol. III, p. 130.
82. Ibid., p. 140.
83. Ibid., pp. 143-144.
84. Ibid., p. 209.
85. Ibid., p. 723.
86. Ibid., p. 724, foot-note.
87. Ibid., p. 142.
88. Marx, *Writings of the young Marx on Philosophy and Society*, p. 304.
89. Ibid., p. 379.
90. Ibid., p. 135.
91. Marx, *Capital*, vol. I, p. 15.
92. Ibid., Engels' Preface, pp. 31-32.

# BIBLIOGRAPHY

Engels, Frederick.
———*Socialism: Utopian and Scientific.* (A part of Anti-Duhring.) Written in 1877-1878. Charles H. Kerr and Co., Chicago, 1905.
———*Engels on Capital.* Translated and edited by Leonard E. Mins. New York International Publishers, 1937.

Marx, Karl.
———*Capital, A Critique of Political Economy.* In 3 Volumes. Volume I, first published in 1867. Translated from 3rd German edition by Samuel Moore and Edward Aveling. Edited by Ernest Untermann. The Modern Library, New York. Volume II, first published in 1893. Translated from 2nd German edition by Ernest Untermann. Edited by Frederick Engels. Charles H. Kerr and Co., Chicago. Volume III, first published in 1894. Translated from first German edition by Ernest Untermann. Edited by Frederick Engels. Charles H. Kerr and Co., Chicago.
———*The Civil War In France.* An address of the General Council of the International Workingmen's Association, 1871. A part of The Paris Commune, Labor News Co., New York, 1920.
———*Critique of the Gotha Programme,* with appendices by Marx, Engels and Lenin. A revised translation. New York International Publishers, 1938.
———*The Poverty of Philosophy.* Translated by H. Quelch, Charles H. Kerr and Co., Chicago.
———*Theories of Surplus Value.* Selections from the volumes published between 1905 and 1910 as Theorien uber den Mehrwert, edited by Karl Kautsky. Translated from the German by G. A. Bonner and Emile Burns. New York International Publishers, 1952.
———*Value Price and Profit.* An address delivered in 1863. The Essentials of Marx, with introduction and notes by Algernon Lee, Rand School Press, New York, 1946.
———*Wage Labor and Capital.* A collection of articles written in 1849 for the Neue Rheinishe Zeitung, and rewritten by Engels in 1891. The Essentials of Marx, Rand School Press, New York, 1946.
———*Writings of the young Marx on Philosophy and Society.* A collection of Marx's early writings in translation from the German to make available in English what he actually said in the twelve years before the Communist Manifesto (1848). Edited and translated by Lloyd D. Easton and Kurt H. Guddat, with preface, introduction, and chapter introductions by both editors. Doubleday & Company, Inc., Garden City, New York, 1967.

Marx and Engels.

———*The American Journalism of Marx and Engels.* A selection from The New York Daily Tribune edited by Henry M. Christman. Introduction by Charles Blitzer, with appendix list of Marx/Engels articles in The New York Daily Tribune prepared by Louis Lazarus. The New American Library, Inc., New York, 1966.

———*Manifesto of the Communist Party.* First published in 1848. Preface by Engels, 1888. The Essentials of Marx, Rand School Press, New York, 1946.

———*Selected Correspondence 1846-1895 Karl Marx and Frederick Engels.* Translated by Dona Torr. New York International Publishers, 1942.

# APPENDIX A

## A New Social Contract Between
## Workers and Management

At the risk of being considered utopian, I have decided to explain what Karl Marx only hinted at, that is, materialize his views on how government should best be organized under the cooperative method, as distinguished from the capitalist one. The essentials of this treatise also appeared in my first book *Confessions of a Girl Economist*, although this is a more advanced version of it. But since I did explain the economic organization of cooperative enterprise, it would seem I had left it incomplete without giving some insight into its possible political organization.

Because Marx did not detail this part of his theory, I have had to go elsewhere for the necessary explanation. The other sources I have used are *The Federalist* by James Madison, Alexander Hamilton, and John Jay; and *Handbook of Business Administration* edited by H. B. Maynard. Also, economist Eduard Heimann had some influence on my ideas that follow. It can be shown that his ideas were similar to mine on the question of political organization in his writing, "Democratic Freedom and the Organization of Labor."

What has resulted from a combination of these different ideas is something practical, not utopian, and it will be wondered why it has not been understood before. An apathetic satisfaction with capitalism is the main cause of the confusion, as well as a mistaken understanding as to what "freedom" means. The quotations I have used from *The Federalist* to explain "freedom" might appear idealistic at first, but when substantiated later by similar views from Marx and other experts on the subject of business administration, they become practical as well as ideal.

Besides mentioning the sources which aided in my explanation which follows, it should also be told that this addition to the book

225

might never have existed without my incentive to include the portion on "justice for the workers" which forms a part of the whole. If I had not realized from experience that a need for such justice exists, I would have assumed the book was complete with only an explanation of the economics of cooperative enterprise. But whatever incentive influenced it, this addition could prove valuable as a further explanation of Marx's cooperative production.

————————————————

Just as the economic organization of cooperative enterprise was found by means of a comparison with capitalism and a discarding of whatever was wrong in the old system, so the political organization of cooperative enterprise must be discovered in the same way. That which is useful under the business administration of capitalism should be maintained, while that which is unfree in it should be abandoned.

The right of the capital owner to purchase wage labor is, of course, the primary evil of capitalism. But another evil in the system is its lack of political freedom for the majority. By this is meant there is no control over the management in industry; that is, management can be good or bad because it exists without the consent of the governed. It is not that management itself is evil; it does perform a useful service. But it is evil in that it is uncontrolled.

The way to destroy this evil under a new economic system is to give political freedom to the majority, while at the same time maintaining the stability of a management hierarchy. It is my intention to show how this problem would be solved, assuming that each enterprise is organized on a cooperative basis; that is, the private capital owner is eliminated from business and borrowed capital is used in his place. Also, there is group ownership of the means of production and profits by the workers and management.

With an abolition of separate economic classes under the cooperative method, it is possible to solve the problems of government under it without prejudice for workers or management. But before we can answer this question of administration under the new economic society, we must first know what the republican method of government includes.

According to James Madison, "We may define a republic to be . . . a government which derives all its powers directly or indirectly from the great body of the people, and is administered by persons holding their offices during pleasure for a limited period or during good behavior.[1] The federal and state governments are in fact but different agents and trustees of the people, constituted with different powers and designed for different purposes."[2]

Now this government that is chosen by the people consists of legislative, executive, and judicial departments, separate and distinct from each other. If this republican method is to function in industry— taking into account, of course, certain differences due to the fact that the cooperative enterprise is a productive or working organization— each company should have similar separate and distinct departments of government which serve individually as a check on abuses of power by either of the other departments.[3] We will begin with an analysis of the legislative branch of government in industry, or that portion of the administration which makes those laws for the enterprise which express the will of the people in it.

In the first place, this branch would consist of a legislature that would meet periodically when called. It would be elected by the people (including both workers and management) working in the enterprise to represent them. The size of the legislature should be limited in order to avoid the problems of a multitude, but at the same time it should not be so small that several individuals can exert too much control.[4] And most important, its size should be controlled by proportionate representation; that is, according to the number of people in a given division of the company, there would be more or fewer representatives of them.

By comparison, this meeting would no doubt be like the stockholders' "called" meeting under the capitalist corporation, with the difference that instead of the capital owners there would be a gathering of those at work in the organization. Instead of stockholders it would be workers who make the company by-laws, etc.

---

[1] Madison, *The Federalist*, volume I, Walter Dunne, Washington and London, 1901, p. 257.
[2] Ibid., p. 321.
[3] Hamilton or Madison, *The Federalist*, p. 353.
[4] Madison, *The Federalist*, p. 68.

There should also be a definite term of office for all members of the law making body. James Madison writes, in reference to the problem of time in government service: "The period of service ought to bear some proportion to the extent of practical knowledge requisite to the due performance. A certain degree of knowledge of the service can only be attained or at least thoroughly attained by actual experience in the station which requires the use of it."[1]

While the legislative branch of government in industry makes its laws, the executive branch performs the necessary management functions. The highest executive in each company would be chosen by free election in the particular company, probably at the time when the legislative body meets. And once chosen, this executive controls all management working downward; all minor executives are accountable to the highest one, so that there is one single will and purpose controlling the management as a whole.

In a similar way, under the capitalist corporation, the stockholders elect a board of directors, and the board of directors then elect a chairman. This chairman of the board is the president of the corporation and controls all management working downwards.[2] The difference is that the chief executive would be elected by worker owners not capital owners under the cooperative method. Also, since according to Marx a board of directors is superfluous management, this would imply they should not exist after a change in ownership. There would only be a chief executive elected. Marx writes that the amount of actual management the board of directors do under capitalism is usually in an inverse proportion to their high salaries, and that management in their case is an excuse for "plundering stockholders and amassing wealth." Even the cooperative enterprises under capitalism have a board of directors, so that in some cases there is a "plundering" of the worker owners the same as the capitalist stockholders.

But aside from this, it should be remembered that the corporation method of ownership (and assuming also its political form or business administration) is, according to Marx, the beginning of the new group kind of business enterprise. It is profit sharing without workers own-

[1] Ibid., p. 367.
[2] See *Handbook of Business Administration*, edited by H. B. Maynard, New York, p. 3-16, p. 2-36.

ership, and at least for stockholders, an elective type of administration. Again on the question of superfluous management as it now exists, there is no doubt that it will eventually be done away with through the passage of time, if for no other reason than to increase the profits for the majority, just as under capitalism a minimum number of workers are used for the same purpose. However, under the cooperative method it can be imagined that what had been money spent on excess management could be used for additional workers to make the labor of the majority easier.

The question arises as to whether the abolition of a board of directors under the cooperative method would solve all problems of dishonesty in it. Such dishonesty might also occur with management under the cooperative method without the necessary precautions, since it, too, is a system based on money as a means of exchange. Theoretically, in the case of cooperative enterprise, management is brought under control, because it is the people working who make the laws, etc.; whereas under capitalism the stockholders are separate from production and management goes by uncontrolled. It should be mentioned, however, that even though board members are left unmanaged, there is a system set up within the business organization of capitalism to guard against a loss of money, etc., and this same system would continue to exist under the cooperative method. For instance, here is a quotation on this from *Handbook of Business Administration*: "The prime burden of the responsibility to protect the assets of the business is on the financial function. The general principle of 'checks and balances' therefore should be applied in meticulous detail so that there actually is a check and balance in each area where neglect, theft or natural hazards might cause loss of the companies' resources."[1]

Assuming, then, that the abolition of a board of directors—as well as this application of a system of checks and balances—would eliminate most problems of dishonesty under the cooperative method, let us go on to answer further questions regarding the executive department.

---

[1] From *Handbook of Business Administration*, edited by H. B. Maynard, copyright 1967 by McGraw-Hill Book Company. Used with permission of McGraw-Hill Book Company. Chapter written by George L. Chamberlin, Controller, Scott Paper Co., p. 9-5.

For instance, it might be asked why only the office of the chief executive should be elective and not that of lower management as well. This problem is answered as follows by James Madison: He writes that if higher and lower executives were all elective, government would have "as much affinity to a legislative assembly as to an executive council. And being once exempt from the restraining of an individual responsibility for the acts of the body, and deriving confidence from mutual example and joint influence, unauthorized measures would, of course, be more freely hazarded, than where the executive department is administered by a single hand, or by a few hands.[1] . . . Wherever a general power to do a thing is given, every particular power necessary for doing it is included."[2]

This top management that would be chosen by the company as a whole under the cooperative method should be given a definite term of office in order to give the functions of management stability. As James Madison writes, "Stability in government is essential to national character, and to the advantages annexed to it, as well as to that repose and confidence in the minds of the people which are among the chief blessings of civil society. . . .[3] Stability requires that the hands in which power is lodged should continue for a length of time the same; a frequent change of men will result from a frequent return of elections; and a frequent change of measures from a frequent change of men; whilst energy in government requires not only a certain duration of power but the execution of it by a single hand.[4] . . . As every appeal to the people would carry an implication of some defect in the government, frequent appeals would in a great measure deprive the government of that veneration which time bestows on everything, and without which perhaps the wisest and freest government would not possess the requisite stability."[5]

Even under the capitalist corporation the top management is given a definite term of office as a follows: The board of directors is usually elected once a year—in some cases once every two or three years.[6]

---

[1] Madison, *The Federalist*, p. 342.
[2] Ibid., p. 310.
[3] Ibid., p. 240.
[4] Ibid., p. 241.
[5] Ibid., p. 345.
[6] See *Handbook of Business Administration*, edited by H. B. Maynard, p. 3-17.

This could occur in a similar way under the cooperative method, with an election of a president in the company.

The highest executive in each particular business should therefore have a definite term of office between elections. However, since under the conditions assumed the chief executive has a high degree of power, his total term of office should definitely be limited in time, because "the greater the power, the shorter ought to be its duration."[1] Another check to the power of the executive must be the right of the legislative branch to impeach him if sufficient cause be given. At the same time, the executive must be given some check on the legislative by the right of veto power over the laws made, but this veto should not be absolute.

Now that we have defined the legislative and executive branches of government under the new organization of industry, there remains only the judicial branch for us to consider. The judicial branch of government in a company is that group which settles questions pertaining to everyday justice in the enterprise that cannot be settled without outside interference.

For instance, excessive exploitation in the form of overwork, etc., often exists under capitalism and goes by unnoticed. By means of a judicial gathering under the cooperative method, where individuals could go on and speak openly of wrongs done, or done them (the people could also tell of wrongs in written form), the voice of the silent and exploited ones would finally be heard, and higher moral standards would be maintained within the business organization itself. Under capitalism, grievances are taken to the management locally, or if a labor union exists, an advance is made with the union's help. However, an exposure of grievances is either dangerous or impossible for the wronged under capitalism where the workers are not owners.

The judicial branch should be composed of a small number of people chosen for humane qualities of wisdom. For instance, one important characteristic a judicial member should have is "sympathy" for the rights and welfare of his fellow human being. In order to bring justice close to the people, this group would be chosen locally at the

[1] Madison, *The Federalist*, p. 364.

place of work by a majority vote. They would convene on call, the same as the legislative branch; and while the term of office for those serving in the judicial department need not be limited in time, they should be open to impeachment by majority vote if necessary cause be given.

Just as under capitalism the labor union battles injustice, etc., the judicial branch or "works council" (as it could be called) under the cooperative method would do the same thing, although their decisions would be made with authority, since the capital owners would no longer exist. Eduard Heimann in "Democratic Freedom and the Organization of Labor" advocated "works councils" within the boundaries of capitalism, which, of course, is contrary to Marx's idea that whoever owns production also rules it. Still, aside from this, Eduard Heimann's conclusions came close to Marx's view of democracy in industry. Here are his words: "Speaking not in legal but in social terms, the larger plant of production was neither liberal nor democratic but was autocratic in the extreme. . . . This indispensable element of democracy may be provided by works councils. . . . There is . . . a realm of undisputed competence for the councils . . . not management and not collective agreements, not business and not wage rates, but the arrangement of the work in the individual shop. . . . In emphasizing the importance of a decentralized responsibility, exemplified by works councils, it must not be overlooked, of course, that other and more centralized devices are also necessary, in order to provide the indispensable measure of economic security."[1] In other words, a separate executive department is necessary as well as a works council.

It should be noted that Marx, too, did not advocate changing the line of management which exists under the capitalist corporation, as he writes that under this form, production is practically resting on social (or cooperative) enterprise, with all members of production non-owners and the stockholders separate from production. It is only a question of having the people in the company elect top management,

---

[1] From *Political and Economic Democracy*, edited by Max Ascoli and Fritz Lehmann, W. W. Norton and Company, New York, 1937. Chapter by Eduard Heimann, pp. 61, 66, 71, 67.

etc., because the stockholders would be paid off like bondholders, and made separate from profit ownership.

While the separate powers given to the legislative, executive, and judicial departments in the cooperative enterprise serve as a check on their individual powers, "a dependence on the people is no doubt the primary control on the government."[1] As James Madison and Alexander Hamilton write, "The elective mode of obtaining rulers is the characteristic policy of republican government. The means relied on in this form of government for preventing their degeneracy are numerous and various. The most effectual one is such a limitation of the term of appointments as will maintain a proper responsibility to the people."[2]

With an explanation of the legislative, executive, and judicial departments under a cooperative method of industry, we have solved the problem of combining political freedom for the majority with a maintenance of that management hierarchy which is necessary for order in the enterprise as a whole. The legislative department is the republican branch[3] which represents the interests of the majority, while the executive department is the minority division which protects the interests of those who perform management functions. And finally, the judicial department is an impartial branch which serves to interpret justice as it exists in the enterprise. Because the government as a whole in the industry is based on the "elective mode of obtaining rulers," it is in actuality an industrial republic.

This new political organization is a fulfillment of Karl Marx's idea of eliminating the separate economic classes of capital and labor, with its replacement by the majority rule of the workers. It shows that the abolition of classes does not necessarily mean an absolute rule by the workers, as those who perform management functions also fulfill necessary economic duties. In other words, both workers and management are "workers" from the standpoint of the non-working capital owner. Therefore, in the actual political organization of industry after an abolition of capitalism, there is nothing un-Marxist

---

[1] Madison, *The Federalist*, p. 354.
[2] Ibid., p. 389.
[3] Ibid., p. 253.

in a protection of the interests of management as well as those of the majority workers, since productive workers and management are only two different types of wage earners according to Marx's definition of them. It is its elective mode of determining leadership which gives the industrial republic its republican (majority rule) character, not its internal organization.